P9-CCO-189

A SHEARWATER BOOK

NATURALIST

NATURALIST

EDWARD O. WILSON

ISLAND PRESS / Shearwater Books
Washington, D.C. • Covelo, California

A Shearwater Book
published by Island Press

LIBRARY OF CONGRESS
CATALOGING-IN-PUBLICATION DATA
Wilson, Edward Osborne, 1929–
Naturalist / Edward O. Wilson.
p.   cm.
Includes index.
ISBN 1-55963-288-7 (cloth)
1. Wilson, Edward Osborne, 1929–   . 2. Naturalists—
United States—Biography.   I. Title.
QH31.W64A3   1994
508'.092—dc20   94-13111
[B]   CIP

Printed on recycled, acid-free paper

Manufactured in the United States of America

10 9 8 7 6 5 4 3 2 1

FOR RENEE AND CATHY

contents

Prelude   xi

PART I   DAYBREAK IN ALABAMA

CHAPTER ONE   Paradise Beach   *5*

CHAPTER TWO   Send Us the Boy   *16*

CHAPTER THREE   A Light in the Corner   *33*

CHAPTER FOUR   A Magic Kingdom   *47*

CONTENTS

CHAPTER FIVE To Do My Duty *62*

CHAPTER SIX Alabama Dreaming *82*

CHAPTER SEVEN The Hunters *100*

CHAPTER EIGHT Good–Bye to the South *124*

CHAPTER NINE Orizaba *139*

PART 2 STORYTELLER

CHAPTER TEN The South Pacific *163*

CHAPTER ELEVEN The Forms of Things Unknown *197*

CHAPTER TWELVE The Molecular Wars *218*

CHAPTER THIRTEEN Islands Are the Key *238*

CHAPTER FOURTEEN The Florida Keys Experiment *260*

CHAPTER FIFTEEN Ants *282*

CHAPTER SIXTEEN Attaining Sociobiology *307*

CHAPTER SEVENTEEN The Sociobiology Controversy *330*

CHAPTER EIGHTEEN Biodiversity, Biophilia *354*

Acknowledgments 365

Index 369

prelude

I HAVE BEEN, AS THE PHYSICIST VICTOR WEISSKOPF ONCE said of himself, a happy man in a terrible century. My preoccupation was not, however, with nuclear swords and breathtaking technological advances, but of a wholly different kind: I have served as a close witness to fundamental changes in Nature.

Nature, with a capital N, the concept: for me it holds two meanings. When the century began, people could still easily think of themselves as transcendent beings, dark angels confined to Earth awaiting redemption by either soul or intellect. Now most or all of the relevant evidence from science points in the opposite direction:

that, having been born into the natural world and evolved there step by step across millions of years, we are bound to the rest of life in our ecology, our physiology, and even our spirit. In this sense, the way in which we view the natural world, Nature has changed fundamentally.

When the century began, people still thought of the planet as infinite in its bounty. The highest mountains were still unclimbed, the ocean depths never visited, and vast wildernesses stretched across the equatorial continents. Now we have all but finished mapping the physical world, and we have taken the measure of our dwindling resources. In one lifetime exploding human populations have reduced wildernesses to threatened nature reserves. Ecosystems and species are vanishing at the fastest rate in 65 million years. Troubled by what we have wrought, we have begun to turn in our role from local conquerer to global steward. Nature in this second sense, our perception of the natural world as something distinct from human existence, has thus also changed fundamentally.

Because my temperament and profession predispose me, I have followed these changes closely. As a younger scientist and naturalist, my own worldview shifted in concert with the advances of evolutionary biology and the decline that practitioners of this science perceived to be occurring in the natural environment. From childhood into middle age, my ontogeny repeated the larger phylogeny. Nature metamorphosed into something new.

My childhood was blessed. I grew up in the Old South, in a beautiful environment, mostly insulated from its social problems. I became determined at an early age to be a scientist so that I might stay close to the natural world. That boyhood enchantment remains undiminished, but it exists in a Heraclitean stream in which everything else has changed, all that I first thought about how the world works and all that I believed of humanity's place in the world. I have written this account to learn more fully why I now think the way I do, to clarify the elements at the core of my beliefs to you and to myself, and perhaps to persuade.

NATURALIST

PART I

DAYBREAK
IN ALABAMA

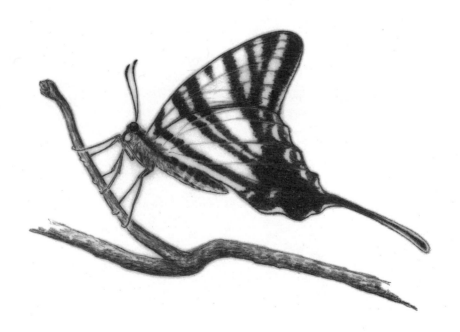

When I get to be a composer
I'm gonna write me some music about
Daybreak in Alabama
And I'm gonna put the purticst songs in it
Rising out of the ground like swamp mist
And falling out of heaven like soft dew.

LANGSTON HUGHES

chapter one

PARADISE
BEACH

WHAT HAPPENED, WHAT WE *THINK* HAPPENED IN DISTANT
memory, is built around a small collection of dominating images. In
one of my own from the age of seven, I stand in the shallows off Paradise Beach, staring down at a huge jellyfish in water so still and clear
that its every detail is revealed as though it were trapped in glass. The
creature is astonishing. It existed outside my previous imagination. I
study it from every angle I can manage from above the water's surface. Its opalescent pink bell is divided by thin red lines that radiate
from center to circular edge. A wall of tentacles falls from the rim to

surround and partially veil a feeding tube and other organs, which fold in and out like the fabric of a drawn curtain. I can see only a little way into this lower tissue mass. I want to know more but am afraid to wade in deeper and look more closely into the heart of the creature.

The jellyfish, I know now, was a sea nettle, formal scientific name *Chrysaora quinquecirrha*, a scyphozoan, a medusa, a member of the pelagic fauna that drifted in from the Gulf of Mexico and paused in the place I found it. I had no idea then of these names from the lexicon of zoology. The only word I had heard was *jellyfish*. But what a spectacle my animal was, and how inadequate, how demeaning, the bastard word used to label it. I should have been able to whisper its true name: *scyph-o-zo-an*! Think of it! I have found a scyphozoan. The name would have been a more fitting monument to this discovery.

The creature hung there motionless for hours. As evening approached and the time came for me to leave, its tangled undermass appeared to stretch deeper into the darkening water. Was this, I wondered, an animal or a collection of animals? Today I can say that it was a single animal. And that another outwardly similar animal found in the same waters, the Portuguese man-of-war, is a colony of animals so tightly joined as to form one smoothly functioning superorganism. Such are the general facts I recite easily now, but this sea nettle was special. It came into my world abruptly, from I knew not where, radiating what I cannot put into words except—*alien purpose and dark happenings in the kingdom of deep water*. The scyphozoan still embodies, when I summon its image, all the mystery and tensed malignity of the sea.

The next morning the sea nettle was gone. I never saw another during that summer of 1936. The place, Paradise Beach, which I have revisited in recent years, is a small settlement on the east shore of Florida's Perdido Bay, not far from Pensacola and in sight of Alabama across the water.

There was trouble at home in this season of fantasy. My parents were ending their marriage that year. Existence was difficult for

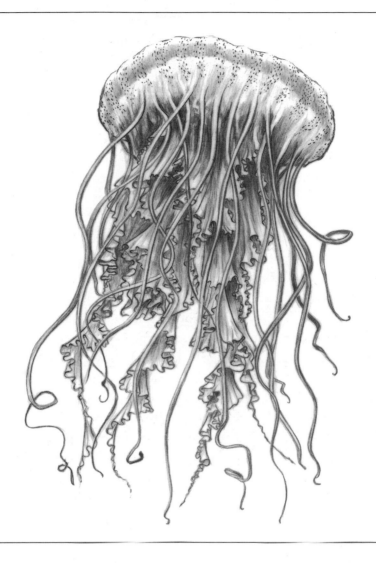

them, but not for me, their only child, at least not yet. I had been placed in the care of a family that boarded one or two boys during the months of the summer vacation. Paradise Beach was paradise truly named for a little boy. Each morning after breakfast I left the small shorefront house to wander alone in search of treasures along the strand. I waded in and out of the dependably warm surf and scrounged for anything I could find in the drift. Sometimes I just sat on a rise to scan the open water. Back in time for lunch, out again, back for dinner, out once again, and, finally, off to bed to relive my continuing adventure briefly before falling asleep.

I have no remembrance of the names of the family I stayed with, what they looked like, their ages, or even how many there were. Most likely they were a married couple and, I am willing to suppose, caring and warmhearted people. They have passed out of my memory, and I have no need to learn their identity. It was the animals of that place that cast a lasting spell. I was seven years old, and every species, large and small, was a wonder to be examined, thought about, and, if possible, captured and examined again.

There were needlefish, foot-long green torpedoes with slender beaks, cruising the water just beneath the surface. Nervous in temperament, they kept you in sight and never let you come close enough to reach out a hand and catch them. I wondered where they went at night, but never found out. Blue crabs with skin-piercing claws scuttled close to shore at dusk. Easily caught in long-handled nets, they were boiled and cracked open and eaten straight or added to gumbo, the spicy seafood stew of the Gulf coast. Sea trout and other fish worked deeper water out to the nearby eelgrass flats and perhaps beyond; if you had a boat you could cast for them with bait and spinners. Stingrays, carrying threatening lances of bone flat along their muscular tails, buried themselves in the bottom sand of hip-deep water in the daytime and moved close to the surf as darkness fell.

One late afternoon a young man walked past me along the beach dangling a revolver in his hand, and I fell in behind him for a while. He said he was hunting stingrays. Many young men, my father among them, often took guns on such haphazard excursions into the countryside, mostly .22 pistols and rifles but also heavier handguns and shotguns, recreationally shooting any living thing they fancied except domestic animals and people. I thought of the stingray hunter as a kind of colleague as I trailed along, a fellow adventurer, and hoped he would find some exciting kind of animal I had not seen, maybe something big. When he had gone around a bend of the littoral and out of sight I heard the gun pop twice in quick succession. Could a bullet from a light handgun penetrate water deep enough to hit a stingray? I think so but never tried it. And I never saw the young marksman again to ask him.

How I longed to discover animals each larger than the last, until finally I caught a glimpse of some true giant! I knew there were large animals out there in deep water. Occasionally a school of bottlenose porpoises passed offshore less than a stone's throw from where I stood. In pairs, trios, and quartets they cut the surface with their backs and dorsal fins, arced down and out of sight, and broke the water again ten or twenty yards farther on. Their repetitions were so rhythmic that I could pick the spot where they would appear next. On calm days I sometimes scanned the glassy surface of Perdido Bay for hours at a time in the hope of spotting something huge and monstrous as it rose to the surface. I wanted at least to see a shark, to watch the fabled dorsal fin thrust proud out of the water, knowing it would look a lot like a porpoise at a distance but would surface and sound at irregular intervals. I also hoped for more than sharks, what exactly I could not say: something to enchant the rest of my life.

Almost all that came in sight were clearly porpoises, but I was not completely disappointed. Before I tell you about the one exception, let me say something about the psychology of monster hunting. Giants exist as a state of the mind. They are defined not as an absolute measurement but as a proportionality. I estimate that when I was seven years old I saw animals at about twice the size I see them now. The bell of a sea nettle averages ten inches across, I know that now; but the one I found seemed two feet across—a grown man's two feet.

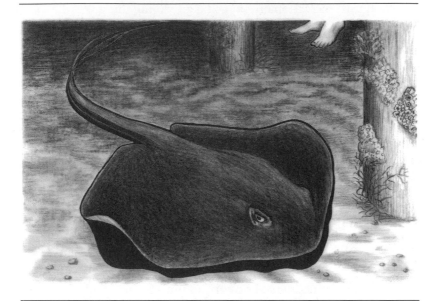

So giants can be real, even if adults don't choose to classify them as such. I was destined to meet such a creature at last. But it would not appear as a swirl on the surface of the open water.

It came close in at dusk, suddenly, as I sat on the dock leading away from shore to the family boathouse raised on pilings in shallow water. In the failing light I could barely see to the bottom, but I stayed perched on the dock anyway, looking for any creature large or small that might be moving. Without warning a gigantic ray, many times larger than the stingrays of common experience, glided silently out of the darkness, beneath my dangling feet, and away into the depths on the other side. It was gone in seconds, a circular shadow, seeming to blanket the whole bottom. I was thunderstruck. And immediately seized with a need to see this behemoth again, to capture it if I could, and to examine it close up. Perhaps, I thought, it lived nearby and cruised around the dock every night.

Late the next afternoon I anchored a line on the dock, skewered a live pinfish on the biggest hook I could find in the house, and let the bait sit in six feet of water overnight. The following morning I rushed out and pulled in the line. The bait was gone; the hook was bare. I repeated the procedure for a week without result, always losing the pinfish. I might have had better luck in snagging a ray if I had used shrimp or crab for bait, but no one gave me this beginner's advice. One morning I pulled in a Gulf toadfish, an omnivorous bottom-dweller with a huge mouth, bulging eyes, and slimy skin. Locals consider the species a trash fish and one of the ugliest of all sea creatures. I thought it was wonderful. I kept my toadfish in a bottle for a day, then let it go. After a while I stopped putting the line out for the great ray. I never again saw it pass beneath the dock.

Why do I tell you this little boy's story of medusas, rays, and sea monsters, nearly sixty years after the fact? Because it illustrates, I think, how a naturalist is created. A child comes to the edge of deep water with a mind prepared for wonder. He is like a primitive adult of long ago, an acquisitive early *Homo* arriving at the shore of Lake Malawi, say, or the Mozambique Channel. The experience must have been repeated countless times over thousands of generations, and it was richly rewarded. The sea, the lakes, and the broad rivers served as sources of food and barriers against enemies. No petty boundaries could split their flat expanse. They could not be burned or eroded into sterile gullies. They were impervious, it seemed, to change of any kind. The waterland was always there, timeless, invulnerable, mostly beyond reach, and inexhaustible. The child is ready to grasp this archetype, to explore and learn, but he has few words to describe his guiding emotions. Instead he is given a compelling image that will serve in later life as a talisman, transmitting a powerful energy that directs the growth of experience and knowledge. He will add complicated details and context from his culture as he grows older. But the core image stays intact. When an adult he will find it curious, if he is at all reflective, that he has the urge to travel all day to fish or to watch sunsets on the ocean horizon.

Hands–on experience at the critical time, not systematic knowl-

edge, is what counts in the making of a naturalist. Better to be an untutored savage for a while, not to know the names or anatomical detail. Better to spend long stretches of time just searching and dreaming. Rachel Carson, who understood this principle well, used different words to the same effect in *The Sense of Wonder* in 1965: "If facts are the seeds that later produce knowledge and wisdom, then the emotions and the impressions of the senses are the fertile soil in

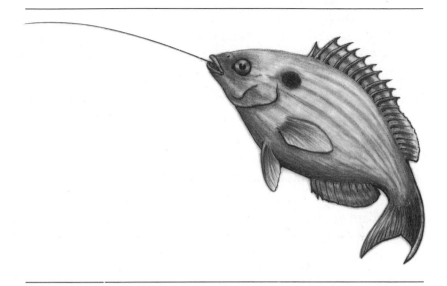

which the seeds must grow. The years of childhood are the time to prepare the soil." She wisely took children to the edge of the sea.

The summer at Paradise Beach was for me not an educational exercise planned by adults, but an accident in a haphazard life. I was parked there in what my parents trusted would be a safe and carefree environment. During that brief time, however, a second accident occurred that determined what kind of naturalist I would eventually become. I was fishing on the dock with minnow hooks and rod, jerking pinfish out of the water as soon as they struck the bait. The species, *Lagodon rhomboides*, is small, perchlike, and voracious. It carries ten needlelike spines that stick straight up in the membrane of the dorsal fin when it is threatened. I carelessly yanked too hard when one of the fish pulled on my line. It flew out of the water and into my face. One of its spines pierced the pupil of my right eye.

The pain was excruciating, and I suffered for hours. But being anxious to stay outdoors, I didn't complain very much. I continued fishing. Later, the host family, if they understood the problem at all

(I can't remember), did not take me in for medical treatment. The next day the pain had subsided into mild discomfort, and then it disappeared. Several months later, after I had returned home to Pensacola, the pupil of the eye began to cloud over with a traumatic cataract. As soon as my parents noticed the change, they took me to a doctor, who shortly afterward admitted me to the old Pensacola Hospital to have the lens removed. The surgery was a terrifying nineteenth-century ordeal. Someone held me down while the anesthesiologist, a woman named Pearl Murphy, placed a gauze nose cone over my nose and mouth and dripped ether into it. Her fee for this standard service, I learned many years later, was five dollars. As I lost consciousness I dreamed I was all alone in a large auditorium. I was tied to a chair, unable to move, and screaming. Possibly I was screaming in reality before I went under. In any case the experience was almost as bad as the cataract. For years afterward I became nauseous at the smell of ether. Today I suffer from just one phobia: being trapped in a closed space with my arms immobilized and my face covered with an obstruction. The aversion is not an ordinary claustrophobia. I can enter closets and elevators and crawl beneath houses and automobiles with aplomb. In my teens and twenties I explored caves and underwater recesses around wharves without fear, just so long as my arms and face were free.

I was left with full sight in the left eye only. Fortunately, that vision proved to be more acute at close range than average—20/10 on the ophthalmologist's chart—and has remained so all my life. I lost stereoscopy but can make out fine print and the hairs on the bodies of small insects. In adolescence I also lost, possibly as the result of a hereditary defect, most of my hearing in the uppermost registers. Without a hearing aid, I cannot make out the calls of many bird and frog species. So when I set out later as a teenager with Roger Tory Peterson's *Field Guide to the Birds* and binoculars in hand, as all true naturalists in America must at one time or other, I proved to be a wretched birdwatcher. I couldn't hear birds; I couldn't locate them unless they obligingly fluttered past in clear view; even one bird singing in a tree close by was invisible unless someone pointed a finger straight at it. The same was true of frogs. On rainy spring nights my college companions could walk to the mating grounds of frogs guided only by the high-pitched calls of the males. I managed a few, such as the deep-voiced barking tree frog, which sounds like someone thumping a tub, and the eastern spadefoot toad, which wails like a soul on its way to perdition; but from most species all I detected was a vague buzzing in the ears.

In one important respect the turning wheel of my life came to a halt at this very early age. I was destined to become an entomologist, committed to minute crawling and flying insects, not by any touch of idiosyncratic genius, not by foresight, but by a fortuitous constriction of physiological ability. I had to have one kind of animal if not another, because the fire had been lit and I took what I could get. The attention of my surviving eye turned to the ground. I would thereafter celebrate the little things of the world, the animals that can be picked up between thumb and forefinger and brought close for inspection.

chapter two

SEND US
THE BOY

WHO CAN SAY WHAT EVENTS FORMED HIS OWN CHARACTER?
Too many occur in the twilight of early childhood. The mind lives in
half-remembered experiences of uncertain valence, where self-
deception twists memory further from truth with every passing
year. But of one event I can be completely sure. It began in the winter
of 1937, when my parents, Edward and Inez Freeman Wilson, separated and began divorce proceedings. Divorce was still unusual at
that time and in that part of the country, and there must have been a
great deal of gossiping and head-shaking among other family mem-

bers. While my parents untangled their lives, they looked for a place that could offer a guarantee of security to a seven-year-old. They chose the Gulf Coast Military Academy, a private school located on the shore road four miles east of Gulfport, Mississippi.

So one January morning I traveled with my mother to Gulfport on a westbound bus out of Pensacola by way of Mobile and Pascagoula. We arrived at GCMA in the afternoon. I looked around and judged the landscape, which was classic leisured-Gulf-Coast, instantly inviting. Brick buildings with verandas and borders crowded by ornamental shrubs were dispersed over beautifully tended grass lawns. Old live oaks (I grant that all live oaks *look* old) and towering loblolly pines offered generous shade. U.S. 90, then a quiet two-lane road, bordered the campus on the south. A few dozen feet beyond, at the bottom of a seawall, peaceful waves rolled in from the Gulf of Mexico. I brightened at this ocean view. Paradise Beach again? It was not to be. We entered the Junior Dormitory to meet the housemother and some of the other grammar-school cadets. I looked at my military-style cot, the kind you can bounce a coin on when properly made. I listened to an outline of the daily regimen. I examined my uniform, patterned after that at West Point. I shook hands with my roommate, who was inordinately stiff and polite for a seven-year-old. All dreams of languor and boyhood adventure vanished.

GCMA was a carefully planned nightmare engineered for the betterment of the untutored and undisciplined. It was a military academy of the original mold, all gray-wool clothed and ramrod-straight. The school prospectus guaranteed—it did not "offer" or "make available"; it *guaranteed*—a solid traditional education. Some of its graduates went on to civilian colleges and universities across the country. But at heart GCMA was a preparatory school for West Point, Annapolis, and private equivalents such as the Virginia Military Academy whose central purpose was to train America's officer corps.

All of this was consistent with white middle-class culture in the

South of 1937. Young men could aspire to no higher calling than officer rank in the military. The South continued her antebellum dream of the officer and gentleman, honorable, brave, unswerving in service to God and country. He comes to our mind, the newly graduated second lieutenant, clad in dress white, escorting his bride, pretty and sweet, out of the church beneath the raised crossed sabers of his classmates, as his proud family watches. His conduct will henceforth affirm the generally understood historical truth that we lost the War Between the States for lack of arms and the exhaustion of battle-depleted troops. Our men, and especially our officers, were nonetheless individually the finest soldiers in the world at that time. They were southerners, men not to be trifled with.

Now you understand why commanding officers interviewed on television at Vietnam firebases so often spoke with southern accents. They had thin lips and highway eyes, and they didn't joke around. Medicine, law, and engineering made admirable careers for a southern man, and business and the ministry were all right of course. Golf champions and quarterbacks who came from Alabama were heroes, and we were all real proud when one of our relatives (his nickname was Skeeter or T. C. or something like that, in any case your third cousin Hank's oldest boy) was elected to Congress. But military command was the profession that bore the cachet of strength and honor.

The Gulf Coast Military Academy was classed each year without fail as an Honor School by the United States War Department. In other words, it was a boot camp. Its regimen was designed to abrade away all the bad qualities inhering in the adolescent male, while building the kind of character that does not flinch at a whiff of grapeshot. "Send Us the Boy and We Will Return the Man" was its motto. The 1937 yearbook, from which my childish face stonily gazes, explains the formula with pitiless clarity:

— The daily work is a systematic routine in which every duty has its place in the day and, therefore, will not be overlooked.

— By association with other cadets, each cadet begins to recognize himself as an integral part of a body and, with this in view, he assumes the correct attitude toward the rights of others.

— By being thrown on his own resources, a boy develops initiative and self-dependence and grows away from the helpless, dependent spirit into which many boys have been coddled.

The systematic routine the author had in mind (and was he, I wonder, square-faced Major Charles W. Chalker, Professor of Military Science and Tactics, whose photograph gazes out at me from the yearbook?) emulated those of the adult service academies. It could be used today, if softened a bit, at the Marine training camp on Parris Island. For seven days a week real bugles, played by cadets proud of their job, led us lockstep through the Schedule. First Call 6:00, Reveille 6:05, Assembly 6:10, Sick Call 6:30, Police Inspection 6:40, Waiter's Warning 6:45, Assembly and March to Mess 7:00, School Call 7:40. Then, without bugles, came calls to change class, Chapel Assembly 10:20, Intermission 4 minutes, Warning Call, Return to Class. And so tramp forward through the day, finally to dinner. The bugles resumed with Call to Quarters 6:50, Study (no radios!) 7:00, Tattoo 9:15, and Taps 9:30. No talking afterward, or you go on delinquency report.

On Saturday the schedule was similar but lighter, with time off for leisure, athletics, and delinquency reports. On Sunday we really snapped to life: shined our shoes, polished our buttons and belt buckles (uniforms mandatory at all times, formal gray and white on Sunday), and attended church. Then we prepared for Battalion Parade, which kicked off at 3:30. We marched out in formation, to be watched and graded by unit and individual, past officer-instructors, visiting parents, and a few curious, respectful townspeople. The youngest boys, of whom I was one, brought up the rear.

The curriculum was laid before the student in resonant single words: arithmetic, algebra, geometry, physics, chemistry, history, English, foreign language. No art, nature field trips, and certainly no enterprises with wimpy titles like "introduction to chemistry" or "the American experience." Some electives were allowed, but only in cheerless subjects such as Latin, commercial geography, and business ethics. There was an implication that if you could not cut the mustard in the military, there was always commerce. Older cadets were trained in rifle marksmanship, mortar and machine-gun fire, surveying, and military strategy. Horsemanship was encouraged. We grammar-school students looked forward to someday enjoying these manly activities.

The school's coat of arms was an Eagle Volant grasping crossed sabers and rifles with bayonets and lances; the shafts of the lances were hung with matched dexter and sinister forty-eight-star American flags. The Navy was represented by a triangular escutcheon enclosing a three-masted barkentine.

All boys at GCMA, from first through twelfth grades, followed the same daily routine and worked their way up the vertically stacked curriculum. We junior cadets, boys in the first six grades, were given a few concessions. There was a dormitory mother, Mrs. R. P. Linfield, whose first name I never knew and whose stiffly composed face in the catalog photographs makes her look exactly like what she was, dormitory mother in a military school. We did not carry a rifle on parade, nor were we trained in weapons and horsemanship. The occasional dances held with young ladies from nearby Gulf Park College were of course irrelevant. In the interests of preserving discipline, parents were urged not to coddle their sons by the dispatching of inappropriate gifts: "Do not send him eatables that will upset his digestion. Send fruit."

Disputes among cadets that could not be talked through were expected to be settled manfully, under adult supervision and in a boxing ring formed by standing cadets. Occasionally fistfights were quietly arranged behind buildings with no instructors or student officers present, but in general all aggression was effectively channeled according to regulations.

Misbehavior of any kind brought time in the bull ring, an activity not mentioned in the brochures. Regular cadets marched with rifles at shoulder arms around a circular track for one to several hours, the length of time depending on the seriousness of the charge. Longer terms were broken up and spread over a succession of days. Junior cadets "marched"—actually, most of the time we just strolled— without rifles. It was a good time to get away from the others and daydream. I was a frequent rule breaker, and spent what seems in retrospect to have been an unconscionable amount of my time at GCMA traveling in circles. As I recall, most of my sins involved talking with other cadets during class. If so, the lesson did not take. Now, as a university professor, I spend almost all of my time talking in class.

In my heart I know that I was a reasonably good kid. I was neither laggard nor rebellious, and time in the bull ring usually came as a surprise. Little or nothing was said to us junior cadets directly about discipline and punishment. We learned mostly by example and word of mouth. Infractions and sentences were posted each Saturday afternoon at 1:50 on the bulletin board next to the mail window, under "Delinquencies." We ran there each time to see who would play and who would march. No further recreation was allowed until all bullring time was completed. We heard rumors of legendary sentences imposed on older boys for unspeakable violations.

Wednesday afternoons were for fun, in the GCMA way of thinking. From 1:30 to 5:30, all cadets free of punishment went on leave. Buses conveyed us the four miles west to Gulfport for milkshakes, movies, and just walking around.

This dollop of frivolity was all well and good, but I pined for my beloved Gulf of Mexico, always in full sight from the front lawn of the Academy. I could not go down to the water; cadets were sensibly forbidden to cross the two-lane highway that separated the school grounds from the seawall and beach. On several occasions toward the end of the term, I joined a group of other boys with the housemother for a supervised swim in the surf. A photograph in the catalog shows us filing down in our regulation swimsuits, complete with shoulder straps. Its caption reads, "Boys going out on the beach under supervision where in the warm sunshine they can frolic on the clean white sand and bathe in the sparkling briny water of the Gulf." No fishing, no time during the frolic to wander dreaming along the strand, no chance to see stingrays or other monsters rising from the deep.

The most notable event during my stay at the Gulf Coast Military

Academy was a visit by President Franklin Delano Roosevelt. Fresh into his second term of office, he came to Mississippi and Louisiana to press the flesh and extend thanks to his constituents in the most solidly Democratic of all the states. Along the coast schools were let out and businesses closed. Storefronts were painted and streets cleaned. Even the "negro kiddies turned out in their best attire," as the *Biloxi-Gulfport Daily Herald* unselfconsciously reported. Upward of 100,000 people converged along the route to be followed by the President and his entourage. In those days chief executives were rarely seen in person, and the New Deal had made Roosevelt a demigod in the Deep South. He brought relief to what was then in many respects a Third World country.

Arriving in Biloxi by train from Washington on the morning of April 29, the President and his staff were escorted to a motorcade of twenty-four cars already packed with local politicians, military officers, and journalists. The party visited Biloxi's high spots, including a lighthouse painted black after Lincoln's assassination, the Veterans Administration Hospital, and Beauvoir, Jefferson Davis' Mississippi home, where a band struck up "Dixie" and the last eight surviving Confederate veterans of the city greeted the President with rebel yells. At frequent intervals Roosevelt lifted his fedora and flashed his famous grin. Finally, the motorcade headed west on U.S. 90 toward Gulfport, passing the Gulf Coast Military Academy at ten o'clock. The entire cadet corps stood at attention in dress gray and white, forming a single line shoulder to shoulder at roadside. Roosevelt at first believed that he was to inspect the corps, and so instructed his military officers to don the formal gold braid worn by presidential aides. On learning that the schedule was too tight to allow a pause of this length, he directed the motorcade instead to slow down as it passed the Academy. We all saluted as the long line of automobiles rolled by. Somehow I failed to distinguish the President among all the passing faces, but I like to think he saw me, standing at the end of the line, one of the two smallest cadets.

To all this strange new life I adjusted reasonably well. For the first

few days after arrival I was seized with confusion and black loneliness, crying myself to sleep when the lights were out—quietly, however, so no one would hear. But after a while I came to feel that I belonged, that GCMA was a family of sorts, one moved by benevolent intention. I hated the place then but came to love it later, savoring it ever more in memory as the years passed and recollections of my distress faded. I stayed just long enough to be transformed in certain qualities of mind. I still summon easily the images of a perfect orderliness and lofty purpose. In one of those least faded, a cadet officer approaches on a Sunday morning as we gather for parade, a teenager mounted on a horse, resplendent in boots, Sam Browne belt, sheathed saber, and a cap cloth-covered in spotless white. He is poised to move in intricate maneuvers. He works his mount slowly through a tight circle, turning, turning, as he speaks to a group of other cadets on foot. He has fallen silent now in my mind, but his visual presence still shines with grace, decent ambition, and high achievement. I ask, What achievement? I cannot say, but no matter; the very ambiguity of his image preserves the power.

I left at the end of the spring term, carrying an inoculum of the military culture. Up to college age I retained the southerner's reflexive deference to elders. Adult males were "sir" and ladies "ma'am," regardless of their station. These salutations I gave with pleasure. I instinctively respect authority and believe emotionally if not intellectually that it should be perturbed only for conspicuous cause. At my core I am a social conservative, a loyalist. I cherish traditional institutions, the more venerable and ritual-laden the better.

All my life I have placed great store in civility and good manners, practices I find scarce among the often hard-edged, badly socialized scientists with whom I associate. Tone of voice means a great deal to me in the course of debate. I try to remember to say "With all due respect" or its equivalent at the start of a rebuttal, and mean it. I despise the arrogance and doting self-regard so frequently found among the very bright.

I have a special regard for altruism and devotion to duty, believing them virtues that exist independent of approval and validation. I am stirred by accounts of soldiers, policemen, and firemen who have died in the line of duty. I can be brought to tears with embarrassing quickness by the solemn ceremonies honoring these heroes. The sight of the Iwo Jima and Vietnam Memorials pierces me for the witness they bear of men who gave so much, and who expected so little in life, and the strength ordinary people possess that held civilization together in dangerous times.

I have always feared I lack their kind of courage. They kept on, took the risk, stayed the course. In my heart I admit I never wanted it; I dreaded the social machine that can grind a young man up, and somehow, irrationally, I still feel that I dropped out. I have tried to compensate to erase this odd feeling. When I was young I made it a habit to test myself physically during field excursions, pushing myself just enough in difficult or dangerous terrain to gain assurance. Later, when I had ideas deemed provocative, I paraded them like a subaltern riding the regimental colors along the enemy line. I asked myself fretfully over and again: Could I have measured up if ever I had been put to a *real* test, with my life at stake, at Château-Thierry or Iwo Jima? Such are the fantasies imposed by egoism and guilt.

I have spent a good deal of time during my career as a scientist thinking about the origins of self-sacrifice and heroism, and cannot say I understand them fully in human terms. The Congressional Medal of Honor I find to be more mysterious and exalting than the Nobel Prize. In leisure reading I browse through the stories of those who won it. I am pleased to know one of them personally, James Stockdale, winner of the Medal of Honor and among this country's most celebrated military heroes. A copy of my book *On Human Nature*, which addresses the biological foundations of altruism and leadership and the possible meaning of the Medal of Honor, rests by his arm in his formal portrait as vice admiral.

Jim Stockdale endured eight years in a North Vietnamese prisoner-of-war camp. During much of that time he was tortured by his captors, who wanted information about his air missions at the time of the Gulf of Tonkin incident. He never broke. Once, feeling that his will might not hold, he slashed his wrists with broken window glass to stop the questioning. The tactic worked; he was given better treatment afterward. All the while, as the senior ranking American officer, he organized his fellow prisoners with secret "tap codes" passed from cell to cell, and pulled them together in semblance of a wartime unit. It would have been as easy to rationalize, to say, I have done my part; I am just a little cog and a forgotten player; why risk my life?

I do not doubt that the steel in Stockdale's spine was put there in

part by the self-discipline and sense of honor the best of the military academies aim to instill. True, the qualities of military heroism can easily be hardened into blind obedience and suborned. But they remain in my eyes the codification of certain virtues necessary for civilization. Their acceptance sacralizes unfurled colors, serried ranks, and ribbons of honor.

You will understand, then, that the people I find it easiest to admire are those who concentrate all the courage and self-discipline they possess toward a single worthy goal: explorers, mountain climbers, ultramarathoners, military heroes, and a very few scientists. Science is modern civilization's highest achievement, but it has few heroes. Most is the felicitous result of bright minds at play. Tricksters of the arcane, devising clever experiments in the laboratory when in the mood, chroniclers of the elegant insight, travelers to seminars in Palo Alto and Heidelberg. For it is given unto you to be bright, and play is one of the most pleasurable of human activities, and all that is well and good; but for my own quite possibly perverse reasons I prefer those scientists who drive toward daunting goals with nerves steeled against failure and a readiness to accept pain, as much to test their own character as to participate in the scientific culture.

One such was Philip Jackson Darlington, for many years Curator in Entomology at Harvard University's Museum of Comparative Zoology. In the spring of 1953, when I was twenty-three and preparing to leave on a collecting trip to Cuba and Mexico, my first into the tropics, I called upon Darlington seeking advice. We met at his cluttered bench in the far corner of the Coleoptera Room.

Phil was held in deep respect by young entomologists. A private and single-minded man, he chose, as his wife, Libbie, once put it, to live an unfragmented life. He devoted his career to the study of beetles and the geographic distribution of animals. He conducted research around the world in an era when foreign travel was difficult and expensive. Darlington was a collector of legendary prowess, unmatched in the field. He would zero in on just the right habitat, then toil hour after hour, day after day and sometimes into the evenings, to bottle hundreds of specimens, many belonging to species rare or new to science. If his scholarly interests seem recondite, it should be recalled that Charles Darwin was also an impassioned beetle collector with a special interest in the geographic distribution of animals.

Darlington was pleased to see me but not inclined to waste words. His manner was professional and reserved, eased by a frequent ironic smile and pursed lips—the scholar's look. He had thick, black eyebrows that sheltered his eyes, pulled attention slightly upward, and made it easier to hold contact with his face as he spoke. He came quickly to the point.

"Ed, don't stay on the trails when you collect insects. Most people take it too easy when they go in the field. They follow the trails and work a short distance into the woods. You'll get only some of the species that way. You should walk in a straight line through the forest. Try to go over any barrier you meet. It's hard, but that's the best way to collect."

He then mentioned some good collecting spots he had worked himself, described the best way to drink Cuban coffee, and the interview was over.

It was exactly what I wanted to hear. How to do it the right way, the *hard* way. Words from a master to chosen disciple: grit, work, determination, some pain, and new species—success—await the tough-minded. No admonitions to watch my health or to have a good time in Havana. Just collect in straight lines and get it right. Bring back the good stuff to the M.C.Z.

As a young man Darlington lived that advice. He climbed the Sierra Nevada de Santa Marta of northern Colombia, collecting all along the 6,000 meters of elevation. He toiled up in an almost straight line to the summit of Pico Turquino, Cuba's highest mountain, in the Sierra Maestra, the backcountry made famous by Fidel Castro's guerrilla campaign of the 1950s. Darlington repeated the feat on La Hotte, Haiti's highest peak, in the remote massif of the Tiburon Peninsula. He covered the last 1,000 meters of elevation alone, cutting his way straight through the undergrowth of virgin cloud forest, twisting his body through narrow breaks between tree trunks. At the summit he was disappointed to find that a team of Danish surveyors had already ascended the opposite slope, hacked out a clearing, and set up cloth targets for their transects. He had supposed that this would be the wildest spot in Haiti, free and safe for a while from the teeming human population below. He hoped in any case that rare endangered native mammals, possibly new to science, might still live on the summit. That night he searched for them with a jacklight and found none. All that appeared was one black rat, an Old World species accidentally introduced to the West Indies in early European cargo and the scourge of the native fauna. But the trip was rewarding just the same. Darlington was indeed the first biologist to visit the top. While working across La Hotte's upper slopes he collected many new kinds of insects and other animals, including a new genus of snakes, later named *Darlingtonia* in his honor.

His adventures continued. Shortly after Pearl Harbor, Darlington enlisted in the Army Sanitary Corps Malaria Survey as a first lieutenant. He served in the Sixth Army during the campaigns on New Guinea, Bismarck Archipelago, central Philippines, and Luzon, retiring as a major in 1944. Before leaving New Guinea, he managed to collect great numbers of ground beetles and other insects in several regions of the country, including the summit of Mount Wilhelm, the highest peak in the Bismarck Range.

One Darlington exploit from that adventure has become a standard of zoology lore. Alone in the jungle looking for specimens, he ventured out on a submerged log to sample water from the middle of a stagnant jungle pool, when a giant crocodile rose from the depths and swam toward him. As he edged back gingerly toward shore, he slipped from the slimy log into the water. The crocodile rushed him, mouth gaping, huge teeth bared. He tried to grasp its jaws, got one grip, then lost it.

"I can't describe the horror of that instant," he told an Army reporter at the time, "but I was scared and I kept thinking: What a hell of a predicament for a naturalist to be in."

The thirty-nine-year-old Darlington was six feet two inches tall and weighed 190 pounds; the crocodile, weighing several hundred pounds, was in its element. It spun him over and over, finally carrying him to the bottom.

"Those few seconds seemed hours," he said. "I kicked, but it was like trying to kick in a sea of molasses. My legs seemed heavy as lead, and it was hard to force my muscles to respond." Whether because of a well-placed kick or for some other reason, the animal suddenly opened its jaws, and Darlington swam free. Flailing his legs and torn arms, he made the shore, scrambled frantically up the bank, and tried to keep going, knowing that crocodiles sometimes pursue prey onto land. At the last moment he slipped in the mud and rolled back again toward the water. The predator closed once again.

"It was a nightmare. That's the first time I've ever hollered for help," he said. "But there was no one to hear me." He scrambled up the bank again and this time made it into the shelter of the jungle. Only then did he become aware of the pain in his arms and his weakness from loss of blood. "That hike to the hospital, which I knew was nearby, was the longest I've ever made." The muscles and ligaments of both arms were lacerated, and bones in his right arm were crushed. The crocodile's teeth had also pierced both his hands. Only his left arm and hand were marginally functional.

I grant that to fight off a crocodile is an act of survival, not proof of character. But to go where crocodiles live is, and especially to do what Darlington did next. He was in a cast for several months, convalescing at Dobadura, Papua. But nothing could stop this driven man. He perfected a left-handed technique for collecting insects. Have someone tie a vial to the end of a stick. Walk out into the forest, jam the stick into the ground, pull the cork out with the left hand, drop the specimens into the vial, replace the cork. Over several months he eventually regained full use of his hands and arms, pursuing his collecting and research all the while. He was able during that time to assemble a world-class collection. After returning to Harvard he continued to work year after year, expanding our knowledge of the insects of New Guinea and other parts of the world.

The standards I use for my heroes were first implanted by a tough military academy, whose instructors believed that little boys should be treated essentially like big boys. It was an accident of timing with an odd result. I thought the academy presaged real life. For the rest of my childhood and through adolescence I assumed, despite mounting evidence to the contrary, that hard work and punishingly high standards are demanded of all grown men, that life is tough and unforgiving, that slipups and disgrace are irreparable.

31

This ethic stirs faint and deep within me even now, although I know it is not entirely reasonable. Nothing will change. There are certain experiences in childhood that surge up through the limbic system to preempt the thinking brain and hold fast for a lifetime to shape value and motivation. For better or for worse, they are what we call character.

I have told you of two such early formative experiences, the embracing of Nature and military discipline in turn, very different from each other in quality and strangely juxtaposed. There were three such episodes during my early childhood. I now come to the last, which in the genesis of a scientist may seem the most peculiar of them all.

chapter three

A LIGHT IN
THE CORNER

ON A SUNDAY MORNING IN JANUARY 1944, I SAT ALONE IN A
back pew of Pensacola's First Baptist Church. The service was almost over. The pastor, Dr. Wallace Roland Rogers, walked from the
pulpit to the center aisle, raised his arms with palms turned up, and
began to intone the Invitation:

> Won't you come? Jesus is calling; Jesus is our friend; let us weep with Him;
> let us rejoice with Him in knowledge of everlasting life.

As he repeated the cantorial phrases with variations, a familiar
hymn rose from the organ behind him in muted reinforcement. The

congregation did not need to sing the words. They are graven in the hearts of every born-again Baptist. Loved like scripture, the text teaches the suffering and redemption of evangelistic Christianity.

> *On a hill far away stood an old rugged cross,*
> *the emblem of suffering and shame.*
> *And I love that old cross where the dearest and best*
> *For a world of lost sinners was slain.*

Rogers as I beheld him was a dignified, friendly man in his mid-forties, with the broad, open face, the steel-rimmed glasses, the quick smile of a Rotary Club president. A leader of the Pensacola community, he was also much respected at the nearby naval air base for his religious leadership during the early months of the war. He was a builder of his church, a warm but disciplinarian friend of youth, a crusader against alcohol and legalized gambling, and a surprising progressive in a racist city in racist times. He represented northwest Florida actively in the national affairs of the Southern Baptist Conference. His sermons and lectures were intelligent and well crafted.

This morning as always the service began at eleven, and as always the choir and congregation rose to sing the Doxology: *Praise God from whom all blessings flow*. Rogers offered a prayer, and we sang another hymn. The congregation resumed their seats. Then came announcements from the pastor, of parish news, special church events, and the names of ill members to be included in the prayers of the congregation. A second hymn followed, and a welcome to visitors. Ushers proceeded down the aisle to collect the offering, with organ music in the background. Next the choir sang; then a soloist rendered "Amazing Grace," in achingly pure soprano. The hymn captured the central theme of redemption: *How precious did that Grace appear, The hour I first believed*.

Finally Rogers rose to deliver the sermon, starting, in traditional form, with a reading from the Bible.

Sorrowful, yet always rejoicing; poor, yet making many rich; having nothing, yet possessing everything.

Second Corinthians, chapter 6, verse 10. After the reading he told a story, lightly humorous in tone as usual, this one about two young farm boys who had come to the big city in order to enlist. Having risen as was their habit just before daybreak, they were wandering somewhat bewildered through the still-empty city streets between tall buildings, lost, unable to find anyone for directions. One turned to the other and said, "Where do you reckon they all go in the morning?"

The congregation chuckled in appreciation. The sermon had been personalized, brought to earth. We were now relaxed, in friendly contact. Rogers paused, grew serious. He began the homily, leading off from the quoted scripture and his story. We Americans, like these boys, may be simple people, he intoned; we may be innocent, but we are winning the war, because this country was founded on faith in God and Christian values, on the pioneers' courage in adversity, and on a willingness to sacrifice for others. If the cause is just, if Jesus is truly in our hearts, no one can stop us. That is the way it was with the disciples, simple men who left all behind them and abandoned all their material desires to suffer unto death if need be in the name of Jesus Christ. They were not the mighty rulers of Rome or rich Sadducees of Jerusalem. They were not men of steel and power. But they changed the world! They came as little children in their hearts to serve the Lord.

And Jesus said, Whosoever shall not receive the Kingdom of God as a little child, he shall not enter therein. And Jesus said, Except a man be born again, he cannot see the Kingdom of God. And Jesus said, over and over, to each of us, Hold fast till I come.

Now came the Invitation, the call to those not yet saved and those who wished to reaffirm their fellowship in Jesus Christ. Several rose in response and walked forward down the aisle. They shook the pastor's hand, took his embrace, and turned to pray with the congregation. There were tears in their eyes. I was one of them, fourteen years old, able and ready to make this important decision on my own. The choir sang "In the Garden," sweetly, adagio,

> And He walks with me, and He talks with me,
> And He tells me I am His own,
> And the joy we share as we tarry there,
> None other has ever known.

Evangelical Protestantism does not waste time with philosophy. It speaks straight to the heart. The message draws power from the simplicity of the story of Christ expressed as a mythic progression. From the pain and humiliation of earthly existence, the soul can be redeemed by union with the sacred fellowship and thereby enter eternal life in heaven.

Instruction and ritual are minimal, belief all. Jesus is with you al-

ways, in the spirit; He waits to comfort you. He will return in the flesh on the appointed day, which will be soon, perhaps in our lifetime. Our Lord is the incarnation of the fellowship and the perfect eternal patriarch. Suffer the little children to come unto me, He said, and hinder them not. Of the Trinity, He is the personal God. Each Christian must find Him individually, out of free choice, and be guided thereafter by readings of the Bible and in communion with others who have also found Grace. The Southern Baptists have no bishops. The pastor can do no more than advise and lead. Members of the congregation form the priesthood of the believer. They learn to speak in a scripture-laced discourse called the language of Zion.

The service codifies the morals of the believers. It makes explicit what the consensus holds to be decent and right. But it is much more, and those who do not grasp that added dimension will always underestimate religious faith. It catches the *power*. It is the parabolic mirror that bends the rays of tribalism to one white-hot focus: Saved by Jesus Christ, united in the fellowship of the Lord. Born again!

There was no question I would be raised in this faith, which is today shared by 15 million people in the United States and ranks second in numbers only to Roman Catholicism. Virtually all my forebears on both sides of the family as far back as the mid-1800s, close to the founding of the denomination in 1845, were Southern Baptists. All lived in Alabama and Georgia, the fundamentalist Bible Belt. Theirs was an activist religion. How well I remember sitting as a six-year-old in the Sunday School class, held at the Pensacola First Baptist Church just before service, learning to sing the heart-thumping refrain,

> *Onward, Christian soldiers, marching as to war,*
> *With the cross of Jesus going on before.*

When I was sprung from the Gulf Coast Military Academy in the summer of 1937, my religious training acquired a new dimension. I was now eight years old. My parents had separated and divorced. My relationship with my mother, who retained custody, remained loving and close, but the divorce had shorn her of support. Pensacola was gripped by the Depression, and times were hard. My mother found work as a secretary, but the wages were marginal, and it was several years before she acquired the additional training and experience to move to a better job. During that first year she placed me in the care of a trusted family friend.

Belle Raub, Mother Raub as I quickly came to call her, lived on

East Lee Street in Pensacola with her husband, E. J., a retired carpenter. She was a heavyset, bosomy woman in her late fifties. She eschewed makeup and favored long, floral-print dresses. She wore a cougar-claw pendant that I found fascinating. ("Where did you get it? Where are cougars found? What do they do?" Monsters of the land.)

Mother Raub was in fact the perfect grandmother. She was forever cheerily working in and around the house, from before I woke in the morning to after I fell asleep, gardening, cleaning, cooking, and crocheting spokewheel-patterned bedspreads that she gave to friends and neighbors. She was attentive to my every need and listened carefully to every story of my life, which I considered to have been both long and filled with meaning. I gave her no problems with my manners or discipline; the Gulf Coast Military Academy had taken care of that.

Mother Raub had edged the porch with a small botanic garden of ornamental plants. I set out to learn the many kinds as best she could teach me. I found the living environment fascinating: elephant-ear arums the size of kitchen tables sprang from the soil along the front of the porch; a persimmon tree next to the street yielded winter fruit; and in the vacant lot behind the Raub property, second-growth turkey oaks formed a miniature forest. All this and the surrounding neighborhood I enthusiastically explored, freed from the twenty-four-hour discipline of the military school.

I acquired a black cat and planted a small garden of my own in the backyard. In a soft sandy spot nearby I began to dig a hole to China or to wherever else the shaft might lead, a project never completed. I learned the joy of fried grits at breakfast time: Mother Raub indulged me in this and in all other things. E. J., who had a drinking problem and was periodically scolded by his wife, was kindly in a gruff, distracted way.

In the fall I entered the nearby Agnes McReynolds Elementary School, located beyond the vacant lot and one block west, each day

carrying my lunch of a sandwich and banana in a tin pail and finding, miraculously, that by noon the banana was always squashed and oozing out of its skin onto the bottom.

Soon judged by my teacher at Agnes McReynolds to be too advanced for the third grade, I was given a written test and skipped to the fourth. This was a serious misdetermination for me socially. I was already small for my age, and growing more shy and introverted all the time. For the rest of my school years I was destined to be the runt of my class. (Upon entering Murphy High School in Mobile four years later, I was the only boy still wearing short pants. I soon switched to the brown corduroy knickers then in vogue, the ones whose legs rubbed together and squeaked when you walked.)

Mother Raub was a Methodist, not a Baptist. This meant that the services she and E. J. attended weekly, after dropping me off at the First Baptist Church, were a bit more sedate and less evangelical. She was nothing, however, if not a fierce moralist in the stricter Methodist tradition. Smoking, drinking, and gambling were in her eyes among the gravest of sins. She was undoubtedly aware that my father zealously overindulged in all these vices. She asked me to swear that I would never in my whole life give in to the same temptations, and I gladly agreed. It was easy: eight-year-old boys then were not prone to vices beyond occasionally betting marbles on games of mumblety-peg. In the nearly sixty years since I have kept my promise, except for the odd glass of wine or beer with meals—not because of piety, but rather because I don't much care for the taste of the stuff, and, at a deeper and probably more cogent level, because of the later downward spiral of my father's life as a result of alcoholism, which I witnessed with helpless despair.

Mother Raub was a woman with a steadfast heart and a mystic soul. Holiness was for her a state to be ardently sought. She told me a story about a very religious friend who wished to unite with Jesus through prayer. One day this good woman looked up from her devotions and saw a strange light in the room. It was a sign from God.

"Where in the room?" I interrupted.

"Well, in the corner."

"Where in the corner?"

"Well . . . in the upper part of the corner, next to the ceiling."

My mind raced. Her friend had seen God! Or, at least, she had received a Sign. Therefore, she must have been a chosen person. Maybe the light gives you the answer to everything, whatever that is. It was the *Grail*! The leap was possible if you prayed in some special way.

So I prayed long and hard many evenings after that, glancing around occasionally to see if the light had arrived or if any other change had occurred in the room. Nothing happened. I decided I just wasn't up to bringing God into my life, at least not yet. I would have to wait, maybe grow a little more.

At the end of that school year I left Mother Raub, this time to rejoin my father. My interest in the mysterious light faded. Perhaps (I cannot remember exactly) I stopped believing altogether in the existence of the light. But I never lost faith in the immanence of the Lord. He would come soon as a light unto the world.

In the fall of 1943, when I was fourteen, I came back to spend another year with Belle Raub. I was old enough to be baptized and born again by my own free will. No one counseled me to take this step; I could have waited for years before the weekly altar call struck home. One evening it just happened. Mother Raub and I had walked over to the McReynolds School to attend a recital of gospel hymns sung a cappella by a traveling tenor soloist. I have forgotten his repertoire as a whole. But one song, delivered in measured, somber tones, deeply moved me. It was a dissonant piece that gripped the listener in Pentecostal embrace:

> *Were you there when they crucified my Lord?*
> *Were you there when they nailed Him to the cross?*
> *Sometimes it makes me to tremble, tremble.*
> *Were you there when they crucified my Lord?*

An otherwise restless and free-spirited adolescent, I wept freely in response to the tragic evocation. I wanted to do something decisive. I felt emotion as though from the loss of a father, but one retrievable by redemption through the mystic union with Christ—that is, if you believed, if you really believed; and I did so really believe, and it was time for me to be baptized.

Dressed in my Sunday clothes and accompanied by Mother Raub, I called on the Reverend Wallace Rogers at the First Baptist Church to announce my decision and to select a time for baptism. For a teenager to meet the pastor of a large congregation was an exceptional event. I was tense and nervous as we walked into Rogers' office. He rose from his desk to greet us.

He was dressed in sports clothes and *smoking a cigar*. A cigar! In his friendly, casual way he congratulated me on my decision, and together we chose a date for the baptism. I filled out the application form as he watched and drew on his cigar. Mother Raub said nothing, then or later, about his transgression. But I knew what was on her mind!

One Sunday evening in February 1944, I stood in the line of the newly converted in a room behind the pulpit. While the congregation watched, we came out one by one to join the pastor in a large tank of chest-deep water in the choir loft at the front of the church. I was dressed in a light gown over my undershorts. When my turn came Rogers recited the baptismal dedication and bent me over once like a ballroom dancer, backward and downward, until my entire body and head dipped beneath the surface.

Later, as I dried off and rejoined the congregation, I reflected on how totally physical, how somehow common, the rite of passage had been, like putting on swimming trunks and jumping off the tower at the Pensacola Bay bathhouse the way it was done in 1943, letting your toes squish in the bottom mud for a moment before you kicked back up to the surface. I had felt embarrassed and uncomfortable during the baptism itself. Was the whole world completely physical, after all? I worried over Dr. Rogers' comfortable clothing and cigar. And something small somewhere cracked. I had been holding an exquisite, perfect spherical jewel in my hand, and now, turning it over in a certain light, I discovered a ruinous fracture.

The still faithful might say I never truly knew grace, never had it; but they would be wrong. The truth is that I found it and abandoned it. In the years following I drifted away from the church, and my attendance became desultory. My heart continued to believe in the light and the way, but increasingly in the abstract, and I looked for grace in some other setting. By the time I entered college at the age of seventeen, I was absorbed in natural history almost to the exclusion of everything else. I was enchanted with science as a means of ex-

43

plaining the physical world, which increasingly seemed to me to be the complete world. In essence, I still longed for grace, but rooted solidly on Earth.

My fictional heroes in late adolescence were the protagonists of *Arrowsmith*, *The Sea Wolf*, and *Martin Eden*, the Nietzschean loners and seekers. I read Trofim D. Lysenko's *Heredity and Its Variability*, a theory officially sanctioned by Stalin as sound Marxist-Leninist doctrine, and wrote an excited essay about it for my high school science class. Imagine, I scribbled, if Lysenko was right (and he must be, because otherwise why would traditional geneticists be up in arms against him?), biologists could change heredity in any direction they wished! It was rank pseudoscience, of course, but I didn't know it at the time. And I didn't care by then; I had tasted the sweet fruit of intellectual rebellion.

I was exhilarated by the power and mystery of nuclear energy. Robert Oppenheimer was another far-removed science hero. I was especially impressed by a *Life* magazine photograph of him in a porkpie hat taken as he spoke with General Leslie Groves at ground zero following the first nuclear explosion. Here was Promethean intellect triumphant. Oppenheimer was a slight man, as I was a slight boy. He was vulnerable in appearance like me, but smilingly at ease in the company of a general; and the two stood there together because the physicist was master of arcane knowledge that had tamed for human use the most powerful force in nature.

Shortly afterward, during my first year at college, someone lent me a book that was creating a sensation among biologists, Erwin Schrödinger's *What Is Life?* The great scientist argued not only that life was entirely a physical process, but that biology could be explained by the principles of physics and chemistry. Imagine: biology transformed by the same mental effort that split the atom! I fantasized being Schrödinger's student and joining the great enterprise. Then, as an eighteen-year-old sophomore, I read Ernst Mayr's *Systematics and the Origin of Species*. It was a cornerstone of the Modern Synthesis of evolutionary theory, one of the books that combined genetics with Darwin's theory of evolution by natural selection. Mayr's writing reinforced in my mind the philosophy implicit in Schrödinger. He showed that variety among plants and animals is created through stages that can be traced by the study of ordinary nature around us. Mayr's text told me that I could conduct scientific research of a high order with the creatures I already knew and loved. I didn't need to journey to a faraway place and sit at the feet of a Schrödinger or a Mayr in order to enter the temple of science.

Science became the new light and the way. But what of religion? What of the Grail, and the revelation of purest ray serene that gives wholeness and meaning to life? There must be a scientific explanation for religion, moral precepts, the rites of passage, and the craving for immortality. Religion, I knew from personal experience, is a perpetual fountainhead of human emotion. It cannot be dismissed as superstition. It cannot be compartmentalized as the manifestation of some separate world. From the beginning I never could accept that science and religion are separate domains, with fundamentally different questions and answers. Religion had to be explained as a material process, from the bottom up, atoms to genes to the human spirit. It had to be embraced by the single grand naturalistic image of man.

That conviction still grips me, impelled and troubled as I am by emotions I confess I do not even now fully understand. There was one instructive moment when the subterranean feelings surfaced without warning. The occasion was the visit of Martin Luther King Sr. to Harvard in January 1984. He came under the auspices of a foundation devoted to the improvement of race relations at the university. Its director, Allen Counter, an old friend with a similar Southern Baptist background, invited me to attend a service conducted by the father of the martyred civil rights leader, and to join a small group at a reception afterward.

It was the first Protestant service I had sat through in forty years.

It was held in Harvard's Memorial Church. Reverend King gave a quiet hortatory address organized around scripture and moral principle. He omitted the altar call—this was, after all, Harvard. But at the end a choir of black Harvard students surprised me by singing a medley of old-time gospel hymns, with a professionalism equaling anything I ever heard in the churches of my youth. To my even greater surprise, I wept quietly as I listened. My people, I thought. My people. And what else lay hidden deep within my soul?

chapter four

A MAGIC KINGDOM

COME BACK WITH ME NOW TO OCTOBER 1935, TO PENSA-
cola, for a walk up Palafox Street. Let's start by peeking over the seawall that closes the south end of the street. Down there on the rocks,
kept wet and alga-covered by the softly lapping water of the bay, sits
a congregation of grapsid crabs. They resemble large black spiders,
with crustaceous skins, carapaces the size of silver dollars, and claw-
like legs that spread straight out from the sides of the body. They rest
on needle-tipped feet, alert and ready to sprint forward, backward,

or sideways at the slightest disturbance. Drop a pebble among them, and those closest to impact scurry for cover.

Let's turn and stroll north along the street, just looking around. On the right is the Childs Restaurant, where the courthouse crowd gathers for lunch. Stop for a moment and pass your hand through the light beam across the entrance. The door swings open, a miracle of modern technology. Do it again; this time let the couple waiting behind you walk on through. People don't seem to mind kids' playing with the beam. A little farther along is the Saenger Theater, Pensacola's premier palace of pleasure, in summer "cooled by iced air." This Saturday's matinee bill is an episode of the Flash Gordon serial (Flash escapes from the lair of the fire dragon), followed by Errol Flynn in *Captain Blood*. You've seen the feature; there's a scary scene near the end in which Flynn skewers Basil Rathbone in a duel on the treasure island, and the treacherous French pirate falls dying in the surf.

This section of lower Palafox, west to Reus and east to Adams, is the busy part of town. Model A Fords are on the street, a pretty good crowd of shoppers on the sidewalks. Be careful when you cross Romana Street up ahead; a kid on a bicycle got run over there last year; that's what they told me.

It's hot, as always. North Florida is still a tropical place in the early fall. Afternoon thunderheads are gathering to the south and west across the bay. No breeze has kicked in yet; the air hangs heavy and moist and laced with engine fumes. Let's cross Palafox over to the courthouse, on your left. On the lawn next to the sidewalk a fire ant colony is swarming. The ants are pouring out of a mound nest, here no more than an irregular pile of dirt partly flattened by the last pass of a lawnmower. Winged queens and males are taking off on their nuptial flight, protected by angry-looking workers that run up and down the grass blades and out onto the blistering-hot concrete of the sidewalk. The species is unmistakably *Solenopsis geminata*, the native fire ant, I can tell you now. Another fifteen years will pass before the

infamous *Solenopsis invicta*, imported from South America, will spread this far east from its point of introduction, Mobile, Alabama. I'll be here as a college student to watch that happen.

Walk a few more blocks, on past the old San Carlos Hotel (they've torn it down since), and cut left on West Gregory Street. My parents' apartment, one of two on the second floor of a stucco Spanish-style building, is several blocks farther down. There is a large live oak in the side yard where bluejays land and shriek at one another. Their call

49

is like a fire engine's siren, always announcing some emergency or other.

On the sidewalk (please turn your gaze downward occasionally and look with me for insects on the ground) lion ants of the genus *Dorymyrmex* run like whirligigs on the stove-hot surface. Crush one, and the unmistakable smell of a dolichoderine ant hits your nose. I can tell you now that the odor of this species comes from a mix of heptanone and methylheptenone, secretions from the pygidial glands the workers use to defend the colony against enemies and alarm nestmates to approaching danger.

Forty years later I will return to within a few feet of this exact spot. I will get down on my knees (an elderly black man passing by will ask me if I need help) and look again for the lion ants. The dirt and cracked concrete slabs will look the same, but this time the ants running around will be *Pheidole dentata*, which lack a strong odor. Same thing fifteen years later. I'll keep coming here from time to time whenever I visit Pensacola, to see if the *Dorymyrmex* have returned to this special square yard or two of space. So far, my surveillance has lasted for nearly sixty years; if I am fortunate, it will last for eighty. Meanwhile, I can tell you that the ant present in 1935 was a *Dorymyrmex*.

You will think this a strange journey and a stranger obsession, but not I. Consider how long-term memory works. With each changing moment, the mind scans a vast landscape of jumbled schemata, searching for the one or two decisive details upon which rational action will be based. The mind with a search image is like a barracuda. The large predatory fish pays scant attention to the rocks, pilings, and vast array of organisms living among them. It waits instead for a glint of silver that betrays the twisting body of a smaller fish. It locks on this signal, rushes forward, and seizes the prey in its powerful jaws. Its singlemindedness is why swimmers are advised not to wear shiny bracelets or wrist watches in barracuda waters.

The human mind moving in a sea of detail is compelled like a questing animal to orient by a relatively few decisive configurations. There is an optimum number of such signals. Too few, and the person becomes compulsive-obsessive; too many, and he turns schizophrenic. Configurations with the greatest emotional impact are stored first and persist longer. Those that give the greatest pleasure are sought on later occasions. The process is strongest in children, and to some extent it programs the trajectory of their lives. Eventually they will weave the decisive images into a narrative by which they explain to themselves and others the meaning of what has happened to them. As the Talmud says, we see things not as they are, but as we are.

Our remembered images are reinforced like pictures improved by one overlay upon the next, each adding finer detail. In the process edges are sharpened, content refined, emotional colors nuanced. In this way, for me Pensacola on a hot autumn day in 1935 has evolved into a network of vividly remembered small animals. There is a backdrop of people, streets, a theater marquee, and houses; but although these parts of my world were important then, they have faded since.

I was a normal boy, within reason. I had friends, played rough-and-tumble games in the yard of nearby P. K. Yonge Elementary School, was ashamed and tearful when kept after class for misbehavior, had a wonderful Christmas that year, obeyed my parents but had to be forced to eat asparagus, and in the gentle Gulf winter, when leaves had fallen and a scum of paper-thin ice coated the gutter puddles, I searched the ground with other boys for pecans and chinquapins. But sixty years have drained these memories of most of their importance, and the fine details and emotional force have largely eroded away to nothing.

They have done so, and natural history has been reinforced, because at an early age I resolved to become a naturalist and a scientist. And I took that course in part, if there must be an explanation, because I was an only child who lived something of a gypsy's existence.

NATURALIST

My mother had legal custody, and we were to remain thereafter very close, but she allowed my father, who had a better job, to care for me on a provisional basis. He remarried in 1938. I acquired a devoted stepmother named Pearl, and the temporary arrangement was extended. My father, a government accountant, for some reason preferred road assignments. He began an odyssey across the southeastern United States, changing his job and the location of his home every year or two. My itinerary from the fourth grade to high school graduation circled round and about the South as follows: Pensacola, Mobile, Orlando, Atlanta, the District of Columbia, Evergreen (Alabama), back to Mobile, back to Pensacola, and finally Brewton and Decatur in Alabama, with intervening summer sojourns in Boy Scout camps and homes of friends in Alabama, Florida, Virginia, and Maryland. Over eleven years I attended fourteen different public schools. In the summer before I started college we finally came back to Mobile, my father's birthplace, which he had said earlier he hated and had "taken off the map"; but now he changed his mind, and it was there he was to remain until he died, in 1951.

A nomadic existence made Nature my companion of choice, because the outdoors was the one part of my world I perceived to hold rock steady. Animals and plants I could count on; human relationships were more difficult. With each move I had to insert myself into a new group of peers, mostly boys. At first, before my father remarried, we lived in boardinghouses, from which I ventured cautiously. In Orlando, our first port of call, I avoided schoolmates for a few weeks, out of fear. I conversed silently with myself, creating three boys in my head: I, me, and myself. I rescued bits of Spanish moss that had fallen to the ground and replaced them on the low branches of the schoolyard oaks. They were my friends, I thought; but the emotion I felt was self-pity.

I studied plants and insects around the streets of Orlando, a beautiful little city in 1938. I kept harvester ants in a jar of sand under my bed and watched them excavate. I discovered fairy tales in the school

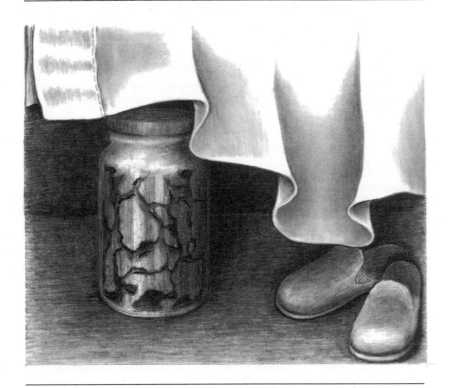

library, and took to reading every one I could find. I was transfixed by the magical choices between grisly death or eternal happiness. I did well in class, and came close to winning the school spelling bee ("Indain" instead of "Indian" was my undoing, still burned on my brain). No one paid any attention to my eccentricities. There were no programs for gifted or disturbed children in those days.

Nor was there any educational theory in 1938 to suggest that loneliness in a beautiful environment might be a good if risky way to create a scientist, at least a field biologist. After a few weeks in Orlando I discovered to my joy that one of the city lakes was within walking distance. I started fishing there for minnows and bream, taking care with the hook I baited and the fins of the fish I caught to protect the one eye I had left after the accident at Paradise Beach. I spent hours admiring a large alligator gar held captive in a cement pool in the small waterfront park. I went back and forth to the lake alone, keeping my own company and organizing my thoughts. Lantana hedges, laden grapefruit trees, and men in Panama hats still float through my surviving memories.

In towns and cities we settled in later I learned how to adapt more quickly in my perpetual role as new kid on the block. Once, early on in Mobile, I pretended to be deaf and dumb until I had a small, fascinated group of boys and girls following me in an attempt to read my ersatz sign language. When I admitted the hoax, all was well. They were relieved, and still fascinated enough to make me a popular new member of the gang. Usually I approached the problem straight on, by working myself into baseball games as an extra, or talking with other boys I saw standing alone at the edges of the schoolyard or lunchroom.

My worst difficulties came from the fistfights. They were merciless and brutal. I suspect that most adults, especially those reared in middle-class suburbs, cannot bring themselves to acknowledge the innate savagery of preadolescent boys. From the ages of nine to fourteen they are naturally predisposed to set up blockwide territories, run in gangs, and bully to gain acceptance, to swagger, boast, dare, and call back and forth to one another in the loud honking voices of emerging male adolescence. Strange kids in the neighborhood, especially those without brothers or parents in view, are fair game. In the South of the 1930s and 1940s—here I have enough experience to speak like a sociologist—there was a certain protocol to the combat. One boy, usually the local bully or the "champion" of a group, challenged another boy, usually the newcomer. The fight was held after school in some secluded spot in the neighborhood where both lived. It was stand-up combat with fists, fought the way we saw Joe Louis do it in the newsreels. Except there were no rounds, and no conclusion until one boy gave up or an adult broke in. Word got around in advance, and a circle of boys gathered to hoot the pugilists on.

"One of 'em's scared and the other's glad of it!"

"Hey, that was just a love tap; wait'll he gets goin'."

Most of the fights I watched, I was in, maybe a dozen up to the age of fourteen. After that time boys of my age found other outlets for aggression, most commonly football or hunting. I can recall these battles like a sports historian ticking off rounds in the Dempsey-Tunney fight. I was deeply anxious about challenges, especially in a new neighborhood, and tried to steer clear of the more aggressive-seeming boys, always without success. My father told me never to back down, and the Gulf Coast Military Academy ethos forbade it. It was unmanly to refuse a fight. I did decline, however, twice, because the boys were too big to beat, and with a gang and from different schools anyway, and I knew I wouldn't see them again. I retreated before their taunts, to my everlasting shame. It is ridiculous, of course, but I still burn a little when I think about my cowardice. I never picked a fight. But once started I never quit, even when losing, until the other boy gave up or an adult mercifully pulled us apart.

"Hey, hey, he's had enough!"

"Okay, okay, let's stop; I wanna stop."

"This is a lot of shit, anyhow. I got to get home."

I couldn't stop. Somehow I felt that, having invested this much of my limited store of courage to take on a challenge, I must never throw it all away and suffer the added shame of losing. My face was sometimes a bloody mess; I still carry old lip and brow split scars, like a used-up club fighter. Even my father, proud that I was acting "like a little man," seemed taken aback. But later I savored the memories of my combat, and especially the victories. There is no finer sight on green Earth than a defeated bully.

My childhood was nevertheless relatively serene. Most of the time I simply found a best friend in new neighborhoods, a boy the same age and physical size who enjoyed riding bikes and exploring the nearest woods for snakes and insects. I was drawn to conspicuous introverts, and they to me. We stayed away from social activities at the school and the clubs and from the roving gangs of boys. Throughout, I was just as happy to be entirely alone. I turned with growing concentration to Nature as a sanctuary and a realm of boundless adventure; the fewer people in it, the better. Wilderness became a dream of privacy, safety, control, and freedom. Its essence is captured for me by its Latin name, *solitudo*.

So inevitably, and given that I was looking at the world with only one visually acute eye, I came to be an entomologist, a scientist who specializes in insects. To put the matter as simply as possible: most children have a bug period, and I never grew out of mine. But as in the lives of scientists generally, there is more to the story. Every child wants to visit a magic kingdom. Mine was given to me at the age of ten, when my father moved Pearl and me to Washington, D.C. We took up residence in a basement apartment on Fairmont Street near Fourteenth Street, within walking distance of the National Zoo and a five-cent streetcar ride to the National Museum of Natural History. A year later (possibly not wanting to risk putting down roots), my father moved us again, to a second apartment six blocks away, on Monroe Street. For me the central-city location, in what is now an all-black neighborhood, was an extraordinary stroke of good luck.

Here I was in 1939, a little kid, nine years old, tuned to any new experience so long as it had something to do with natural history, with a world-class zoo on one side and a world-class museum on the other, both free of charge and open seven days a week. Unaffected by the drabness of our working-class neighborhood, I entered a fantasy world made weirdly palpable by federal largesse. I spent hours at a time wandering through the halls of the National Museum, absorbed by the unending variety of plants and animals on display there, pulling out trays of butterflies and other insects, lost in dreams of distant jungles and savannas. A new vision of scientific profes-

sionalism took form. I knew that behind closed doors along the circling balcony, their privacy protected by uniformed guards, labored the curators, shamans of my new world. I never met one of these important personages; perhaps a few passed me unrecognized in the exhibition halls. But just the awareness of their existence—experts of such high order going about the business of the government in splendid surroundings—fixed in me the conception of science as a desirable life goal. I could not imagine any activity more elevating than to acquire their kind of knowledge, to be a steward of animals and plants, and to put the expertise to public service.

The National Zoo, the second focus of my life, was a living museum of equal potency with the National Museum of Natural History. It was and is administered as part of the same umbrella organization, the Smithsonian Institution. Here I spent happy days following every trail, exploring every cage and glass-walled enclosure, staring at the charismatic big animals: Siberian tigers, rhinoceros, cassowaries, king cobras, reticulated pythons, and crocodiles big enough to consume a boy in two bites. There were also smaller animals that eventually became equally fascinating. I developed a liking for lizards, marmosets, parrots, and Philippine tree rats.

Close to the zoo was Rock Creek Park, a wooded urban retreat, into which I ventured on "expeditions." In those confines, within earshot of passing automobiles and the conversations of strollers, I found neither elephants to photograph nor tigers to drop-net. But insects were everywhere present in great abundance. Rock Creek Park became Uganda and Sumatra writ small, and the collection of insects I began to accumulate at home a simulacrum of the national museum. During excursions with a new best friend, Ellis MacLeod (who was later to become a professor of entomology at the University of Illinois), I acquired a passion for butterflies. Using homemade nets made of broomsticks, coat hangers, and cheesecloth bags, we captured our first red admirals and great spangled fritillaries and sought the elusive mourning cloak along the shaded trails of Rock Creek. We were inspired by Frank Lutz's *Field Guide to the Insects* and W. J. Holland's *Butterfly Book*. Poring over R. E. Snodgrass' *Principles of Insect Morphology*, which we could barely begin to understand but revered because it was *real* science, we decided we would devote our lives to entomology.

The course of my life had been set. While sorting through dusty files I recently discovered a letter to my parents written by my fifth-grade teacher at the Hubbard School on February 2, 1940, when I was ten years old: "Ed has genuine writing ability, and when he combines this with his great knowledge of insects, he produces fine results."

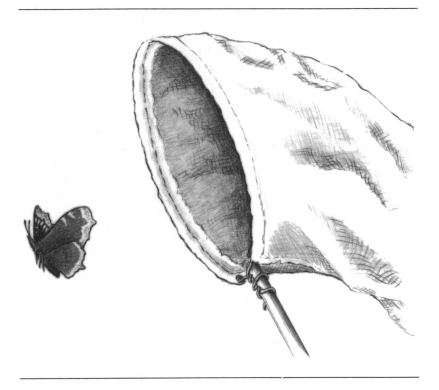

About this time I also became fascinated with ants. One day as Ellis and I clambered over a steep wooded slope in the park, I pulled away the bark of a rotting tree stump and discovered a seething mass of citronella ants underneath. These insects, members of the genus *Acanthomyops*, are exclusively subterranean and can be found only in the soil or in fallen pieces of decaying wood. The worker ants I found were short, fat, brilliant yellow, and emitted a strong lemony odor. The smell was the chemical citronellal, which thirty years later (in my laboratory at Harvard) I discovered is secreted by glands attached to the mandibles of the ants and, like the pygidial substances of the Pensacola *Dorymyrmex*, is used to attack enemies and spread alarm through the colony. That day the little army quickly thinned and vanished into the dark interior of the stump heartwood. But it left a vivid and lasting impression on me. What netherworld had I briefly glimpsed? What strange events were happening deep in the soil?

I devoured an article titled "Stalking Ants, Savage and Civilized," by William M. Mann, in the August 1934 issue of the *National Geographic*. In what was to be one of the more remarkable coincidences of my life, Mann was at that time director of the National Zoo. Like the still anonymous keepers of the museum, he became my hero from afar. To run a great zoo while writing about his adventures around the world with ants—what a role model! In 1957, when I was a beginning assistant professor at Harvard and Mann was in the last year of his directorship, he gave me his large library on ants (an important source for my later research) and escorted me and my wife, Renee, on a special tour of the zoo. In 1987 I was awarded the silver medal of the National Zoological Park for my work on ants and other animals; at the ceremony I came home in a deeply satisfying way.

Always prone to closing and repeating circles in my life, I have often returned to the National Museum of Natural History. The denizens of that Olympus, all a new generation since 1940, have acquired names and faces and become friends and colleagues. The great collections they attend behind the closed doors are familiar ground.

There is today a quickening of purpose, a sense of rising importance and responsibility, at both of the institutions that influenced me fifty years ago. Michael Robinson, the director of the National Zoo as I write, in 1994, prefers to speak of his domain as a biopark, where animals will be released from the isolation of cages and terraria and placed in natural settings of plants and animals from their place of origin. The public can then view them not as caged curiosities but as parts of ecosystems, on which biological diversity—and the health of the planet itself—ultimately depend.

A short distance away, on the Mall, the curators of the National Museum of Natural History continue building one of the world's largest collections of plants and animals. They too must feel the future in their bones. Recent studies indicate that between 10 and 100 million species of plants, animals, and microorganisms exist on Earth, but only about 1.4 million have been studied well enough to receive scientific names. Many of these species are vanishing or being placed in imminent danger of extinction by the reduction of habitat and other human activities. The loss in tropical rain forests in particular, thought to contain a majority of the species on Earth, may exceed half a percent a year.

So there is a lot for those who study the diversity of life to do, a new respectability, and a great responsibility. But that is not the reason I am wedded to the subject. The boy who experienced the magic of the zoo and museum is still strong inside me. He is the puppet master of the man. I would have followed the same path regardless of what happened in the rest of the world.

chapter five

TO DO
MY DUTY

———————————————————————————
———————————————————————————
———————————————————————————

IN THE SPRING OF 1941 MY GRANDMOTHER MARY EMMA JOY-
ner Wilson, known to her family as May, died in Mobile of a heart attack in the house where she had been born in 1868, married, attended
a private school run by her mother, raised four sons, and stayed the
remainder of her life. Since 1916, when her husband died, she had
lived in the company of her bachelor son, Herbert. During all those
seventy-three years she had seldom journeyed beyond the edge of
the city.

My father brought Pearl and me to live in the large rambling struc-

ture that he and Herbert inherited from my grandmother. The house had a long history, at least for the young state of Alabama. Built by May's grandfather in 1838, it was for a few years the only house on Charleston Street, though located only a dozen blocks from Bienville Square and the commercial heart of the old city. Here then, if anywhere, were the roots of my peregrine family.

Alabama's seaport was a small town in the early 1800s when my father's forebears arrived, a junior version of New Orleans complete with muddy streets, balcony grillwork, creole cooking, and epidemics of yellow fever. In 1815, two years after American troops took it from the Spanish on orders from President Madison, Mobile was nothing more than fourteen city blocks grouped in a large square north of Fort Charlotte. By the 1830s and 1840s the town was growing rapidly, but many of the streets, including Charleston, still led down to what an early map labeled "low and miry land"—mud banks—lining the Mobile River estuary. The Hawkinses, Joyners, and Wilsons could ride there by carriage in a few minutes and walk over long wharves to reach the ferry slips. Often, no doubt, they just went to fish and net blue crabs lured with soup bones. The wildlands south of the city still existed in a remnant condition. Large stretches of hardwood and pine forest extended south all the way to Cedar Point, the southernmost tip of mainland Alabama on the west side of Mobile Bay. Beyond that, across Mississippi Sound, a mostly uninhabited Dauphin Island formed a line along the horizon.

When my father was a teenage boy, just before the First World War, he was able, he told me, to step out the front door of the Charleston Street house, stroll down the road a mile or two with a .22 rifle under his arm to the wooded terrain now occupied by Brookley Airport, and hunt quail, rabbits, or whatever else took his fancy. When I was the same age in the 1940s, I often rode my bicycle around Brookley to reach uninhabited woodland and pitcher plant and pine savanna along the Dog and Fowl rivers. I sometimes paused to eat sandwiches and drink Royal Crown Colas on the two-lane wooden bridges spanning these two streams. Around midday an hour or more might pass without the approach of a single automobile. I leaned on the wooden rails in reverie, looking deeply into the slow-moving and limpid water for glimpses of gars and soft-shelled turtles. Today this land is thickly settled, and heavy traffic rumbles all the way down to a bridge running from Cedar Point to Dauphin Island.

My father was proud of his family history. The Hawkinses and Joyners had emigrated from New England to the Mobile Bay area not long after it became American territory; one, my great-great-grandmother Mary Ann Hawkins, was born there in 1826. They prospered as marine engineers, pilots, and shipowners. My great-grandfather James Eli Joyner, who married Mary Ann's daughter Anna Amelia, operated a ferry that serviced the Baldwin County shore out of Mobile. One November day in 1870 his ship caught fire and sank close to Mobile, and he drowned while attempting to swim ashore. His young wife was holding my grandmother May in her arms on the porch of the Charleston Street house as she gazed at the distant plume of smoke, not realizing that it meant she would be a widow. To make ends meet thereafter, she opened a private school in the house, the first in Mobile. I own her pendant containing a portrait of her mother, as well as the heavy gold watch chain with dolphin catch taken from her husband's body.

In the War Between the States virtually every able-bodied male on both my father's and mother's sides fought for the Confederacy. Of the two paternal great-grandfathers, James Joyner served for the duration of the war as artilleryman and teamster; the other was a special case, the undoubted star of all my forebears as far back as I have been able to trace them: William Christopher Wilson.

Black Bill, as his friends called him, was a man whose blood I like to imagine coursing through my veins, even though after three generations I carry only one-eighth of his genes. He was born William Christopher O'Conner in 1816 in a family of Dublin printers, whose customers I was told included the Bank of England. He must have been a rebel of considerable fire. His parents wanted him to train for the Episcopal ministry, but he yearned for a life at sea. So he left home as a teenager, took a job as a cabin boy on a ship bound for Baltimore, and changed his name to Wilson en route when a passenger by that name died.

In Baltimore he proceeded to take a Jewish bride named Maria Louise Myers, daughter of Jacob Myers and Sarah Solomon Myers, late of Germany. The newlyweds soon moved to Mobile to seek their fortune. Black Bill—his name came later from the color of his long beard and not from a Black Irish complexion—found employment as a bar pilot. He advanced to master's status and eventually acquired his own boat, with which he guided merchant ships through the treacherous shallows between Fort Morgan and Fort Gaines. In the early 1840s he became a founding member of the Mobile Bar Pilots Association, a guild still in operation today. He moved his family to Navy Cove, on Fort Morgan Peninsula, where the sails of approaching merchantmen could first be sighted on the Alabama coast as they approached across the open Gulf.

In 1863, when Admiral Farragut blockaded Mobile Bay, Black

Bill and his fellow pilots used their fast ships to run supplies in from Havana. Often pursued, Wilson was finally cornered on a small island outside the harbor. Instead of being simply thrown in irons, he was brought before Farragut and his staff, who made an offer: if Wilson would lead the fleet into Mobile Bay so that it could move swiftly past the guns of Fort Morgan and Fort Gaines without running aground on the shoals, he would receive a large monetary reward and be resettled with his family somewhere in the North. He refused, crying, according to his own account, "I'd see the whole Yankee fleet damned in hell before I'd betray my country!" Not exactly the famously historical flourish of Farragut's authenticated "Damn the torpedoes! Go ahead!" that followed soon afterward (or it might have been "Damn the torpedoes, full speed ahead!" or, most likely and least euphoniously, "Damn the torpedoes, Jouett, full speed!"), but good enough for a southern family in a city in which, even into this century, a sign of respect to an older man was to call him "Cap'n." Oddly, William Christopher Wilson was still an Irish citizen at the time of his capture and remained so. And he never legally changed his name to Wilson. Had I known that as a young man, I might have changed my own back to O'Conner, the sound of which has a nice swing around the apostrophe and a pleasing consonantal bark at the hard C, in contrast to the whispery syllables of Wil-son.

Black Bill was sent off to a succession of federal prisons in New York and Maryland for the remaining two years of the war, and Farragut and his men soon got what they wanted anyway. They captured another Mobile bar pilot who was at that time fishing for a living off the coast at nearby Pascagoula, the legitimate pilot business having been pretty well closed down. His name was Martin Freeman (no relation to my mother's people of the same surname, who were then living in northern Alabama). He and other fishermen were armed and prepared to resist a Yankee invasion, but one salvo from the Union guns offshore changed their minds. Freeman agreed to pilot the fleet, and on August 5, 1864, when a double column of mon-

itors and wooden frigates charged into the bay, he was coolly riding
the main top of the flagship *Hartford*. Members of Black Bill's family
watched from their Navy Cove house as Federal shells burst on
nearby Fort Morgan. Among Freeman's rewards after Mobile had
been captured was the Congressional Medal of Honor, making
him—I hope I do not put too heavy a spin on it after 130 years—the
only traitor ever to receive America's highest military honor.

When we arrived in Mobile in 1941, the old house was dilapidated
and the surrounding neighborhood in decay. Most of the men in the
Wilson clan had either died or dispersed, leaving behind widows and
spinster daughters sprinkled about the city. We addressed them all as
either Aunt or Cousin, depending on their blood ties and age. These
survivors were of surprising interest to my father, who at this point
turned out to be a family historian seized by nostalgia and a yearning
for reflected glory. On Sunday afternoons we visited these living
monuments of the treasured past—Aunt Nellie, the younger Cousin
Nellie, Aunt Vivian, and Cousin Mollie—in their respective par-
lors. Obedient to instructions, cleaned up and dressed in my visiting
clothes, I kissed each on the cheek and sat on a chair to one side until I
could slip away without notice. The reminiscing droned on, a recy-
cling of the stories and sketches of the late Grandma May, Aunt
Hope, Aunt Georgia, Aunt Sarah, and all their stalwart departed
husbands and brothers and sons, and what happened in the lamented
War Between the States, and the many things families did in Old Mobile. Occasionally we visited Magnolia Cemetery, where our forebears and their multitudinous relations and friends lay at rest. Pearl
and I stood patiently by as my father located graves, checked dates,
and reconstructed lives and genealogies.

I had no interest in this world of ghosts. I considered my father a
bore and my great-aunts and cousins an ordeal. For me Mobile was a
place of vibrant life—not of spirits, however, nor of people, and certainly not of relatives, but of *butterflies*. At twelve years of age, I had
arrived with a burning desire to collect and study butterflies. I was

keenly aware that the city is on the edge of the subtropics and home to many species not found in Washington, D.C.

At every opportunity I charged out on my balloon-tired, single-gear Schwinn bicycle, pumping my way down Charleston Street to the rubble-strewn weedlots of the riverfront, west to the scattered pine-and-hardwood copses of Spring Hill, south on the Cedar Point road as far as Fowl River, and east across the Mobile-Tensaw delta on old U.S. 90 to Spanish Fort in Baldwin County. I greeted the sight of each new species of butterfly with joy, and when I caught my first specimen I thought myself a big-game hunter with net. The zebra and golden-winged julia, northernmost representatives of a group that abounds in tropical forests; the goatweed butterfly, bright orange-red with a swift erratic flight, hard to net; the little fairy sulfur, average-sized dog face sulfur, outsized cloudless sulfur, all tropical looking with the flamboyant flashing of their yellow wings; giant swallowtail (and what a thrill to see how different it looked in life from the common tiger swallowtail of the North); zebra swallowtail in the shadowed woods; great purple hair-streak, a stunning iridescent gem I first spotted resting on a weed in a vacant lot; and the large Brazilian skipper, which I reared from translucent gray-green caterpillars feeding on canna lilies in our backyard—all these I added to my butterfly life list.

During the next two years, before we hit the road again, as it seemed inevitably we must, my interest in natural history soared. I went looking for pileated woodpeckers rumored to nest at Spanish Fort, and on the way saw my first wild alligators, in the marshes of the Tensaw estuary. I scoured the riverine hardwood forests for holly trees and orchids. I built a secret outdoor shelter partly from the stems of poison oak and paid for it with an agonizing rash over a large part of my body (afterward I could identify *Rhus quercifolia* at a hundred paces). I hunted reptiles: stunned and captured five-lined skinks with a slingshot, and learned the correct maneuver for catching Carolina anole lizards (approach, let them scuttle to the other side of the tree trunk and out of sight, peek to see where they are sitting, then take them by grabbing blind with one hand around the trunk). One late afternoon I brought home a coachwhip snake nearly as long as I was tall and walked into the house with it wrapped around my neck. Pearl sent me back out with instructions to release it as far from the house as could be traveled round-trip during the remaining daylight hours. I owned a machete and used it to chop my way through tangled undergrowth, imagining myself to be in the jungles of South America. One day I misjudged the downward stroke and slashed my left index finger to the bone. Blood streamed down my arm on the long bicycle ride home. Pearl let me keep the knife, nonetheless, figuring I'd learned the hard way to be more careful.

When America entered the war in December 1941, the tempo of life in Mobile picked up sharply. Tanker traffic in and out of the harbor increased, and overflights of B-17 bombers and other warplanes became commonplace. Poor rural whites—peapickers we deri-

sively called them—and blacks poured into the city looking for work. Jobs were plentiful and labor was short. One anecdote making the rounds at the time involved a white woman who stopped a local Negro woman (to use the idiom of 1942) near her house, saying that she was looking for domestic help. The other responded: "Why, so am I." If you were white you were supposed to gasp with amused surprise. Change was in the air.

I was sanguine about the war, knowing that since Franklin Delano Roosevelt had already fixed just about everything else in the country, and since the Democratic Party and Joe Louis, both of whom enjoyed my allegiance, had always won for as far back as I could remember, this new crisis would also work out all right. In my insouciance I retrieved an identity card discarded by my father, doctored it with swastikas and pseudo-German phrases, and dropped it on the sidewalk in front of our house. Someone found it and took it to the district office of the Federal Bureau of Investigation. My father was called in and questioned by agents. All quickly agreed on the explanation, and my father, to his credit, found the incident hilarious. Indeed, he dined out on it for a while.

My friends and I were indignant about the Japanese attack on Pearl Harbor, of course, and we knew the Nazis to be evil incarnate. As cartoonist for the Barton Academy junior high school newspaper, I depicted a bestial Japanese soldier stabbing Uncle Sam in the back. In school assembly we sang "The White Cliffs of Dover" and other songs in solidarity with the British war effort. But mostly my mind was elsewhere. I was absorbed in my own interests and never tried to follow the course of the war.

In June 1942 Ellis MacLeod came down from Washington to stay with me for the summer. We visited my favorite haunts, shared again our old fantasies, and renewed our intention to become entomologists. That fall after he returned home, I set out to collect and study all the ants in a vacant lot next to the Charleston Street house. I still remember the species I found, in vivid detail, enhanced by the knowledge acquired in later studies: a colony of the trap-jawed *Odontomachus insularis*, whose vicious stings drove me away from their nest at the foot of a fig tree; a colony of a small yellowish-brown *Pheidole*, possibly *Pheidole floridanus*, found nesting beneath an amber-colored whiskey bottle in midwinter and which I kept for a while in a vertical observation nest of sand between two glass plates. And colonies of imported fire ants, unmistakably *Solenopsis invicta*, were there. The vacant lot discovery was the earliest record of the species in the United States, and I was later to publish it as a datum in a technical article, my first scientific observation.

My energies and confidence were gathering. By the fall of 1942, at the age of thirteen, I had become in effect a child workaholic. I took a job with backbreaking hours of my own free will, without adult coercion or even encouragement. Soon after the start of the war there was a shortage of carriers for the city newspaper, the *Mobile Press*

Register. Young men seventeen and over were departing for the service, and boys aged fifteen to sixteen were moving up part-time into the various jobs they vacated. On the lowest rung of unskilled labor, many paper routes came open as the fifteen- and sixteen-year-olds moved up. Somehow, for reasons I do not recall, an adult delivery supervisor let me take over a monster route: 420 papers in the central city area.

For most of that school year I rose each morning at three, slipped away in the darkness, delivered the papers, each to a separate residence, and returned home for breakfast around seven-thirty. I departed a half-hour later for school, returned home again at three-thirty, and studied. On Monday nights from seven to nine I attended the meeting of my Boy Scout troop at the United Methodist Church, on Government and Broad streets. On Sunday mornings I went to service at the First Baptist Church. On Sunday evenings I stayed up through Fibber McGee and Molly on the radio. On other nights I set the alarm soon after supper, went to bed, and fell asleep.

Four hundred and twenty papers delivered each morning! It seems almost impossible to me now. But there is no mistake; the number is etched in my memory. The arithmetic also fits: I made two trips to the delivery dock at the back of the *Press Register* building, each time filling two large canvas satchels. When stacked vertically on the bicycle front fender and strapped to the handlebars, the bags reached almost to my head and were close to the maximum bulk and weight I could handle. The residences receiving the papers were not widely spaced suburban houses but city dwellings, apartment buildings with two or three stories. It took perhaps a maximum of one hour to travel back and forth to the *Press Register* dock, load the papers twice, and make two round trips in and out; the delivery area was only a few minutes' ride away. That leaves three and a half hours for actual on-the-scene work, or an average of two papers a minute—during which I reached down, pulled out the paper, dropped it, or threw it rolled up for a short distance, and passed on, moving faster and more easily after one satchel was emptied.

The supervisor collected the week's subscription money from the customers on Saturday, twenty-five cents apiece, so I didn't have to work extra hours that day and had time to continue my field excursions. I made thirteen dollars a week, from which I bought my Boy Scout paraphernalia, parts for my bike, and whatever candy, soft drinks, and movie tickets I wanted.

At the time it did not occur to me that my round-the-clock schedule was unusual. I felt fortunate to have a job and to be able to earn money. It was the kind of regimen I had learned to expect as normal from my brief experience at the Gulf Coast Military Academy. I still assumed, without any real evidence, that the same level of effort would be required of me as an adult. And what of my father and Pearl, asleep in their bed as I headed out in the predawn hours in all kinds of weather? Pearl, who came from a hardscrabble life in rural North Carolina, seemed well pleased that I showed the kind of spunk it takes to survive. And the feelings of my father, who never worked that hard in his life—who can say?

But the labor over long hours did not really matter; I had discovered the Boy Scouts of America. All that I had become by the age of twelve, all the biases and preconceptions I had acquired, all the dreams I had garnered and savored, fitted me like a finely milled ball into the socket of its machine when I discovered this wonderful organization. The Boy Scouts of America seemed invented just for me.

The 1940 *Handbook for Boys*, which I purchased for half a dollar, became my most cherished possession. Fifty years later, I still read my original annotated copy with remembered pleasure. Richly illustrated, with a cover by Norman Rockwell, it was packed with useful information on the subjects I liked the most. It stressed outdoor life and natural history: camping, hiking, swimming, hygiene, semaphore signaling, first aid, mapmaking, and, above all, zoology and botany, page after page of animals and plants wonderfully well illustrated, explaining where to find them, how to identify them. The public schools and church had offered nothing like this. The Boy Scouts legitimated Nature as the center of my life.

There were rules, uniforms, and a crystal-clear set of practical ethics to live by. If I jog my memory today by raising my right hand with the middle three fingers up, thumb and little finger down and crossed, I can still recite the Scout Oath:

On my honor I will do my best:
To do my duty to God and my country,
    and to obey the Scout law;
To help other people at all times;
To keep myself physically strong,
    mentally awake and morally straight.

And the Scout Law: A Scout is trustworthy, loyal, helpful, friendly, courteous, kind, obedient, cheerful, thrifty, brave, clean, reverent. Finally, there was the Scout Motto, *Be Prepared.*

I drank in and accepted every word. Still do, as ridiculous as that may seem to my colleagues in the intellectual trade, to whom I can only reply, Let's see you do better in fifty-four words or less.

The work ethic was celebrated from cover to cover. There was a clearly marked Boy Scout of America route to success through virtue and exceptional effort. In the chapter titled "Finding One's Life Work," I read: "A Scout looks ahead. He prepares for things before they happen. He therefore meets them easily." Never be satisfied, the instructions warned. Just to wait and hope and accept whatever comes is the road to failure. Reach high, strive long and hard toward honorable goals, and keep ever in mind Longfellow's invocation:

The heights by great men reached and kept, were not attained by sudden flight; but they, while their companions slept, were toiling upward in the night.

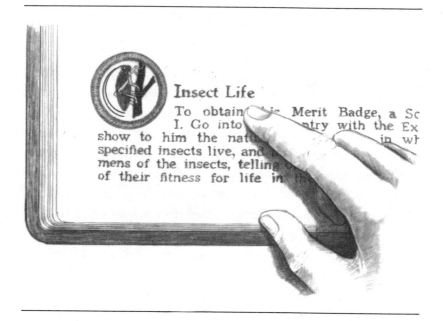

Insect Life
To obtain this Merit Badge, a Sc
I. Go into the country with the Ex
show to him the nat...   ...in wh
specified insects live, and ...
mens of the insects, telling ...
of their fitness for life in ...

I found something else the public schools never offered, a ladder of education to be taken at your own pace, better fast than slow, with each new step successively harder. I saw the whole challenge of scouting as a competition I would enjoy and surely win. The Scout program was my equivalent of the Bronx High School of Science.

I plunged into the new regimen. In three years I advanced to Eagle Scout with palm clusters, the highest rank, and was made junior assistant scoutmaster of my troop. I earned forty-six merit badges, almost half of those available in the organization. I happily crunched through the programs for subjects as diverse as Bird Study, Farm Records and Book-Keeping, Life Saving, Journalism, and Public Health. I pored over the requirements of all the badges at night to see which one I could best do next. My heart sang when I first read the prescription for Insect Life, beginning: "To obtain this Merit Badge, a Scout must: 1. Go into the country with the Examiner and show to him the natural surroundings in which certain specified insects live, and find and demonstrate living specimens of the insects, telling of their habits or of the nature of their fitness for life in their particular surroundings."

All the time I attended to my schoolwork in an adequate but desultory manner. The subjects were relatively easy, and I maintained passing grades. But most of the curriculum seemed dull and pointless. My most memorable accomplishment in my freshman year at Murphy High School in Mobile was to capture twenty houseflies during one hour of class, a personal record, and lay them in rows for the next student to find. The teacher found these trophies instead, and had the grace to compliment me on my feat next day in front of the class. I had developed a new technique for catching flies, and I now pass it on to you. Let the fly alight, preferably on a level and unobstructed surface, such as a restaurant table or book cover. Move your open hand carefully until it rests twelve to eighteen inches in front of the sitting fly's head. Bring the hand very slowly forward, in a straight line, taking care not to waggle it sideways; flies are very sensitive to lateral movement. When your hand is about nine inches away, sweep it toward the fly so that the edge of the palm passes approximately one or two inches above the spot where the fly is resting. Your target will dart upward at about the right trajectory to hit the middle of the palm, and as you close your fingers you will feel the satisfying buzz of the insect trapped inside your fist. Now, how to kill the fly? Clap your hands together—discreetly, if you are in a restaurant or lecture hall.

Scouting also proved to be the ideal socializing environment for an undersized and introverted only child. Our gangs were the Scout patrols, groups about the size of an army squad, several of which made up the larger troop. We automatically became members of one when we joined the Scouts, and we were esteemed or criticized on our own merits according to Scout rules. I never met a bully in the Scouts, and relatively few braggarts. The questions before each boy were: Can you walk twenty miles, tie a tourniquet, save a swimmer

in Red Cross lifeguard exercises, build a sturdy sapling bridge with nothing but ax and rope? For me the answers were yes, yes, *yes*!

Scouting added another dimension to my expanding niche. I became a teacher. In the summer of 1943 I was asked to be the nature counselor at Camp Pushmataha, the Boy Scout summer camp near Citronelle used by the Mobile Area District. At fourteen, I was the youngest counselor, with no experience at instruction, but I quickly figured out what interested other boys, what would get them talking about natural history and make them respect the subject: snakes. Several volunteers and I built cages and searched the surrounding woods for as many different kinds of snakes as we could find. Somehow in the process I learned how to capture a poisonous snake. Pin its body with a staff as close to the head as you can manage, then roll the staff forward until the head is pressed firmly to the ground and the neck clear, grasp the neck closely behind the posterior jaw angles, and lift the whole body up. Few boys would touch a snake of any kind, so when one was discovered the word was brought to me by yelling messengers: "Snake! Snake!" And off I would go to perform my derring-do, which I followed with a brief lecture on the species discovered. In a short time we had a row of cages filled with a partial representation of the rich fauna that inhabits the Gulf states. I worked like a zoo director, talking to visitors about the diversity of species. I could then segue into discourses about the insects and plants of Greater Pushmataha. I had become a successful natural history instructor.

But before long my inexperience and reckless pride did me in. It happened one afternoon when I was cleaning a cage containing several pygmy rattlesnakes, my star attractions. The adults of this cryptically colored species (*Sistrurus miliarius*) grow to no more than fifty centimeters in length. They are less deadly than their larger cousins found in the same region, the diamondback and canebrake rattlesnakes, but they are still poisonous and moderately dangerous. In a moment of carelessness I moved my left hand too close to one of the coiled rattlers. Like a quarrel sprung from a crossbow, it uncoiled and struck the tip of my index finger. The two fang punctures felt like a bee sting. I knew I was in trouble. Off I went with an adult counselor to a nearby doctor in town, who administered the old-fashioned first-aid treatment as quickly as he could: deep X-shaped scalpel incisions centered on each of the fang punctures, followed by suction of the blood with a rubber cup. I knew the drill; I had learned it when I earned the merit badge for Reptile Life. I didn't cry during the operation, which was performed without anesthesia. I held my hand steady and cursed loudly nonstop with four-letter words, at myself for my stupidity and not at the innocent doctor or the snake, in order to keep my mind off the procedure. I knew a great deal of off-color language at fourteen and must have surprised the adults helping me. The next morning I was sent home for convalescence. I lay gloomily on a couch for a week, holding my swollen left arm as still as possible.

It was a bad time for herpetology at Camp Pushmataha. When I returned to resume my duties, I found that the camp supervisor had wisely disposed of the pygmy rattlesnakes. I was forbidden to touch any more poisonous species, and nothing more was said to me about the matter.

Contrary to the impression this account may have created, the Boy Scouts of America in southern Alabama in the early 1940s was not an ideal organization in all respects. It retreated helplessly from the Gorgons of sex and race.

Sex education was not on the agenda of the Boy Scouts of America, or of any school or other youth organization for that matter. The 1940 *Handbook for Boys* went no further than to caution that boys of a certain age have nocturnal seminal emissions once or twice a week. Scouts were not, it said, to worry about these episodes, which were normal. They were not to "excite" themselves to produce the emissions; the practice was "a bad habit." If urges became too troublesome to handle, one should try a cool hip bath, 55° to 60°F. If more help on this or related matters was required, "Seek advice from wise, clean, strong men." No warnings were given about pederasts. They surely lurked somewhere in the ranks of the adult leaders. I heard rumors of one, but never met him personally.

Then where did I learn all my filthy language? From other boys, who spiced their conversation whenever they were beyond adult earshot. Because sex was taboo and bizarre enough to be conceptually exciting, boys of Scout age talked about it all the time. We approached the subject obliquely, with Rabelaisian humor. A substantial fraction of campfire and trailside conversation consisted of raucous jokes that dwelled on every imaginable sexual perversion and grotesquerie: homosexuals trying to have babies, necrophiliac undertakers carrying the severed genitalia of female corpses as trophies, sex with animals, impossibly large sexual equipment on both men and women, insatiable appetites and marathon infidelities, and so on through a fantastical *Psychopathia Sexualis*. Every teenage Alabamian male, it seemed, was a budding Krafft-Ebing. But of normal heterosexual relations scant was known and nothing spoken. We could not cross the barrier to what we guessed our parents and married sisters did each night, or what we ourselves hoped to experience with girls. To discuss such matters would be a shocking invasion of privacy. So we left orthodoxy alone, and sketched the vague outline of acceptable behavior by circumscribing it with everything that was explicitly forbidden. Normalcy was like the image in a photograph created in silhouette by developing its chromatically sensitive background.

Race was also emphatically not on the official agenda. All the boys in the *Handbook for Boys* were white, and so were all the Scouts I knew. So were the students in the school I attended and the people in our church. I grew up mostly unconcerned about segregation and its dehumanizing effects. The impact of discrimination entered my mind only secondhand. But not entirely. In 1944 I was invited by a senior counselor to put on my Eagle Scout regalia and visit a troop of Boy Scouts just starting up in a black rural area near Brewton, Alabama. Standing in the front of the church meeting room I gave a short talk on the many advantages of Scouting. When we left I did not feel pride in the example I was supposed to have set; I felt shame. I was depressed for days. I knew in my heart that those boys, mostly two or three years younger than I, would have few real advantages no matter how gifted or how hard they tried. The doors open to me were shut to them.

Then I gradually forgot about the matter. What could I do? My mind was on other things. I was filled with ambition and anxiety and did not have a strong social conscience. Twenty years later the Old South came to an end. The civil rights activists who risked their lives to break segregation were heroes to my liking: singlemindedly true to a moral code, physically courageous, enduring. That was enough to make me look again at this part of my social heritage. And by then I had left Alabama. The world changed; I changed. But I cannot claim to have been a liberal as a boy and young man, certainly not one with any foresight or courage. The trajectory that took me into science would have been the same regardless; and I will not now be so presumptuous or hypocritical as to offer an extraneous apology for the proud and tortured culture through which I passed to the naturalist's calling.

chapter six

ALABAMA
DREAMING

IN AUGUST 1944 I WEIGHED 112 POUNDS. I KNOW THIS TO BE
true because in that month I reported with my best friend, Philip
Bradley, for football practice at Brewton High School, and we were
put on the scales in the locker room. At fifteen years, I was probably
the youngest, and certainly the smallest, of the players. Bradley was
a bit heavier, at 116 pounds, every ounce of which I envied, while the
largest member of the team came in at a hulking 160 pounds. I was
allowed to strap on my ridiculously oversized uniform because the
team needed every man (well, every boy) it could get. And I was

there despite my obvious lack of qualifications because this was Alabama. In small towns across the state, football was what young males between the ages of fifteen and nineteen aspired to do when not in class or occupied with part-time jobs. At the other end of the statistical curve of athletic promise from me, boys with heavy shoulders and quick hands could hope for college athletic scholarships. There happened to be, however, none in our school well enough endowed for college play that year.

Brewton was and still is a town of about five thousand on the Alabama side of the border with Florida, forty miles north of Pensacola. It has changed very little since 1944. I have returned twice in middle age while on my way by automobile across the state, to drift like a phantom through the grid of residential streets down to the main commercial section that runs parallel to the railroad tracks, and to pause at the grounds of the high school, where I summoned the memory of boys hitting the worn tackle bag, grunting, and joking back and forth in reasonably close imitations of grown men. Once I stopped to ask a young fireman for directions, and when I mentioned that I had attended the high school in 1944, he said, "Boy, that was a l-o-o-ng time ago!" I replied that it didn't seem very long to me, not in a pleasant little town that had conceded so little to the rush of the twentieth century. And not when I could close my eyes and summon uniforms caked with dried mud and turned aromatic by stale sweat.

There were twenty-three on the football squad that year, composing the first and second teams of eleven each, each member playing both offense and defense, plus me, the third-string left end and, by accident of numbers, the entire third string. I couldn't catch the football half the time, I couldn't even see a pass coming with my one good eye, and I was too light to block. About all I could manage was a shoestring tackle. If I dived to the ground and threw my arms around both ankles of the onrushing ball carrier, I could trip him, hoping he wouldn't fall onto me too hard. Somehow, perhaps because the opposing teams were even punier than our own, we managed to defeat every one of the other ten high schools we played except archrival Greenville. I was allowed on the field just once all season, in the fourth quarter of the final game, played at home, and this once because it was toward the end of the fourth quarter and the enemy had been crushed beyond all hope of recovery. How warmly I remember and cherish the command, "Wilson, take left end!" It was an act of charity on the part of the coach, whose name I have forgotten but toward whom I will always feel gratitude. Because of him I was thereafter authorized to say in that part of Alabama, "I played football for Brewton," in the same way a New York corporate executive in a Century Club dining room says, "I rowed for Yale."

Most of the players had nicknames such as Bubba (it was not a joke then; Bubbas were future good old boys and managers of Chevrolet dealerships; they were big, heavyset, and good-natured), J. C., Buddy, Skeeter, Scooter, and Shoe. Mine was Snake, not because of my body shape, which would have been apropos, and certainly not because I could weave magically through crowds of tacklers head down with the ball tucked hard on my waist, as in my dreams, but because I had maintained my enthusiasm for real snakes. After our sojourn in Mobile, my father had left me with Belle Raub in Pensacola and gone on the road with Pearl, to a destination I never knew. The three of us reunited in a small house in Brewton in the early spring of 1944. That summer I served as Boy Scout nature counselor at Camp Bigheart, on the shore of Pensacola Bay. Once again I relied on snakes to enliven accounts of natural history.

By this time reptiles and amphibians had become my central interest. The fauna of the region would excite passion in a herpetologist of any age. Forty species of snakes, one of the richest assemblages in the world, are native to the western Florida panhandle and adjacent border counties of Alabama. Over a period of a year I managed to capture most of them. And a majority of those I could not take alive I either saw at a distance, such as the marsh-dwelling flat-

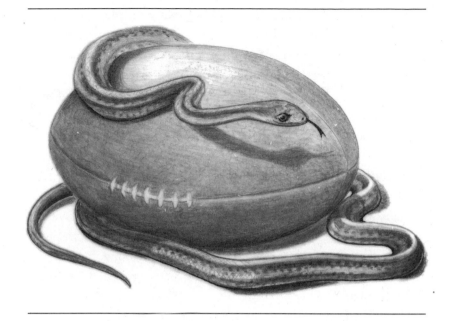

tailed water snake (*Natrix compressicauda*), or else were brought to me dead, most memorably a large diamondback rattlesnake killed by a group of men not far from our house.

On the western edge of Brewton, next to a dense swamp, was a goldfish hatchery run by an affable sixty-year-old Englishman named Mr. Perry. I never learned his first name; polite southern youth did not address their elders in such familiar terms. Nor did I ask him how he came to such an unusual occupation in a backwater southern town. But we became good friends and spent hours talking freely on many subjects. He was always glad to see me when I rode my bicycle up to the edge of the property. He never had other visitors that I saw, lived quietly with his wife in a small house on the property, and always worked alone. His water came from artesian wells that have since dried up, and he fed his goldfish cornmeal mixed with pig blood received weekly from a local slaughterhouse. The goldfish were sold for bait, both locally and out of town. His canisters of young fish, some monochromatic gold, others gold marbled with white, departed at regular intervals by rail from the Brewton station.

Perry had excavated the ponds, each twenty to thirty feet square, in an irregular double row along the edge of the swamp. Thick weeds choked their borders, and tall trees walled them in on the swamp side. A six-foot-wide stream of artesian water flowed into the swamp from each end of the hatchery. The whole ensemble was a textbook diagram from an ecology textbook made literal: the rich nutrients pumped in continuously gave birth to an exuberance of algae, aquatic plants, and fish. The net produce of biomass fed swarms of insects and thence of frogs, snakes, herons, and other larger predators; and all the excess food and all the waste draining into the exit streams fructified the biota of a deep swamp that stretched east for an indeterminate distance.

Into this paradise I threw myself with abandon. The hours I spent there were among the happiest of my life. At every opportunity I came down to the hatchery ponds. After talking with Mr. Perry for a while, mostly about his pisciculture and my own explorations, I donned calf-length rubber boots from the row of pairs he kept in his equipment shed and walked into my private world. At home I politely ignored the nagging of my stepmother, who seemed almost distraught at my failure to find a job after school. I in turn grew increasingly abashed and resentful at her singleminded efforts to prepare me for the grim Depression-era life she had experienced. I had already worked longer hours than she, I had proved myself, and now I needed space. Pearl saw little value in my swamp expeditions, and, looking back, I cannot blame her.

Adults forget the depths of languor into which the adolescent mind descends with ease. They are prone to undervalue the mental growth that occurs during daydreaming and aimless wandering. When I focused on the ponds and swamp lying before me, I abandoned all sense of time. Net in hand, khaki collecting satchel hung by a strap from my shoulder, I surveilled the edges of the ponds, poked shrubs and grass clumps, and occasionally waded out into shallow stretches of open water to stir the muddy bottom. Often I just sat for long periods scanning the pond edges and vegetation for the hint of a scaly coil, a telltale ripple on the water's surface, the sound of an out-of-sight splash. Then, sooner on hot days than otherwise, I worked my way down for a half-mile or so along one of the effluent streams into the deep shade of the swamp, crossed through the forest to the parallel stream, and headed back up it to the hatchery. Sometimes I cut away to explore pools and mudflats hidden in the Piranesian gloom beneath the high closed canopy. In the swamp I was a wanderer in a miniature wilderness. I never encountered another person there, never heard a distant voice, or automobile, or airplane. The only tracks in the mud I saw were those of wild animals. No one else cared about this domain, not even Mr. Perry. Although I held no title, the terrain and its treasures belonged entirely to me in every sense that mattered.

Water snakes abounded at abnormally high densities around the ponds and along the outflow streams, feeding on schools of blood-gorged fish and armies of frogs. Mr. Perry made no attempt to control them. They were, he said, no more than a minor source of gold-fish mortality. Although neither of us had the vocabulary to express such things, we shared the concept of a balanced ecosystem, one in which man could add and take out energy but otherwise leave alone without ill consequence. Mr. Perry was a natural-born environmentalist. He trod lightly upon the land in his care.

A swamp filled with snakes may be a nightmare to most, but for me it was a ceaselessly rotating lattice of wonders. I had the same interest in the diversity of snakes that other fifteen-year-old boys seemed automatically to develop in the years and makes of automobiles. And knowing them well, I had no fear. On each visit I found something new. I captured live specimens, brought them home to cages I had constructed of wood and wire mesh, and fed them frogs and minnows I collected at the hatchery.

My favorites included the eastern ribbon snakes, graceful reptiles decorated with green and brown longitudinal stripes, which spent their time draped in communal bunches on tree limbs overhanging the pond waters. With their bulging, lidless eyes they could see at a considerable distance and were wary. I stalked them to within a few feet by wading in the shallow water of the pond edges and seized one or two at a time as they plunged into the water and tried to swim away. They grew tame in captivity and fed readily on small frogs. Green water snakes were memorable in another way. Found lying half-concealed in vegetation at the edge of the ponds, they were big, up to four feet in length, and heavy-bodied. Catching one was an unpleasant experience unless I could take them quickly back of the head. Most larger snakes try to bite when first handled, and many can break the skin to leave a horseshoe row of needle pricks; but green water snakes have an especially violent response, and their sharp teeth can slash the skin and make blood run freely. They were also difficult to maintain in captivity. Once I found a mud snake, a species that uses the hardened tip of its tail to help hold giant amphiuma salamanders while subduing and swallowing them. The tip can prick human skin; hence the species' alternate name of stinging snake.

One species, the glossy watersnake *Natrix rigida*, became a special target just because it was so elusive. The small adults lay on the bottom of shallow ponds well away from the shore and pointed their heads out of the alga-green water in order to breathe and scan the surface in all directions. I waded out to them very slowly, avoiding the abrupt lateral movements to which reptiles are most sensitive. I needed to get within three or four feet in order to dive and grab them by the body, but before I could close the distance they always pulled their heads under and slipped quietly away into the deeper, opaque waters. I finally solved the problem with the aid of the town's leading

slingshot artist, a taciturn loner my age who liked me because I praised his skills as a hunter. He aimed pebbles at the heads of the snakes with surprising accuracy, stunning several long enough for me to seize them underwater. After they recovered, I kept the captives for a while in the homemade cages, where they thrived on live minnows offered in dishes of water.

The tigers and lords of this place were the poisonous cottonmouth moccasins, large semiaquatic pit vipers with thick bodies and triangular heads. Young individuals, measuring eighteen inches or so, are brightly patterned with reddish-brown crossbands. The adults are more nearly solid brown, with the bands mostly faded and confined to the lower sides of the body. When cornered, moccasins throw open their jaws, sheathed fangs projecting forward, to reveal a conspicuous white mouth lining, the source of their name. Peterson's *A Field Guide to Reptiles and Amphibians of Eastern and Central North America*, written by the herpetologist Roger Conant, warns, "Don't ever handle a live one!" I did so all the time, with the fifteen-year-old's naive confidence that I would never make a mistake.

Immature cottonmouths were never a problem, but one day I met an outsized adult that might easily have killed me. As I waded down one of the hatchery outflow streams, a very large snake crashed through the vegetation close to my legs and plunged into the water. I was especially startled by the movement because I had grown accustomed through the day to modestly proportioned frogs, snakes, and turtles quietly tensed on mudbanks and logs. This snake was more nearly my size as well as violent and noisy—a colleague, so to speak. It sped with wide body undulations to the center of the shallow watercourse and came to rest on a sandy riffle. It was the largest snake I had ever seen in the wild, more than five feet long with a body as thick as my arm and a head the size of my fist, only a bit under the published size record for the species. I was thrilled at the sight, and the snake looked as though it could be captured. It now lay quietly in the shallow clear water completely open to view, its body stretched along the fringing weeds, its head pointed back at an oblique angle to watch my approach. Cottonmouths are like that, even the young ones. They don't always undulate away until they are out of sight, in the manner of ordinary watersnakes. Although no emotion can be read in the frozen half-smile and staring yellow eyes, their reactions and postures give them an insolent air, as if they see their power reflected in the caution of human beings and other sizable enemies.

I moved into the snake handler's routine: pinned the body back of the head, grasped the neck behind the swelling masseteric muscles, and lifted the snake clear of the water. The big cottonmouth, so calm to that moment, reacted with stunning violence. Throwing its heavy body into convulsions, it twisted its head and neck slightly forward through my tightened fingers and stretched its mouth wide open to unfold inch-long fangs. A fetid musk from its anal glands filled the air. In the few seconds we were locked together the morning heat became more noticeable, reality crashed through, and at last I awoke from my dream and wondered why I was in that place alone. If I were bitten, who would find me? The snake began to turn its head far enough to clamp its jaws on my hand. I was not strong even for a boy of my slight size, and I was losing control. Reacting as by reflex, I heaved the giant out into the brush, and it thrashed frantically away, this time until it was out of sight and we were rid of each other.

This narrow escape was the most adrenaline-charged moment of my year's adventures at the hatchery. Since then I have cast back, trying to retrieve my emotions to understand why I explored swamps and hunted snakes with such dedication and recklessness. The activities gave me little or no heightened status among my peers; I never told anyone most of what I did. Pearl and my father were tolerant but not especially interested or encouraging; in any case I didn't say much to them either, for fear they would make me stay closer to home. My reasons were mixed. They were partly exhilaration at my entry into a beautiful and complex new world. And partly possessiveness; I had a place that no one else knew. And vanity; I believed that no one, anywhere, was better at exploring woods and finding snakes. And ambition; I dreamed I was training myself someday to be a professional field biologist. And finally, an undeciphered residue, a yearning remaining deep within me that I have never understood, nor wish to, for fear that if named it might vanish.

Too quickly the enchanted interlude came to an end. In the late spring of 1945, a few weeks after sirens blew across the little town to celebrate the surrender of Germany, we moved again, to the city of Decatur, in north central Alabama. This time I yielded to the pertinacity of my stepmother and found work. In the ensuing year I held a series of jobs: paperboy, lunch-counter attendant and short-order

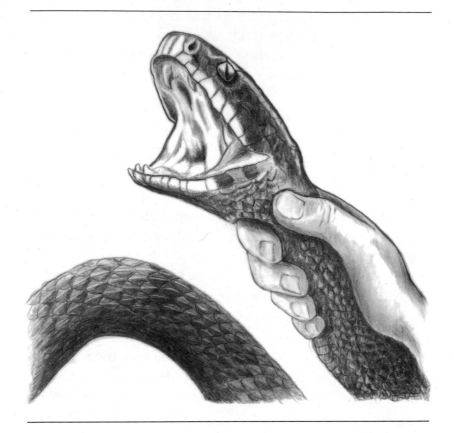

cook at a downtown drugstore, stock clerk at a five-and-ten department store, and finally, in the summer of 1946, just before leaving for
college, office boy in a nearby steel manufacturing plant. My income
rose steadily with each step, to about twenty-five dollars a week. All
this was good for my soul—maybe. I know it made Pearl happy; but,
more important, it persuaded me to strive thereafter to my limit in
order to go any distance, master any subject, take any risk to become
a professional scientist and thereby avoid having to do such dull and
dispiriting labor ever, ever again.

I managed to continue my relationship with Nature on a part-time
basis that summer and fall. On warm days when I could get away

from school and work I wandered the banks and tributary streams of the Tennessee River to the north and east of Decatur. Surrounded by one of the richest variegations of aquatic environment in North America, I took an interest in freshwater ecology. I discovered and studied sponges and the odd larvae of the spongillaflies that live in them. Soon after my arrival I learned, to my delight, that a local research station of the Tennessee Valley Authority had a complete collection of local freshwater fishes (Alabama has more kinds than any other state). After ingratiating myself with the personnel, I set out to learn this fauna species by species. The Tennessee Valley is also riddled with limestone caverns. I heard of one cave close enough to reach by bicycle and began exploring it in search of bats and blind subterranean insects. I shed most of my immediate interest in snakes, those in the Tennessee Valley being less diverse and harder to find than the ones in southern Alabama.

To my relief, there was no hope of playing football; the high school in Decatur was much larger than the one in Brewton and well peopled with natural athletes. There was no point in even showing up for practice; most male students did not. Thus I was spared the humiliation of my physical inadequacy.

Suddenly, in the fall of 1945, having reached sixteen years of age and with college only a year away, I recognized that I must get serious about my career as an entomologist. The time had come to select a group of insects on which I could become a world authority. Butterflies were out; they were too well known and were being studied by a great many obviously capable scientists. Flies looked much more promising. They occur everywhere in dazzling variety, and they have environmental importance. I liked their clean looks, acrobatics, and insouciant manner. Although houseflies and dung flies, not to mention mosquitoes, have given the dipterous clan a bad name, most species are little jewels in nature's clockwork, fastidious, unobtrusive, and efficient at what they do, which is scavenging, pollinating flowers, or preying on other insects. I was especially taken by

93

long-legged flies of the family Dolichopodidae, many of which are metallic green and blue and skitter about on leaves in the sunshine like animated gemstones. More than a thousand species in North America were known at that time, and hundreds more were undoubtedly waiting to be discovered. I set out to order the equipment I needed to collect these insects: killing jar, Schmitt specimen boxes, and the special long black insect pins made chiefly in Czechoslovakia. But it was 1945; Czechoslovakia had recently been a war zone and was soon to fall under Soviet occupation. No pins were available.

Without pause I cast about for another group of insects in which to invest my energies, one that could be preserved in small bottles of alcohol obtained locally. I quickly hit upon ants. Of course, ants: my old acquaintances, the source of some of my earliest passions. From a local drugstore I purchased dozens of five-dram prescription bottles, the old-fashioned glass ones with metal screwtops, and filled them with rubbing alcohol. I ordered a copy of William Morton Wheeler's 1910 classic *Ants: Their Structure, Development, and Behavior* from a Decatur bookstore, built glass observation nests to the author's specifications, and prepared to launch my career as a myrmecologist. I rode my bicycle into the woods and fields all around Decatur, building a sizable collection of species and annotating the habitat and nests of each. Such museum series have lasting value. To this day, nearly fifty years later, I still occasionally consult my early Alabama specimens and notes on questions of classification and ecology. I have studied ants in European museums that were collected as early as 1832. They are all beautifully preserved, their exoskeletons as complete and finely sculptured as in life.

About this time I learned of a myrmecologist named Marion R. Smith who worked at the National Museum of Natural History. I knew that he was a middle-aged gentleman who had grown up in Mississippi and devoted his early research to the ants of that state. In a laboriously typed letter I announced my intention to conduct a survey of the ants of Alabama. Without a pause Smith wrote back to say, *Good idea!* He himself, he informed me, had surveyed the ants of

Mississippi, and he enclosed a copy of a binary taxonomic key he had written to identify the species known from that state. In such keys you follow the specimen through a succession of two-way choices until you arrive at one that tells you the name of the species. Here, for example, is the beginning of the key to the ant genus *Monomorium* from William S. Creighton's classic 1950 monograph on the ants of North America. I have changed some words to make the language less technical:

1. The three terminal joints of the antenna ("feeler") thicken successively toward the tip of the antenna; workers in a given colony are all about the same size .... Go to **2**

OR

The first two of these joints are about equal in size; workers in each colony are of two sizes .... *Monomorium destructor*

2. The head is densely covered with small punctures, which make its surface dull; a common house ant in the United States ("Pharaoh's ant") .... *Monomorium pharaonis*

OR

The head has only scattered punctures, its entire surface shiny.. Go to **3**

And so on until all the known species are covered from a particular geographic area, say Mississippi or all of North America or even the whole world. I got busy, put names on the specimens I had collected, and sent them to Smith for verification. He responded quickly: You got half of them right. You are off to a *good start!* He didn't say, You got half of them wrong. And he did not say, Why don't you study a few years more and see me then? He said, Keep up the good work and write me soon. With each passing year I cherish yet more warmly the memory of Dr. M. R. Smith, myrmecologist of the National Museum of Natural History.

I redoubled my efforts and began to discover unusual and interesting species. One day I found a marching column of army ants in my backyard—not the famous voracious hordes of South American rain forests, but miniature army ants of the genus *Neivamyrmex*, whose colonies of 10,000 to 100,000 workers search for prey through grass clumps around human habitations and across leaf-carpeted forests in the southern United States. At first glimpse a *Neivamyrmex* raiding group resembles nothing more than a large column of slender, dark-brown workers of some other species, running back and forth between nest and a dead animal or spilled sugar. A close examination, however, reveals them to be armies on the march, invading the nests of other kinds of ants, often changing their own nest site from one day to the next. I tracked the *Neivamyrmex* colony for several days until finally, on a rain-soaked afternoon, they marched across the street and out of sight into the tangled weeds of a neighbor's yard. In future years I would encounter and study *Neivamyrmex* colonies many times, in many places, from the Carolinas to the Amazon. I would write on army ants from all around the world.

During my senior year in high school this late-adolescent idyll was invaded by a rising anxiety: to be a scientist, one must go to college, and no member of my family on either side had ever progressed that far. They had been successful businessmen, farmers, shipowners, even engineers in an era when a high school diploma sufficed for such occupations. College was still thought of as a costly luxury, and the ordinary middle-class life trajectory up to that time was to pass directly from high school graduation to gainful employment. To further my ambitions I had to enter uncharted waters.

Unfortunately, my father's health was failing. A thin, frail-looking man, his 130 pounds stretched over a five-foot, nine-inch frame, he had been sickly for years, worn down by bouts of alcoholism and bronchitis. The latter was made chronic and severe by chain smoking, two to three packs a day. Now, in the winter of 1945, he was stricken with a bleeding duodenal ulcer. He checked into the Naval Hospital in Charleston, South Carolina, where treatment was free to him as a veteran of the First World War. The operation, during which a large section of his small intestine was removed, was nearly fatal. He returned home for a long convalescence, never complaining to me, never expressing anything but optimism about our future; but I knew better.

Although I loved my father, my concern at this point was mostly selfish. I realized I could not depend on him for further support and feared that I might have to postpone college and take work to assist him and Pearl (who never took a job of her own). Later I learned that my mother, now married to a successful businessman and herself a civilian employee of the Army Quartermaster Corps, would have been more than willing to cover all my expenses. She was soon to supply partial support in any case. But I was a proud, closemouthed kid, frankly ignorant in such matters, and did not tell her of my father's troubles or my own anxieties.

NATURALIST

How, then, to get to college? Grades. For the first time I focused on my course work and began to receive straight As. Financial aid. I competed for a scholarship from Vanderbilt University, a respected private institution in nearby Nashville, Tennessee. The application consisted of a written test, transcripts, and letters from teachers. As a newcomer at Decatur High School with a spotty previous academic record, I must have seemed easily dismissible to the Vanderbilt scholarship committee. There was no way to convey my passion and special expertise in natural history, nor did I think these qualities should weigh much in comparison with formal classroom performance. Probably I was right. In any case I was turned down.

The GI Bill of Rights offered a way to college. If I enlisted in the Army immediately after my seventeenth birthday, I would be technically a veteran of the Second World War and eligible for veterans' benefits, including financial support for later college attendance. Three years in the service, four years of college, graduate at the age of twenty-four. My father and Pearl enthusiastically approved. So in June 1946 I rode a Greyhound bus to the induction center at Fort McClellan near Anniston, Alabama, where I intended to enlist. I hoped to train and qualify as a medical technician, to learn all the biology possible during my period of servitude, perhaps to travel, and to spend all my spare time improving my skills in entomology.

At the end of the physical examination the attending physician and a recruitment officer took me aside. They informed me that I could not be accepted into the Army because I was blind in my right eye. Physical standards, they said, had tightened with the end of the shooting war. Once again the little pinfish of Paradise Beach, whose dorsal spine had pierced my eye, changed the course of my life. I stood on the veranda of the administration building, my hands on the railing, enviously watching successful recruits drill on the field below, as I waited for transportation back to Anniston. Bitterly disappointed by this unfair outcome, I wept. I vowed that although I had failed here, I would go on, make it through college and succeed some other way, work on the side as needed, live in basements or attics if I had to, keep trying for scholarships, accept whatever help my parents could give, but regardless of what happened, let nothing stop me. In a blaze of adolescent defiance against the fates, I swore I would not only graduate from college but someday become an important scientist.

chapter seven

THE HUNTERS

THE UNIVERSITY OF ALABAMA SAVED ME. IT WAS OPEN TO all graduates of Alabama high schools, by which I mean all qualified *white* graduates, an exclusion that was to endure two more decades. The expense was minimal: $42 a quarter in tuition and fees, $168 for the full year of four quarters, including summer; room rent $7 a month; laundry costs negligible; textbooks $2 to $10 apiece, less if you got them secondhand. Travel back and forth from home, by either hitchhiking or Greyhound bus, cost less than $20. I found a boardinghouse that offered three meals a day, heavy on eggs, flap-jacks, grits, turnip greens, corn bread, and fried chicken necks and wings, for $30 a month. My total expenses for attending the University of Alabama in the 1946–47 academic year plus an extra summer term were about $700. By finishing in three years through an accelerated program, I earned my bachelor of science degree with an expenditure of a little more than $2,000, somewhat less than the annual salary of a government clerk or schoolteacher at the time.

None of it came from loans and scholarships. All of it came from my parents. My luck was holding as I started classes in September 1946. My father's health had improved somewhat. He moved with Pearl yet once again, this time back to Mobile, where they settled in half of a duplex house owned by one of my aging aunts. My father found a job as an accountant at Brookley Air Field and was able to defray part of my expenses. My mother, alerted by this time to our precarious financial state, gave me the balance. As the only child of four parents, I was blessed, proceeding on safer ground than I had expected. Nevertheless, the generous admission standards and low cost of the University of Alabama were important preconditions of upward mobility for me, as they have been for thousands of others even less well situated. Faithful alumnus I have been ever since. My journey came full circle in 1980, when I was invited to give the spring commencement address. There before me, to my relief, sat black graduates among white, the doors of opportunity by then having been opened to all.

When my father and I rode into Tuscaloosa that first September afternoon in his new Hudson Commodore sedan, the campus was verging on chaos. Veterans were pouring in to the university to use the educational benefits of the GI Bill of Rights. All the physical facilities were overcrowded, traffic around the campus was snarled, and teachers, administrators, and counselors were forced to work overtime to cope with the greatest crisis since that sorry day in 1865 when the teenage Corps of Cadets had marched out to engage an advancing column of Union cavalry, lost, and watched as the Federals burned the university down.

I entered college in the company of men as much as ten years my senior, many of whom had undergone harrowing combat only a year or two before. One, Hugh Rawls, a biology student with whom I became good friends, had seen just ten minutes of action. He had gone ashore at Saipan as commander of an amphibious tank; on the beach Japanese shells fell first left, then right, then dead center on his tank. Only he and the gunner were able to crawl out. As he staggered back to the water's edge, seven sniper bullets struck and permanently disabled him. Another good friend, Herbert Boschung, survived three plane crashes during combat missions over Germany. My companions seldom spoke of these events. They had begun a new life.

Many of the men came from outside Alabama, having found colleges and universities closer to their homes too crowded to admit them. I had no problem in adjusting to their company. They were used to mingling good-naturedly with seventeen-year-old recruits. College life was in any case as strange to them as it was to me, and I found reassurance in their shared bewilderment.

The university solved many of its problems by acquiring and converting part of a military hospital two miles away on the outskirts of Tuscaloosa. Thus was created the Northington Campus, where I lived and at first attended most of my classes in Quonset huts and recreation rooms. Because the hospital had been constructed during the war and was large, many of us were assigned private rooms. Mine was a padded cell in the former mental ward. In 1978, thirty-two years later, I watched the tall smokestack crumple, felled by an explosive charge, and the surrounding buildings destroyed. I viewed the scene on film, at the climax of the motion picture *Hooper*, starring Burt Reynolds and Sally Field. Thus Northington Campus ended its existence in the service of a Warner Brothers Gotterdämmerung.

It was in the university, padded cell notwithstanding, that I found my natural home. Shortly after classes started, I climbed the balustraded steps to the main entrance of Nott Hall, built in the 1920s but antebellum in design. I had come to call on Professor J. Henry Walker, head of the Department of Biology, to introduce myself and to discuss my career plans. I was moved to this bold maneuver not by any sense of self-importance—I was still a timid boy, and hubris was only later to fester in my soul—but by the mistaken belief that college students normally chose their careers immediately, and should therefore at an early point consult the faculty for guidance on research and special study. I was reinforced in my presumption by the manly talk I heard among the returned veterans, most of whom had firm career plans of their own.

Walker was a slenderized replica of Warren Harding, a handsome, middle-aged man with blue eyes, prematurely white hair, and meticulous grooming befitting a gentleman of the Deep South. He communicated with soft accent and precise hand gestures. He was careful in all things, I later learned: he kept the department's postage stamps in his office safe. He nodded encouragingly as he peered into my Schmitt box of specimens and listened to my disquisition on the ants of Alabama. He murmured reinforcement as though it were entirely routine for freshman students to launch entomological careers in his office: "Yes, yes, very interesting, fella, very interesting, you've done very well." (All younger males, it turned out, were called fella.) He then made a telephone call and escorted me one flight up to the office of Bert Williams, a young professor of botany newly arrived from Indiana University.

Williams, a tall, gangling man in his thirties with a slight stoop and Lincolnesque face, greeted me warmly without hesitation, as though I were a fellow academic on sabbatical leave. After we talked ants, natural history, and botany for a while, he took me to a table space in his laboratory where, he suggested, I might wish to conduct my research. His largess knew no bounds thereafter. He lent me a dissecting microscope, glassware, and alcohol. He offered to take me along on future field trips. Later in the year he gave me a part-time research assistantship, tracing radioactive phosphorus through the roots of plants. Perhaps because Williams had no other research students at that time, and certainly in part because he was by nature a modest and caring man, he treated me as though I were a graduate student or postdoctoral fellow. I even came to feel as though I had joined his wife and infant daughter as part of the family, like a favored nephew. I have known no kinder or more effective mentor. Forty-seven years later, in 1993, I had the great pleasure of welcoming his granddaughter to her freshman year at Harvard University and offering her my assistance.

I received less personal but equally cordial treatment from the other half-dozen members of the biology faculty. They were used to devoting their time to large classes of premedical students, whose strictly defined needs in anatomy, physiology, histology, and parasitology called for formal lectures and by-the-book laboratory exercises. Undergraduate students who followed in their own footsteps, who were bent on careers in pure science, were relatively rare. I flourished under the guidance of these multiple elders. In addition to training, they gave me the most priceless gifts an apprentice can receive: they let me know that they did not understand everything, that I might acquire information they did not have, and that my efforts were valued.

I set up an aquarium just inside the lower entrance of the biology building and exhibited a giant amphiuma salamander I had captured on one of our field trips. Fascinated students watched as it slithered back and forth crunching live crayfish. I captured entire colonies of *Neivamyrmex* army ants, seething masses of thousands of workers, housed them in artificial nests I built in Williams' laboratory, and studied the parasitic beetles and flies living with them. One of these guests, a near-microscopic beetle in the genus *Paralimulodes*, rides on the backs of the worker ants like a flea and lives by licking oily secre-

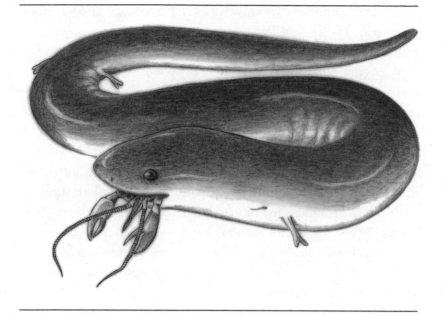

tions from their bodies. My observations later became the basis of one of my early scientific papers. The biology faculty let me know with passing smiles and fragments of corridor conversation that they considered all these efforts useful and important.

To much of the rest of the country the University of Alabama means football, the Rose Bowl in the golden 1930s, the Sugar Bowl in the 1970s and 1980s, the blood feud with Auburn University—Harvard versus Yale with 280-pound tackles—and the legend of Paul William "Bear" Bryant. But those are only the most visible aspects of an excellent public university. The University of Alabama was and is the home of first-rate scholars and teachers, and of abounding opportunity for students who come there, as I did in 1946, to learn about the world, to enter a profession, and, if you will permit an old-fashioned expression, to make something of themselves. I found it as good a place for undergraduate training in my field of science as I would later judge Harvard, Princeton, and Cambridge to be, among other universities I have come to know reasonably well. The personal attention and encouragement I received could not have been surpassed.

What counts heavily in the shaping of a scientist is the accessibility and approval of the faculty. What is truly decisive, however, is the desire and ability of the student. Otherwise, failure awaits regardless of the learning environment, and no excuse can be made for it. If you are a lousy hunter, the woods are always empty.

Unencumbered by the need to hold a job on the side, I devised a time budget that was optimal for my progress through the university; I paid just enough attention to formal courses to get mostly *A*s. I spent the rest of my time doing research, reading, and talking with faculty and other students, usually about evolutionary biology but ranging widely into subjects as diverse as geography, philosophy, and the techniques of creative writing.

I never joined one of the fraternities that dominated social life on the campus, for the simple reason that I was never invited. At the end of my senior year I was inducted into Phi Beta Kappa, the national honor society, as a reward for my overall high grade average. At commencement I hitched a ride to the campus from a middle-aged couple from Tuscaloosa. As they let me off near the president's house, the woman told me her son belonged to Sigma Epsilon Alpha and asked which fraternity I belonged to. "Phi Beta Kappa," I replied. "Why, I never heard of *that* one," she said. Too bad, I thought.

During my first two years I was a part-time cadet in the Reserve Officers Training Corps (ROTC), which was compulsory for all male students at the University of Alabama. I was by then in my late-teens radical period and anxious to see the world rise to meet my own empyrean and wholly untested moral standards. I now held much of American culture in contempt. My guidebooks to radicalism were Philip Wylie's *Generation of Vipers* and *An Essay on Morals*, wonderfully humorous jeremiads against organized religion, Babbitry, Mom worship, and sundry other national foibles. If radical left students had existed and been active then, I might have linked arms on behalf of each week's nonnegotiable demand. At ROTC drill one day, I explained to our sergeant, a regular Army lifer waiting out his retirement in this remote outpost, that marching and rifle practice had been made obsolete by the atom bomb. What we were doing on the parade ground, I declared, was a useless exercise to commemorate the past, like dancing around maypoles. Without changing expression, he growled something inaudible that might have been an expletive.

My feelings about the military were decidedly mixed by this time. On Governor's Day in my sophomore year, His Excellency James Folsom Senior (Junior was also to become governor in the 1990s) traveled from his capital office in Montgomery to review the ROTC cadet corps. A great populist and pro-education governor, referred to fondly as Big Jim because of his towering height and hefty body, and Kissing Jim for reasons ambiguously reported by the press, Folsom was already a legend in the Camellia State. I waited out in front of formation in a special line of cadets to be honored for scholarship, together with others to be recognized for rifle marksmanship. Folsom arrived in a gaggle of state troopers, military officers, and school officials. He was that day conspicuously under the influence of alcoholic refreshments, a common condition for him on public occasions after eight in the morning, and he wove a bit on his feet as he moved from honoree to honoree, speaking to each before handing him a medal. When he came to me he said, "Wheah you from, boy? Mobile? That's a mighty fine place, mighty fine." He reached into a box held by a staff aide and handed me a marksmanship medal. I was delighted to own this unearned award, even for a short while. I much preferred it to the wimpy scholarship medal—it did not seem right for a soldier to be decorated for doing well in English literature. The next day I reluctantly returned my prize to ROTC headquarters.

Leftist radicalism and an uneven passage through ROTC were minor deflections from my chosen trajectory. My resolve to be a biologist was reinforced when I discovered the ideal social environment for developing a scientist—or at least one of several possible ideals. It is the same as for a political revolutionary. Start with a circle of ambitious students who talk and work together and conspire against their elders in order to make their way into a particular discipline. They can be as few as two or as many as five; more than five makes the unit unstable. Give them an exciting new idea that can transform the discipline and with which they can advance their ambitions: let them believe that they own a central truth shared by few others and therefore a piece of the future. Add a distant authority figure, in this case a scientist who has written a revolutionary text, or at least a circle of older revolutionaries who have generated the accepted canon. The farther away these icons are from their acolytes, the better. At midcentury, Europe was best of all. French and German pedants, especially if their texts are hard to translate (and therefore require exegesis by English-speaking disciples) are especially potent. Bring on a local role model, an older man or woman who promotes The Idea and embodies in his character and working habits the ideals of the youthful discipline.

The circle I joined in my sophomore year, though all older than I by two to seven years, were also novices, committed naturalists, and ambitious. They included future successful academics: George Ball from Detroit, later to become professor of entomology at the University of Alberta; Herbert Boschung, a fellow native Alabamian who was to remain at the university first as professor and subsequently as director of the Alabama State Natural History Museum; Hugh Rawls, whose love of mollusks led to a professorship in Illinois; and Barry Valentine, a New Yorker who became a professor of zoology and entomology at Ohio State University.

Our mentor in this formulaic mix was Ralph Chermock, newly arrived from Cornell University as an assistant professor. A relative of Erich Tschermak von Seysenegg, one of the three rediscoverers of the Mendelian laws of heredity, he was a highly competent specialist in butterfly classification and deeply committed to research on evolutionary biology. At thirty, Chermock was physically impressive, an amateur boxer with a compact gymnast's body and thick arms, who occasionally performed one-arm pushups on his office floor to intimidate his followers, but also a tense man who chain-smoked and often snorted and giggled when he laughed. He had the disconcerting habit of listening intently to everything you had to tell him, head cocked and wearing an inviting but quizzical smile, like a psychiatrist or a skeptical job interviewer.

Perhaps I overinterpret Chermock's demeanor from his particular reaction to me. On arriving at the university in 1947 he immediately spotted me as a youngster turning spoiled and overconfident from too much praise. An adjustment was in order. He scandalized me by giving me an $A-$ instead of A in a course on evolutionary theory when I was convinced I had done brilliantly—at least until thirty years later, when I reread my final examination paper. In any case he took every opportunity to grind my ego down to size. When I completed a careful laboratory study of prey selection in the trapjawed ant *Strumigenys louisianae*, using a "cafeteria" technique I had invented myself, and showed him the article I had written on my findings, his response was muted. He gravely informed me that I could never publish the article until I had confirmed the laboratory data by going back into the field and actually finding the same prey captured and dead in undisturbed *Strumigenys* nests. I knew it would be like searching for a needle in a haystack, but out I went, day after day, locating these elusive little ants and carefully opening their nests until finally I discovered one with freshly caught prey that were still intact enough to be identified before the voracious larvae had eaten them; and Chermock relented. The several best teachers of my life, including Chermock, have been those who told me that my very best was not yet good enough.

Ball and Valentine had come to Alabama explicitly to work with Ralph Chermock. With him they brought the Cornell mystique, the

reputation of an entomology department whose history extended back to the great nineteenth-century pioneer John Henry Comstock, and whose reputation for total dedication to insect research at the highest professional level was and remains internationally respected. Awed by the legends, I felt myself to be in the best of company.

The prophets of the Chermock circle were the architects of the Modern Synthesis of evolutionary theory. All were, in 1947, men of middle age who worked in prestigious places like Columbia, the University of Chicago, and New York's American Museum of Natural History. The sacred text of the Chermock circle was Ernst Mayr's 1942 work *Systematics and the Origin of Species*. Mayr was the curator of birds at the American Museum, but his training had been in Germany, a source of added cachet. The revolution in systematics and biogeography that Mayr promulgated was spreading world-wide, but especially in England and the United States, the national strongholds of Darwinian evolutionary theory.

Bear with me while I explain the reason for the extraordinary impact of the new Darwinian movement. By 1920, just a quarter-century before I encountered it as a student, evolutionary biology had dissolved into a jumble of natural history observations, with its best theory consisting of a few rules and geographic trends mounted upon statistical correlations. The principle of natural selection, the core of the Darwinian theory, was itself in doubt. Geneticists thought that evolution might proceed not so much by incremental episodes of natural selection (acting upon continuously varying traits such as size, instinct, and digestion) as by mutations that change heredity in discontinuous steps. In retrospect it seems obvious that both propositions had to be true. Variation, we now understand very well, arises by mutations and also by recombinations of mutations during sexual reproduction; the changes can be large or small in effect; and natural selection—differential survival and reproduction—determines which mutations and combinations survive and reproduce by virtue of the traits they prescribe in such properties as size, instinct, and digestion.

This synthetic view is essentially the Darwinian theory of natural selection with mutating genes added. The close connection to Darwinism is why the modern theory came to be called Neo-Darwinism or, just as often, the Modern Synthesis. In the 1920s and early 1930s a group of population geneticists, most prominently Sergei Chetverikov of Russia, Sewall Wright of the United States, and J. B. S. Haldane and Ronald A. Fisher of England, used mathematical models to demonstrate that one gene form created by mutation can replace another throughout a population even if its advantage in survival and reproduction is quite small, say 1 or 2 percent. In theory at least, the substitution can occur rapidly, with most of it completed in as few as ten generations. Such microevolution, entailing one or a few genes at a time, can accumulate to become macroevolution, producing whole new structures such as eyes and wings. It can also cause the splitting of species into two or more daughter species, a process that is the fount of higher-level biodiversity.

The Modern Synthesis reconciled the originally differing worldviews of the geneticists and naturalists. It empowered scientists in both disciplines to examine the entire evolutionary cavalcade as an extension of Mendelian heredity and, later, to add the refinements of genetics brought by molecular biology.

The natural history phase of the Modern Synthesis followed genetics and natural selection theory. If there was any single moment of birth, it was the publication in 1937 of Theodosius Dobzhansky's landmark *Genetics and the Origin of Species*. For the first time, new data from the field and laboratory defined the differences among species and races with precision, illuminating the nature of variation within populations in chromosomes and genes, and the steps of microevolution. Evolution seemed firmly grounded in genetics, at least to the following extent: nothing the geneticists could say by the late 1940s, when I came along as a student, seemed likely to overturn the Modern Synthesis. Only a complete surprise, something major and out of the blue, could accomplish that. To this day nothing so radical has occurred, although many an ambitious biologist has tried to play the role of revolutionary.

The naturalists were given a hunting license, and for the Chermock circle Mayr's *Systematics and the Origin of Species*, following upon Dobzhansky's book, was the hunter's vade mecum. From Mayr we learned how to define species as biological units. With the help of his written word we pondered the exceptions to be expected and the processes by which races evolved into species. We acquired a clearer, more logical way to think about classification by using the phylogenetic method. This system measures differences between species by the amount of evolution that has occurred since they split apart.

Also in our armamentarium was George Gaylord Simpson's *Tempo and Mode in Evolution*, published in 1944. The great paleontologist argued that the fossil record is consistent with the evidences of ongoing evolution seen in living species. And finally, in 1950, botany entered the mainstream with the publication of Ledyard Stebbins' *Variation and Evolution in Plants*.

RIGHT: *Ed Wilson (left) and his best friend Ellis MacLeod at the Hubbard School, Washington, D.C., in 1940, dressed for duty as student traffic-crossing guards.*
BELOW: *The three-year-old future zoologist, in 1932, with an early animal acquaintance.*

In 1937, when Ed was eight, he lived for several months in an Atlanta boardinghouse with his father, Edward O. Wilson, Sr.

The author, devoted to entomology at the age of thirteen, collects insects in a vacant lot next to his Mobile, Alabama, home, in the summer of 1942. (Photograph by Ellis MacLeod.)

As an Eagle Scout, in Brewton, Alabama, 1944.

ABOVE: *The author with police escort near Gemeheng on April 11, 1955, during the long trek through the mountains of New Guinea's Huon Peninsula.*
LEFT: *With Methuselah, his pet giant Cuban anole, at the Atkins Gardens near Cienfuegos, in July 1953.*

RIGHT: *William L. Brown, Ed's mentor in his early studies of ants, at the Museum of Comparative Zoology in 1955.*
BELOW: *Renee and Ed at Holden Green, Harvard University's housing project for married students and young faculty, in November 1956.*

Field work in the Florida Keys during the 1966–1968 experiment on island biogeography. LEFT: *The author, perched in the crown of a red mangrove tree, identifies insects in and around an abandoned osprey nest.*
BELOW: *His student and collaborator Daniel Simberloff approaches a mangrove islet during the recolonization surveys.*

ABOVE: *Ed Wilson examines ants at Spring Hill, in Trinidad's North Range, in 1961.* RIGHT: *Renee Wilson assists with butterfly net at Gulf Shores, Alabama, in 1956.*

Wilson receives the National Medal of Science from President Carter at a White House ceremony, November 22, 1977.

We thus were equipped with the texts of radical authority. We also had field guides and our own previously acquired expertise: fishes, amphibians, and reptiles for Boschung; mollusks for Rawls; beetles for Ball and Valentine; and ants for me. And providence shone bright on all of us together: Valentine had an automobile. We were scientifically licensed hunters, with the means to roam an ecologically diverse state that had to that time been only partly explored by naturalists.

Chermock encouraged us to collect not only our favored organisms but also amphibians and reptiles for the University of Alabama collection. On weekends and holidays we struck out across the state, to the farthest corners and back and forth. We pulled the car over to roadsides and clambered down into bay-gum swamps, hiked along muddy stream banks, and worked in and out of remote hillside forests. On rainy spring nights we drove along deserted rural back roads, falling silent to listen for choruses of frogs. Sometimes I sat on the front fender of the car as Rawls or Valentine drove slowly. Perched that way, with my left arm curled around a headlight and a collecting jar held in my right hand, I watched for frogs and snakes spotlighted by the high beams of the car. When one was sighted the driver stopped the car, and I dashed ahead to bottle the specimen. On other nights we walked the streets of Tuscaloosa, observing and collecting insects attracted to the lights of storefronts and service stations. During these expeditions I soaked up new information on dryinids, perlids, limulodids, entomobryomorphs, plethodontids, lithobiids, sphingids, libelludids, and so on and on deep into the heart of biodiversity. Chermock was unimpressed by our growing expertise. He told us, half seriously, that we could not call ourselves biologists until we knew the names of 10,000 kinds of organisms. I doubt that he could have passed the test himself, but it didn't matter. Hyperbole from the chief kept our juices flowing.

By the age of eighteen I had been converted to scientific professionalism. Barely out of my Boy Scout years, I was back on the trail

of merit badges, this time through research, discovery, and publication. I came to understand that science is a social activity. Previously I had spent most of my time in natural history to learn about wild creatures and to enjoy personal adventure. I didn't care much what others thought of my activity. Now, as Alfred North Whitehead once said of scientists generally, I did not discover in order to learn; I learned in order to discover. My private pleasure was now tinged with social value. I came routinely to ask: What have I acquired in my studies that is new not just for me but for science as a whole?

The poorly explored Alabama environment offered the Chermock circle boundless opportunity for discovery even with minimal training. One night we drove slowly from the central part of the state into the Florida panhandle, stopping the car frequently to listen to the songs of chorus frogs mating in the accumulated rainwater of road-side ditches. (For a close approximation of a chorus frog call, run the edge of your fingernail along the fine teeth of a pocket comb.) We were searching for the zone where the northern race *Pseudacris nigrita triseriata*, which sings with one trill pattern, meets and interbreeds with the southern race, *Pseudacris nigrita nigrita*, which sings with a different pattern. Near dawn we encountered the changeover close to the Florida border, and then it proved to be very abrupt. We reasoned that the two forms are actually reproductively isolated species, not interbreeding races, and deserved their formal distinction as *Pseudacris triseriata* and *Pseudacris nigrita*. Research by later specialists proved us right.

At another time, wading far up the underground stream of a cave in northern Alabama, we discovered a new kind of blind white shrimp. And again: in mixed hardwood and pine forests, Barry Valentine and I collected the first Alabama specimens of the rare insect order Zoraptera, and soon afterward published our records in an entomological journal. Occasionally I worked alone, an old habit. While digging into soil on the fringes of a swamp near Tuscaloosa, I discovered a new species of a pretty little ant with dark-brown body and yellow legs and described it as *Leptothorax tuscaloosae*.

Scientific discovery at this elementary level was all so easy, all such fun. I could not understand why most of the other students at the university did not also aspire to be biologists.

Meanwhile I developed a strong new research interest in the imported fire ant, which I had first observed in Mobile in 1942. The notorious pest species was beginning to spread out of the city and into the fields and woodlands of the rural countryside. In 1948 Bill Ziebach, the "Outdoors" editor of the *Mobile Press Register*, began a series of articles on the threat by the ant to crops and wildlife. He consulted me on the species and quoted me in the paper. As a result, in early 1949 the Alabama Department of Conservation asked me to conduct a study of the ant and evaluate its impact on the environment. I took leave from the university for the spring term to begin, at the age of nineteen, a four-month stint as entomologist, my first position as a professional scientist. I was joined by James Eads, another biologist, like my other companions a war veteran in his mid-twenties and, most crucially again, owner of a car. Jim and I criss-crossed southwestern Alabama and the western counties of the Florida panhandle, mapping the expanding semicircular range of the ant. We dug up colonies to analyze nest structure, explored fields for crop damage, and interviewed farmers. In July we submitted a fifty-three-page analysis to the Department of Conservation office in Montgomery titled "A Report on the Imported Fire Ant *Solenopsis saevissima* var. *richteri* Forel in Alabama." It contained original findings on the ant still in use today, including the rate of spread (five miles a year along all borders), the partial elimination of native fire ant species, and documentation of moderate crop damage caused by direct consumption of seeds and seedlings.

How this notorious insect got its common name is itself a story worth telling. Up to the time of our first meeting with state officials in Montgomery, the species was called the Argentine fire ant, in recognition of its presumed native origins (it is now known to occur widely through northern Argentina as far as the Paraguayan border). Someone in the Department of Conservation suggested that the name might prove offensive to Argentinians; we already had too many German cockroaches, English sparrows, and the like. We should change it, he said, while we had time. Someone else, I can't remember who, suggested the imported fire ant. That name was used in our report and subsequently by the media and in scientific literature.

In the year following, while working on my master's degree at the University of Alabama, I intensified my studies of the imported fire ant. Eads and I, along with Marion Smith at the National Museum, had observed that workers of the species belonging to different colonies vary in color from dark brown to light reddish brown. I noticed further that the light workers were smaller, and that their colonies appeared to be displacing those of the dark workers. By 1949 the dark form was limited mostly to peripheral areas in Alabama and Mississippi. It had disappeared entirely from Mobile, its point of origin. I set out to test experimentally whether the two forms were genetically distinct. One method I invented was to introduce light queens into dark colonies and observe the color of their offspring reared in a socially altered environment. The color remained true to their mother queen, providing evidence—but not definitive proof—that the difference between light and dark was hereditary.

In the course of my switching experiments I discovered that when more than one queen was introduced into a new colony at the same time, the workers executed all but one by stinging and dismembering them. They never made the mistake of eliminating the final queen, which would have destroyed the colony's ability to produce more workers. This result foreshadowed the discovery, by other entomologists thirty years later, that the workers are able to discriminate among many queens and select the healthiest and most fecund.

In a history of the imported fire ant I published later, in 1951, I considered the color forms to be varieties of the same species. In 1972 William Buren, after an exhaustive new study, confirmed my general findings but elevated the light form to full species rank. He gave it the name *Solenopsis invicta*, meaning the "unconquered" *Solenopsis*. In 1972 the ant was spreading throughout the southern United States in the teeth of intense efforts and the expenditure of over $100 million to stop it. In a widely quoted interview at the time I summed up the futility of the enterprise in a phrase: the fire ant eradication program, I said, is the Vietnam of entomology.

I was exhilarated by the successes of my early fire ant research. I found that the vagrant learning of my boyhood could be focused in a way that was of interest and practical use to the public. The self-confidence I acquired helped to carry me through the critical years of intellectual growth and testing ahead.

Meanwhile, a second obsession intruded briefly into my college training. I was transfixed by the legend of the four-minute mile, the supposedly unbreakable barrier of track and field. In 1945, when Gunder Hägg brought the record down to 4:01.4, there was much talk about whether the great Swedish miler had reached the limit of human endurance. Such speculation was entirely misdirected, of course: an inspection of the history of the event shows that the mile record had been descending in a nearly straight line for eighty years; the curve showed no sign of bottoming out when Hägg led the world, and a simple extrapolation in the late 1940s would have indicated that the four-minute mile could be expected at any time. That moment came on May 6, 1954, when England's Roger Bannister ran the distance in 3:59.4. Thereafter hundreds of athletes repeated the feat, pushing the finishing time steadily downward. As I write, the record stands at 3:46.31.

But in 1948, while athletes around the world prepared for the first postwar Olympic Games, distance running was still in its romantic period. The four-minute mile was the Everest of track and field. In the July 10 issue of the *Saturday Evening Post* I came upon an article declaiming that European athletes would "run Americans ragged" in the distance events. They trained longer, the author said, were willing to endure more discipline and pain than the soft Americans, and would sweep the medal rounds. Gunder Hägg was pictured cruising along a track in six-foot strides, long dark hair flying. I became enchanted by the idea of breaking records by will and discipline. If you were not large in body, I thought, perhaps you could triumph by being large in spirit. It was my kind of activity: do it alone, avoid the drag of teams, have no one witness your trials and failures, until you can accomplish some exceptional feat.

So I bought a pair of surplus Army boots to add weight to my feet and endurance to my body, and started running through the back streets of Mobile, into the countryside, and, back in Tuscaloosa, round and round Northington Campus, which I treated as a giant

track. I trained in solitude, mostly at night, all through the late summer and into the winter of 1948. I scaled the chain-link fence surrounding the University of Alabama athletic grounds in order to run on the cinder track when the regular athletes had left, to get the feel of a quarter-mile. I ran for an hour or two hours at a time. I had neither coach nor training schedule, and spoke to no one about my effort. I just ran in the heavy shoes that I thought would lend wings to my feet when I later switched to lighter gear.

In February I tried out for the track team. I simply reported to the locker room, put on spiked shoes for the first time in my life, walked out on to the track, and ran a trial mile while the coach timed me with a stopwatch. I came in at "a little over five minutes." The coach mercifully didn't tell me the exact time, and I didn't want to hear it. I was bitterly disappointed and humiliated. Not just my body but my philosophy had failed. But—surely if I tried harder I could do better! The coach was kindly disposed. He suggested that I practice for the two-mile race. There were no longer distances, such as 10,000-meter races and marathons, in the Southern Conference programs of 1949. So I started coming to practice for two-mile runs every afternoon, adding speed sprints to my endurance training. But it was too late, and obviously hopeless. At nineteen, I was already a senior, and I must have seemed to the coach his poorest prospect. We were both saved further embarrassment when shortly afterward I was offered the temporary position to survey fire ants in Alabama. I told the coach I was dropping out, and handed back my spiked shoes. He did not burst into tears.

My failure galled me for years afterward. What, I sometimes mused, if I had started at sixteen or seventeen, with proper coaching? Might I have at least made the team? Would Gunder Hägg have found an American rival? In 1970, at the age of forty-one, I started jogging again, then running wind sprints, this time to lose weight and safeguard my health. These goals attained, I felt the old fire re-kindling and crazy hopes rising: maybe I could compete in races at the master's level, for men over forty. Obviously no four-minute miles were in the cards, but perhaps a five-minute mile? As my times dropped in solitary runs, I consulted the world records for different age groups, from childhood to old age. They are kept for all distances, based on times registered from all over the world. I found that even though most of the records from one age to the next, say twenty-nine to thirty to thirty-one years, were made by different individuals at various meets in widely separated parts of the world, they formed a tight line of points for each event. The curves peaked in the early twenties for the hundred-meter dash and in the late twenties for the marathon. This statistical evidence suggested that the best in the world, whoever they were, wherever and whenever they ran, turned in a record time that is precisely predictable once age is known. Age alone accounts for almost all the variation in world record times.

This result impressed me deeply. It seemed to show that heredity is destiny, at least in one important sense: taken to the limit of human capacity, performance follows a predetermined trajectory. No athlete can break away, not even an iron-willed distance runner. I applied the results to my own capacity. I took the ratio of my mile in 1949, "a little over five minutes," to the world record set in that period, a tick over four minutes. Multiplying it by the world record held in 1970 by men in their early forties, I arrived at my own likely best personal time, about six minutes.

Pathetic! In a sport where a tenth of one percent can mean victory or defeat, I was carrying a 25 percent hereditary deficit. Then I felt a last adolescent surge. I would break the apparent genetic bond and wipe away the stain of 1949! This was the period just before the jogging craze of the mid-1970s. I ran the streets of my hometown, Lexington, Massachusetts, in tennis shoes, almost never encountering another jogger. Dogs chased me, neighbors stared, teenage boys hurled taunts. I ran quarter-mile wind sprints on the high school track. I entered races and did time trials. My three best times were 6:01, 6:01, and 6:04. Returning to my track tables, I estimated that my fastest time for two miles would be about 13 minutes. One day I ran my personal best, 12:58. Heredity was destiny after all.

Meanwhile, I witnessed one triumph after another by my friend Bernd Heinrich, a distinguished entomologist and champion master's distance runner. He won the over-forty laurels in the 1980 Boston Marathon, and variously set national or world records in the 50-mile, 100-kilometer, and 24-hour endurance runs, the latter by covering 158 miles in nonstop running. I went out with him one day for a 4-mile practice run, during which he patiently held back as I padded alongside. "Ed," he said, "you could go faster if you ran on the balls of your feet." He might as well have said, you could fly if you flapped your wings. He seemed made of aluminum tubes and wires. His lungs were leather-lined. He was Mozart to my envious Salieri.

The experience has often made me think more objectively about my own limitations and more generally about those of the species to which I belong. For the obsessed and ambitious, the only strategy is to probe in all directions and learn where one's abilities are exceptional, where mediocre, where poor, then fashion tactics and prostheses to achieve the best possible result. And never give up hope that the fates will allow some unexpected breakthroughs.

I am blind in one eye and cannot hear high-frequency sounds; therefore I am an entomologist. I cannot memorize lines, have trouble visualizing words spelled out to me letter by letter, and am often unable to get digits in the right order while reading and copying numbers. So I contrived ways of expressing ideas that others can recite with quotations and formulas. This compensation is aided by an unusual ability to make comparisons of disparate objects, thus to produce syntheses of previously unconnected information. I write smoothly, in part I believe because my memory is less encumbered by the phrasing and nuances of others. I pushed these strengths and skirted the weaknesses.

I am a poor mathematician. At Harvard as a tenured professor in my early thirties I sat through two years of formal courses in mathematics to remedy my deficiency, but with little progress. It was distance running all over again. I remain mathematically semiliterate. When walked through step by step, I have been able to solve partial differential equations and grasp the elements of quantum mechanics, although I soon forget most of what I have learned. I have no taste for the subject. I have succeeded to some extent in theoretical model building by collaborating with mathematical theoreticians of the first class. They include, in successive periods of my research, William Bossert, Robert MacArthur, George Oster, and Charles Lumsden. My role was to suggest problems to be addressed, to combine my intuition with theirs, and to lay out empirical evidence unknown to them. They were my intellectual prosthesis and I theirs. Like my fellow field biologists who waded with me into swamps and climbed forested hillsides, we were civilized hunters searching for something new that might be captured, something valuable enough to take back home and display at the tribal campfire.

I have evolved a rule that has proved useful for myself and might be for others not born with championship potential: for every level of mathematical ability there exists a field of science poorly enough developed to support original theory. The advice I give to students in science is to move laterally and up and down and peer all around. If you have the will, there is a discipline in which you can succeed. Look for the ones still thinly populated, where fine differences in raw ability matter less. Be a hunter and explorer, not a problem solver. Perhaps the strategy can never work for track, with one distance and one clock. But it serves wonderfully well at the shifting frontiers of science.

chapter eight

GOOD-BYE TO THE SOUTH

WHEN I GRADUATED FROM THE UNIVERSITY OF ALABAMA, IN 1949, my father's health had begun to decline steeply. Chronic bronchitis, worsened by two packs of cigarettes a day, racked his body far into the night. As a member of a class and generation of men who took pride in fingers stained yellow by tar, he had no inclination to quit the habit. His alcoholism was also severe, and that addiction he took seriously. He feared becoming, as he put it, "like a Bowery bum." Already a member of Alcoholics Anonymous, he checked himself in at intervals to a rehabilitation center for detoxification and yet another stab at recovery. Nothing worked for long; the problem seemed insoluble. Given that he was already seeking professional help, there was nothing left for Pearl and me to offer but sympathy and attempts at persuasion. I hid the frustration and anger I felt: a son does not easily instruct his father on right behavior and self-control.

In early 1951 my father grew noticeably depressed and his behavior erratic. I was not able to read the signs, and was in any case away from home most of the time. I did not suspect what was coming. Early in the morning of March 26, he wrote a calm note of apology to his family, drove his car to an empty section of Bloodgood Street near the Mobile River, seated himself by the side of the road, put his favorite target pistol to his right temple, and ended his pain. He was forty-eight years old when he died.

He was given a military funeral at Magnolia Cemetery, graced with rifle volleys and the folding of the American flag from atop his coffin. The painful disorder of his life made this strictly prescribed rite of passage deeply comforting to me. My father was laid to rest close to the last of his three brothers, Herbert, dead from heart failure only a year before.

After a few days the shock of grief was infiltrated by feelings of relief, for my father now released, for Pearl whose desperate siege had been broken, and for myself—the filial obligation I had feared might tie me to a crumbling family was now forgiven. The impending tragedy finally took form, and happened, and was over. I could now concentrate entirely on my new life. As the years passed, sorrow and guilt-tinged relief were replaced by admiration for my father's courage. It is easy to say that the greater courage would have been to try again, to pull himself back and struggle toward a normal life. I am reasonably certain, however, that he had considered the matter very carefully and decided otherwise.

No son knows his father well enough to matter until it is too late; then understanding comes in fragments. I can say of him that he was an intelligent man who cheated himself of his own potential. Before he finished high school he ran away from home to go to sea in the boiler room of a cargo ship, made one round trip to Montevideo, and joined the Army. In the Quartermaster Corps he learned his trade as an accountant, which carried him through a long succession of jobs in private business and, in his last twelve years, the federal government. He was by nature loyal, warm, and sympathetic. He was quick-tongued in mixed company, given to frequent bouts of nostalgic and embroidered tales of personal adventure and to little, short-lived flashes of anger. He loved poetry but, like me, could not memorize enough lines to recite it competently. The youngest of four brothers, he lost his father when he was thirteen, and in his remaining time at home was spoiled by a mother whose permissiveness had become a family legend. His lifelong self-indulgence was made worse by a restiveness that never found ease because, I suspect, he had no destination in mind. His dream of retirement was to pilot his own houseboat back and forth on the Intracoastal Waterway of the Atlantic and Gulf Coasts, with no place chosen as home port.

My father's reading was limited to magazines and newspapers. He paid scant attention to music or to history other than that of his family, and he had little interest in current affairs. He loved hunting and fishing but did not take the time to develop his skills. He turned instead to the more quickly satisfying recreation of target practice with his collection of guns. From him I learned how to blow cans and bottles off fence posts with pistols and shotguns at twenty paces, how to fire a U.S. Army Colt .45 with both hands to keep it from bucking too far out of line.

He drew strength from his conception of southern white male honor. Never lie, he told me, never break your word, be always respectful of others and protective of women, and never back down if honor is at stake. He rested his dicta upon the remembered traditions of his family, which he rewove and annotated endlessly. He meant every word of this credo, and he was a physically courageous man. I think he would have died rather than accept humiliation or disgrace as defined by his lights. In truth, he did just that in the end. But otherwise the world in which he chose to live was too confining, too ambiguous, and too nearly obsolete to test his code of honor in any decisive way.

I sometimes reflect on the fact that my father and the old house on Charleston Street are not just physically gone but absolutely gone, except for a handful of photographs, official records, and now this brief memoir. The neighborhood of old trees and sagging Victorian homes has been scraped away and replaced with cinderblock public housing. When I and a few other older family members die, the man and our family home will vanish almost as though they never existed. This observation on the human condition is one that I find both altogether banal and eternally astonishing. When my cousin Jack Wilson, son of my father's oldest brother and a lifelong resident of Mobile, died in 1993, a large section of the cerebral memory of his and my father's generation was erased. I have felt a small pleasure from this, certainly not from Jack's death but from the fact that I am now the sole inheritor of my father's existence. I have been freed to recreate my father not just from his scantily remembered actions but also from what I can reconstruct of his character. Some of that I will keep private and let go to oblivion, when I die.

Strong father, weak son; weak father, strong son; either way, pain drives the son up or down in life. I do not dare to take the full measure of my father's influence on me. But I would say to him if I could that his self-image was a worthy template, and I tried to bring it to fruition.

My mother, Inez Linnette Freeman, had achieved a better life after the divorce, and she encouraged and assisted me to do the same. She had come from a background similar to my father's in many respects, her roots reaching far back in Alabama. Her forebears, all of English descent, had come from the Mississippi Delta and Georgia to settle in the northern half of the state. Several of them helped to found the little towns of Bremen, Falkville, and Holly Pond during the early and mid-1800s. Most were farmers and merchants. One, my great-grandfather Robert Freeman, Jr., was both a farmer and a renowned (I hesitate to use the word notorious) horse trader. His wife, Isabel "Izzie" Freeman, practiced as a country doctor, which I interpret to mean the equivalent of practical nurse and midwife in a rural region where M.D.s were scarce. Being freeholders with property well north of the cotton belt and main river ports, these people by and large held tepid opinions about the Confederacy and the Civil War. When captured by Federal forces, Private Robert Freeman readily forswore further military service in order to return to his family and farm near Falkville.

In 1938 my mother married Harold Huddleston, a native of Stevenson, Alabama, near the Tennessee line. He was a successful businessman, and later advanced by the time of his retirement to a vice presidency of the Citizens Fidelity Bank and Trust, one of the several largest banks in the Southeast. Each September from my early teens until my graduation from college, I lived with my mother and Harold in their home first in Louisville, Kentucky, and then in the adjacent town of Jeffersonville, across the Ohio River in Indiana. They were supportive of my plans to attend college and train to be a biologist. Harold himself had attended the University of Alabama. Upward mobility into the professional class was something both he and my mother embraced as a fundamental ethic. They frequently took me to local parks where I could collect butterflies and ants. In what was a brave expedition on her part, my mother accompanied me when I was fourteen to Mammoth Cave in Kentucky. The cavern system, one of the largest in the world, had recently been set aside as a national park. As we descended into the gloom, I held back from the tour group to search (illegally) along the walkways for blind yellow ground beetles, cave crickets, and any other cave-dwelling insects I could find, giving the specimens to my mother to hold. She lost them somewhere near the cave exit, and I sulked all the way back to Louisville.

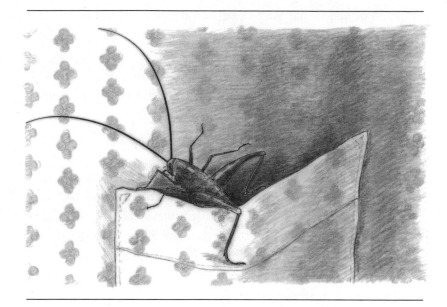

My mother provided not just encouragement but also financial help when I entered college. Later, as I prepared to enter the Ph.D. program at Harvard, she offered to pay my way through medical school. She wanted to be sure, as she put it, that I had not excluded dreams of a medical career for lack of money. But this more traditional profession held no interest for me. An entomologist I would be, and I was confident that I could make it the rest of the way on my own.

I did support myself from the time of my master of science candidacy at the University of Alabama until I completed the Ph.D. at Harvard five years later. I relied on scholarships and teaching assistantships throughout and never incurred debt. Long-term student loans were scarce to absent at the time. In any case the possibility simply never occurred to me.

In 1950 I transferred to the University of Tennessee, in Knoxville, to begin work on the Ph.D., mainly because of the presence there of Arthur Cole, a professor of entomology who specialized in the classification of ants. That year I searched the nearby Chilhowee and Great Smoky mountains for my favored insects, building my personal collection, while studying Cole's collection from the United States, the Philippines, and India. I finished a comprehensive review of the history and genetic change in the imported fire ant and sent it to the journal *Evolution*. While serving as Cole's laboratory teaching assistant, I honed my skills in the anatomy and classification of insects.

The academic challenge was not great at the University of Tennessee, and I grew restive. Out of boredom I also became a bit reckless. I was intrigued by the fact that a statute was still on the books forbidding the teaching of evolution in the state. In 1925 the Tennessee legislature had declared unlawful any doctrine that questioned the divine origin of man. A young high school teacher, John T. Scopes, was brought to trial that same year for presenting the theory of evolution to his biology class. In one of the most celebrated legal proceedings of American history, William Jennings Bryan led the prosecution and Clarence Darrow the defense. Since Scopes was undeniably guilty, he was convicted and fined $100, but not before expert testimony from scientists in favor of evolution and Darrow's scarifying courtroom examination of Bryan on the Bible sent shock waves through the ranks of the Christian fundamentalists. The state supreme court later acquitted Scopes, but only on the ground that the fine was excessive. The law stayed in place and was still untested in the higher courts when I came to Knoxville.

In the fall of that year, while teaching laboratory sessions in the general biology course at the University of Tennessee, I learned about the extraordinary discovery of the first of the South African man-apes. These erect, small-brained hominids seemed to place the origin of humanity one to two million years ago on the African continent. They were the key missing links between remote apelike ancestors and the most primitive true humans of the genus *Homo* known at the time of the Scopes trial, the so-called Javan Man and Peking Man—both of which are now placed in the single species *Homo erectus*.

Here, I thought, was one of the most important scientific discoveries of the century: Eden revealed in Africa by the lights of Darwin! I was intrigued by the prospect of a complete human phylogeny, with its deep significance for the self-image of our species. I also had a mischievous itch to shake things up just to see what would happen. I might get into the same trouble as Scopes, but I would spring out of it immediately—I guessed—because the evidence was so much more solid—I felt sure—and the faculty would support me—I hoped. In any case I could not resist spreading the word about the amazing South African man-apes.

I was granted permission to give a lecture on the subject to the elementary biology class. I told them the matter was settled: we *did* descend from apes, or a close approximation thereof, and scientists knew when these distant ancestors had lived and even something about how they had lived—they were carnivores, and Eden was no garden. The students, some my own age, were mostly Protestants, and many had been raised in fundamentalist families. Some, I am sure, had been taught that Darwin was the devil's parson, the spokesman of evil heresy. They scribbled notes; some glanced at the clock as time wore on. Finally the hour ended, and I waited for a reaction. The students filed out, talking among themselves about this and that but not, so far as I could overhear, about evolution, until only one remained, a large blond boy who looked me in the eye and asked, "Will this be on the final exam?" I told him no, please don't worry. He seemed relieved; one less thing to memorize. Nothing more was heard of my lecture. It was as though I had declaimed for an hour on the life cycle of the fruit fly.

The state legislature, yielding to reason or perhaps just resigned to the inevitable, repealed the anti-evolution law in 1967. The religious movement against the theory of evolution has sputtered on in a few other states, unsuccessfully promoting laws to force the teaching of the biblical account of creationism as an alternative theory. Either way, I learned a lesson of my own in Tennessee: the greater problems of history are not solved; they are merely forgotten.

By early 1951 I had decided to move on to Harvard University. It was my destiny. The largest collection of ants in the world was there, and the tradition of the study of these insects built around the collection was long and deep. To this end I had the support of Aaron J. Sharp, a distinguished botanist and professor at the University of Tennessee, who quietly advised me to apply to Harvard and nominated me for a fellowship there. A second supporter was William L. Brown, then a graduate student in Harvard's Department of Biology. I had first contacted Brown in 1948, when I was still an undergraduate at the University of Alabama, because I had heard from Marion Smith of his interest in the biology of ants. He turned out to be a fellow fanatic on the subject. Brown also was, and is, one of the warmest and most generous people I have ever known. He fueled my already considerable enthusiasm with a stream of advice and urgings. Equally important, he treated me from the start as an adult and a fellow professional. His attention was focused on the good of the discipline. He rallied others to the cause and urged them to take up significant research topics. What you must do, he wrote me in so many words, is to broaden the scope of your studies. Never mind a survey of the Alabama ants; start on a monograph of an important ant group. Make it continentwide, or even global if circumstances warrant. You and I and others who join us must get myrmecology on the move. Right now, you have the advantage of living in the Deep South, where there are a great many dacetine ants. These are extraordinarily interesting insects, and we still don't know much about them. There is an opportunity to do some really original research. See what you can come up with, and keep me posted.

I plunged into the dacetine project at once, tracking down species one after another, turning over rocks and tearing apart decaying stumps and logs, dissecting nests, and capturing colonies to be cultured in the laboratory. The dacetines are slender, ornately sculptured little ants with long, thin mandibles. Their body hairs are modified into little clubs, scales, and sinuous whips. In many species a white or yellow spongy collar surrounds their waists. Clean and decorative, they are under the microscope among the most aesthetically pleasing of all insects. The workers hunt springtails and other soft-bodied, elusive insects by approaching them with extremely cautious movement, legs lifting and swinging forward as though in slow motion. They open their jaws wide during the stalk, in some species by more than 180 degrees, to reveal rows of needle-sharp teeth. When the huntresses draw very close, they are able to touch the prey with the tips of paired slender hairs that project forward from their mouths. The instant contact is made, they snap the jaws shut like a bear trap, impaling the prey on their teeth. Each dacetine species uses a variation on this technique, mostly in the speed and degree of caution of the stalking approach, and each hunts a particular range of prey species.

Largely because I enjoyed grubbing in dirt and rotting wood on hands and knees, I was very successful in my pursuit of dacetine ants. In two articles, published in 1950 and 1953, I presented detailed accounts of the comparative behavior of the dacetine ants found in the southern states. In 1959 Brown and I combined our data to prepare a synthesis of dacetine biology. We correlated the food habits of large numbers of species from around the world with their social organization. We discovered that the anatomically most primitive species, which are native to South America and Australia, forage above ground for larger and more various insect prey, such as flies, grasshoppers, and caterpillars. They form large colonies and often have well-differentiated castes, including large-headed "majors" or "soldiers" and small-headed "minors," each playing a different role in the colony. The majors, for example, are adept at defending the colony against invaders, while the minors are prone to serve as brood nurses and attendants of the queen. As evolution proceeded, its trends evi-

denced by living species that are anatomically more advanced, the ants came to specialize more on springtails and other very small insects. The body size of the workers correspondingly decreased and became more nearly uniform within each colony, and the division of labor was diminished. Colony populations became smaller, and the nests more subterranean and inconspicuous.

Ours was a novel approach to the study of behavior. So far as I am aware, the dacetine study was the first of its kind on the evolution of social ecology in animals. It preceded the work of John Crook and others in the 1960s on primate socioecology; and in some respects it was more definitive, principally because we had more species and could use experiments on food choice. But despite the fact that we published our findings in the *Quarterly Review of Biology*, a premier journal with a worldwide distribution, our summary article was cited only rarely thereafter, and principally by fellow entomologists. It had little effect on the later development of behavioral ecology and sociobiology. Part of the reason is that monkeys, birds, and other vertebrates are more nearly human-sized and more familiar than ants, and therefore textbooks and popular accounts treat them as more "important."

William Brown, Uncle Bill as he was to become affectionately known by younger entomologists in later years, urged me to visit Harvard. I did so in late June 1950, traveling three days and nights on a Greyhound bus from Mobile to Boston. We seemed to stop at every city and town of greater than 50,000 population along the way, and I was exhausted by the time I reached the ant room of the Museum of Comparative Zoology. Bill and his wife, Doris, were gracious hosts. They put me up in their Cambridge apartment, where I slept on a sofa next to the crib of their two-year-old daughter Allison. Early the next morning I watched apprehensively as Allison reached through the crib bars for pages of Bill's newly completed Ph.D. thesis. During the next several days, as Bill made final preparations with Doris to leave for field work in Australia, he took time to guide me through the ant collection. Once again he encouraged me to select large, important projects and to aim for publishable results. Your dacetine and fire ant studies are very promising, he said; but now you should come to Harvard in order to work more effectively with projects of even greater scope. Take a global view; don't sell yourself short with local studies and limited goals. He introduced me to Frank M. Carpenter, the professor of entomology and great authority on insect fossils and evolution, who was later to serve as my doctoral supervisor. Both men urged me to apply to the Ph.D. program at Harvard. I did so, even though I had already enrolled for the coming academic year of 1950–51 at the University of Tennessee.

The following spring I was admitted to Harvard for the coming fall semester with a scholarship and teaching assistantship that covered all expenses. In late August 1951 I sold my only suit to a second-hand store in Knoxville for ten dollars, packed all my belongings, including my research notebooks, into a single suitcase, and traveled by bus to visit my mother and Harold in Louisville. After taking one look at me, dressed—how shall I say it—in Salvation Army grunge, Harold escorted me to a men's clothing store and bought me a wardrobe befitting a 1951 Harvard student. I walked out in an Irish tweed jacket, Oxford button-down white shirt, narrow knit tie, chino slacks, and white duck shoes and socks. With a fresh crew cut added, I was ready to pass into a new life.

I arrived in Boston by bus and took the subway to Harvard Square, crossed over to the Harvard Yard entrance next to Massachusetts Hall, and asked the first person I met for directions across campus. He was evidently a student, and he spoke in a cultured English voice. So this, I said to myself, is the famous Harvard accent. Several weeks later the same student, who was indeed a Harvard sophomore, turned up in a laboratory section of beginning biology I was teaching. I learned then that his name was John Harvard Baker; that he was British, having only recently arrived in this country; and that he was a descendant of the uncle of the legendary John Harvard,

whose donation founded the university in 1636 (Harvard himself had no children). Our meeting was, I think, a fittingly symbolic introduction to the university where I was to spend the rest of my professional life.

I walked on that day in September to Richards Hall, one of the graduate student dormitories in Harkness Commons, picked up my keys at the manager's office, and proceeded to my assigned room, number 101. My roommate had already arrived and posted his name on the door: Hezekiah Oluwasanmi. I thought, what kind of a name is that? Polynesian, maybe Samoan? He was Nigerian, and another Ph.D. candidate. We soon became good friends, continuing on through his eventual tenure as vice-chancellor of the University of

Ife. Through the fall of 1951, as I sat reading at my desk, I half listened to Hezekiah and his friends, some of whom wore tribal scars on their cheeks, discuss the coming liberation of Nigeria. They were among the first intellectuals to plot such a movement in British Africa. I wondered if perhaps I was getting involved in something illegal just by being in the same room. I could see the headline in the *Mobile Press Register*: "Alabamian arrested with African revolutionaries as FBI closes in." It was all exhilarating, a proper introduction to the expanding and infinitely interesting world I had entered.

chapter nine

ORIZABA

ALMOST ALL MY LIFE I HAVE DREAMED OF THE TROPICS. MY boyhood fantasies drifted far beyond the benign temperate zone of Thoreau and Muir. Nor did I have any interest in arctic glaciers or the high Himalayas. I hungered instead for the frontiers of Frank Buck and Ivan Sanderson, hunters of tropical exotic animals, and William Beebe, naturalist-explorer of the Venezuelan jungle. My favorite novel was Arthur Conan Doyle's *Lost World,* which hinted that dinosaurs might yet be found on the flat summit of some unclimbed South American *tepui.* I was besotted with *National Geographic* articles on tortoise beetles and butterflies, winged jewels that entomologists—of the kind I hoped to become when I grew up—netted during journeys to remote places with unpronounceable names. The tropics I nurtured in my heart were the untamed centers of Creation.

When I was a boy most of the tropical forests and savannas were indeed still wildernesses in a nineteenth-century sense. They covered vast stretches of land waiting to be explored on foot, and sprinkled through them were unrafted rivers and mysterious mountains. In the farthest reaches of the Amazon-Orinoco basins and New Guinea highlands lived Stone Age peoples never seen by white men. But more compelling than all these wonders, more than white water, talking drums, arrows quivering in tent poles, and virgin peaks awaiting the flags of explorers' clubs, the fauna and flora of the tropics called to me. They were the gravitational center of my hopes, a vertiginous world of beauty and complexity I longed to enter. When I grew impatient during my late teens, I looked around for some passable equivalent nearer home. The Alabama bay-gum swamps and riverine hardwood forests, I realized, were somewhat like tropical forests writ small. After I entered college I explored the edges of the Mobile-Tensaw delta floodplain with that comparison in mind. I was attracted by the dense shrubby vegetation and meanders of unnavigable shallow mud-bottom creeks. It was a place no field biologist had visited—and was seldom entered by anyone for any reason—and I wondered if it might contain undiscovered species of ants and other insects living in ecological niches new to science. I decided I would conduct a one-man expedition into the interior and thus inaugurate my career as a tropical explorer, at least in spirit.

I never made it into the delta. I was too occupied with the demands of college life at the University of Alabama and my ongoing studies of fire ants and other research projects across the state. Then successive transfers to the University of Tennessee and Harvard to continue graduate studies removed me from the region altogether.

In my first year at Harvard I was delayed further. I settled on a sen-

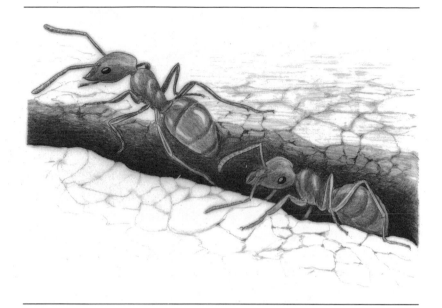

sible thesis project that could be reliably finished in three or four years. *Then*, I figured, I could go to the tropics. My research would be on the ant genus *Lasius*, one of the most abundant but poorly understood assemblages of the north temperate insect fauna. The forty or more species are distributed through the cooler habitats of Europe, Asia, and North America. Their colonies excavate a large percentage of the little crater nests that dot cornfields, lawns, golf courses, and sidewalk cracks across the United States and Canada. If you go out and look for small brown chunky ants along the streets of cities such as Philadelphia, Toronto, and Boise, the first ones you are likely to see are foraging workers of a species of *Lasius*.

My project required a great deal of museum and laboratory work, but my explorer's urge destined me for the open air. I made it back decisively into the field in the summer of 1952 when I teamed up with Thomas Eisner. He was, like me, a first-year graduate student at Harvard. We found we had a great deal of scientific interests in common and soon became best friends. In one sense he was the perfect

Harvard intellectual: multicultural and driven. His father, Hans, was a chemist and German Jew who, with his wife, Margarete, three-year-old Tom, and Tom's older sister Beatrice, left in 1933 when Hitler rose to power. They settled in Barcelona, only to witness the outbreak of the Spanish Civil War and the expansion of fascism. In 1936 Tom, then seven years old, heard the sound of dive bombers attacking the city, as the family prepared to flee to Marseilles and then to Paris. In 1937 the elder Eisner took his family to Montevideo, Uruguay. In this neutral country Tom spent the rest of his childhood in relative peace. The war had been left largely beyond the horizon, but Tom was kept aware of its progress. He was one of the spectators who watched the distant smoke plume rising from the pocket battleship *Admiral Graf Spee* as it was scuttled in the River Plate outside Montevideo after being chased there by British cruisers.

In Uruguay Eisner kindled a lifelong interest in butterflies and other insects. As he approached college age, his family moved to New York. Tom came to Harvard fluent in German, Spanish, French, and English, with a smattering of Italian. He was a virtuoso at the concert piano and, most important to me, a committed entomologist. We were kindred spirits in that one central pursuit. On a grander scale he had repeated the pattern of my own childhood, having been towed from one locality to another, anxious and insecure, turning to natural history as a solace.

Eisner was, and is (he has changed remarkably little over the years), a slender man with wispy hair and a tense and energy-charged manner, spinning in perpetual motion from one research scheme to another. He is a great biologist by virtue not just of extraordinary lifelong dedication but also of a masterly application of what I like to call the pointillist technique, which works wonderfully well in evolutionary biology. Eisner completes one meticulous study after another, usually a pinpoint analysis of some aspect of the way insects and other arthropods use chemical secretions to communicate and defend themselves. Taken separately, any one of the individual contributions may seem to apply to only a few species and hence to be of limited interest. Taken together and viewed from a distance, however, they form a novel evolutionary pattern of biology.

When I met him in the fall of 1951, Eisner was, like me, on the threshold of the serious part of his career. We had the good fortune to fall in together with other students destined for achievement and whose influence on us was immediate and considerable. They included Donald Kennedy, who became president of Stanford University; Howard Schneiderman, in later years vice president for research at Monsanto Company; and Sheldon Wolff, destined for a distinguished career in cytology and medical research.

Tom and I decided to spend the summer of 1952 in search of insects across North America, traveling fast and free. In late June we took off in his 1942 Chevrolet, which he had named Charrúa II after the old Amerindian warrior tribe of Uruguay. We went north from Massachusetts to Ontario, then proceeded across the Great Plains states to Montana and Idaho, from there to California, Nevada, Arizona, New Mexico, through the Gulf states, and, finally, northward home in late August. We were naturalist hobos. We lived on the margin of society. Each night we slept on the ground, sometimes in the feeless camping areas of state parks, more often on the edge of open fields and woodlots off the side of the road. We ate canned food and washed our clothes under campground faucets, putting most of our negligible funds into the care and fueling of Charrúa II. The car required a quart of oil every hundred miles and frequent repairs of its frazzled tires. While I collected and studied ants, Eisner collected ants for his own future thesis research on anatomy, along with dustywings, snakeflies, and other insects of the order Neuroptera.

It was a time when national parks were uncrowded and many of the nation's major highways were still winding two-lane roads. We wandered almost aimlessly through cypress swamps, alpine meadows, and searing deserts, observing and collecting insects. On one ovenlike July night we made a swift traverse of Death Valley, cooled

only by wet handkerchiefs tied around our heads. We saw most of the major ecosystems of North America close up, and all we learned in that remarkable summer cemented our lifelong passion for field biology.

A few months later, in the spring of 1953, I was handed the opportunity of a lifetime: election as a Junior Fellow in Harvard University's Society of Fellows. The Society, patterned after the prize Fellows of Trinity College in Cambridge University, gave three years of unrestricted financial support to young men (and, in later years, young women) who demonstrated exceptional scholarship potential. Junior Fellows were encouraged to study any subject, conduct any form of research, go anywhere in the world their interests directed them. The Society was made up of two dozen Junior Fellows and nine Senior Fellows, the latter being distinguished Harvard professors who served as mentors and dinner companions to the younger men. Each year the Senior Fellows chose eight new members to replace the third-year, graduating class. In 1953, as one of the fortunate few, I found myself lodged free in Lowell House with a generous stipend, a book allowance, and travel funds available upon application.

At the first dinner of the fall term we new Fellows stood as the Society chairman, the historian Crane Brinton, read the statement written by Abbott Lawrence Lowell, who as president of Harvard in 1932 had given a substantial portion of his fortune to found the Society:

> *You have been selected as a member of this Society for your personal prospect of achievement in your chosen field, and your promise of notable contribution to knowledge and thought. That promise you must redeem with your whole intellectual and moral force . . .*
>
> *You will seek not a near, but a distant, objective, and you will not be satisfied with what you have done. All that you may achieve or discover you will regard as a fragment of a larger pattern, which from his separate approach every true scholar is striving to descry.*

Fair enough. On that first evening I savored the expertly selected wine, the rare roast beef, the postprandial cigar, the self-conscious scholar's talk. Like Thackeray's Barry Lyndon, I was a happy indigent admitted to the company of lords. The Society proceeded to transform my self-image and my career. Its greatest immediate impact was a sharp rise in my expectations. I had been examined by first-rate scholars in diverse fields and judged capable of exceptional research across an expanding terrain. I thought, I have three years to justify the confidence placed in me, the same amount of time it took to make Eagle Scout. No problem. The Society's alumni and Senior Fellows were outstanding achievers; they included Nobel and Pulitzer winners. I thought, That's a reasonable standard to shoot for.

The second gift from the Society of Fellows was to place me in the weekly company of other young men, all in their twenties, who had begun to excel in widely diverse fields of learning. My new compan-

ions included Noam Chomsky, with whom I discussed the instinctive behavior of animals; the poet Donald Hall; and Henry Rosovsky, economic historian and future dean of the Faculty of Arts and Sciences at Harvard. Among the many notable dinner guests I met during my three years as a Junior Fellow were Bernard De Voto, T. S. Eliot, Robert Oppenheimer, and Isidor I. Rabi. I spent an especially memorable evening arguing with Rabi about the evolutionary consequences of atomic bomb tests; he defended the position that the explosions were good because radiation increases the rate of mutation, which can speed evolution. And that is a good thing, is it not? Was he serious? I was not completely sure, but the conversation was information-packed and exciting either way.

The final gift of the Society of Fellows was to launch me into the tropics at last. As quickly as I could arrange it, in mid-June, I departed for Cuba. On the flight from Miami to Havana the pilot invited the younger passengers into the cockpit, where I watched the Cuban coast come into view and my dream become reality.

In Havana I joined a small group of other Harvard graduate students to commence a course in tropical botany. We first traveled by

car to the western province of Pinar del Río to visit patches of forest
on the *mogotes*, outcroppings of limestone too rugged to convert into
fields of sugarcane. The rest of the land had been cleared almost
everywhere down to dirt and grass, left dotted for the most part only
by towering royal palms. Several days later we proceeded to the Atkins Gardens, a Harvard-owned property at Soledad, near Cienfuegos on the southwestern coast forty miles east of the Bay of Pigs.

From the Gardens I traveled with three botanists, Robert Dressler,
Quentin Jones, and the course instructor, Grady Webster, to search
for remnants of the Cuban forest in Las Villas Province. The very
difficulty of this quest bore shocking witness to the ecological destruction of the island. For centuries Cuban landowners had relent-
lessly cleared the forests with no concession to the native fauna and
flora. To find the last refuge we had to go beyond the reach of bull-
dozers and chain saws, mostly up onto the slopes of steeper mountains and down the banks of river gorges. Traveling across the west
central part of the island in 1953, I began to undergo a fundamental
change in my view of the tropics.

On one memorable morning, we climbed into a Jeep to visit Blanco's Woods, a locally famous woodlot left uncut because its wealthy
absentee owner had for some reason neglected to "develop" it. Blanco's Woods was one of the few parcels of relatively undisturbed lowland forest remaining in all of Las Villas Province, and probably all
of Cuba. We drove for miles along rutted dirt roads through sugarcane fields and cattle pastures, crossing small fordable streams lined
with corridors of weeds and second-growth woody vegetation. Occasionally we had to stop to open cattle gates and shut them behind
us. We found it next to useless to probe the baked clay ground along
the way for native plants and insects, of which there were few to
none. It was equally pointless to look for endemic Cuban birds and
other vertebrates. Among the few to be seen in the vicinity were the
abundant brown anole lizards on the fence posts and, once in a great
while, a giant Cuban anole in the crown of a royal palm.

NATURALIST

When at last we came to Blanco's Woods it seemed unprepossessing, not a rain forest of popular expectation, but a stand of small to medium-sized trees, mostly torchwood, undergirded by dense shrubby undergrowth. If we had not been able to identify the trees, we might have imagined ourselves to be on the edge of an Iowa woodlot. Still, the little forest proved to be rich in representatives of the original Cuban fauna and flora, and we reveled in the discovery of one native species after another. While mosquitoes feasted on my sweating face and arms, I turned up two treasures of the ant world: the Cuban species *Thaumatomyrmex cochlearis*, its proportionately huge pitchforklike jaws wrapping all the way around the head so that the longest tines stick out beyond the rear border; and *Dorisidris nitens*, one of the rarest ants in the world, a shiny black species of a genus and species also found only in Cuba—and then known from only one previous collection. These specimens and others gathered in a few hours made valuable additions to the Museum of Comparative Zoology ant collection.

We decided to visit next the nearby Trinidad Mountains to study residues of forest still surviving there. Our car trip was even more difficult than the one to Blanco's Woods. We drove southeast along the uncertain two-lane, mostly unpaved highway from Cienfuegos to the town of Trinidad, and we were held up for an hour at a ford on the Rio Arimao jammed with trucks and cars. We had heard that a new road was being cut up the east slopes of the massif, and now we resolved, in order to make up lost time, to take it as a short cut to the vicinity of San Blas, where we knew forest was most likely to be found. The route proved to be a muddy nightmare. We toiled up it, occasionally pushing our four-wheel-drive vehicle out of the deeper ruts. We passed treaded earth-moving equipment and trucks loaded with newly cut logs (our forest!) on the way down. At the top, where we stopped at last to rest and to collect specimens, groups of people came from their houses to offer congratulations: ours was the first vehicle to make it up the new road.

Across the island on this day, young Fidel Castro was preparing to storm the Moncada Barracks in Santiago de Cuba, which was defended by 1,000 of Batista's troops. His near-suicidal attack would be launched a week later. Seven years later the Harvard station would be appropriated and Cuba largely closed to American naturalists.

The groves of trees we encountered in the Trinidad Mountains were mostly *cafetals*, small family-owned coffee plantations. I found and duly sampled a few native Cuban ants and other insects living there. We then hiked off the road to higher slopes, working our way along the edges of bluffs and around spurs of dogtooth limestone. The land was either too steep or too rugged to support agriculture, yet fertile enough to shelter patches of native rain forest and other vegetation. If it were not for mountains and limestone, I reflected, all of Cuba would be a sugarcane field. At Mina Carlota we found ourselves at last in the midst of an abundance of the old fauna and flora of the Cuban mountains. Forty years earlier William Mann, then a Harvard graduate student studying ants and now, in 1953, director of the National Zoo, had traveled to this exact spot. After a few hours of random collecting, he stumbled upon a new species of ants, which he later named *Macromischa wheeleri* in honor of his sponsoring professor, William Morton Wheeler. In 1934 he recounted his discovery thus in the *National Geographic*:

> *I remember one Christmas Day at the Mina Carlota, in the Sierra de Trinidad of Cuba. When I attempted to turn over a large rock to see what was living underneath, the rock split in the middle, and there, in the very center, was a half teaspoonful of brilliant green metallic ants glistening in the sunshine. They proved to be an unknown species.*

Ever since reading that passage as a ten-year-old, I had been enchanted by the idea of prospecting in a faraway place for ants that resembled living emeralds. Now here I was at the very same place, climbing the steep forested hillside of Mina Carlota. Searching for ants, I turned over one limestone rock after another, perhaps a few of the very ones that Mann had handled. Some cracked; some crumbled; most stayed intact. Then one rock broke in half, exposing a cavity from which poured a teaspoonful of the beautiful metallescent *Macromischa wheeleri*. I took a special satisfaction in repeating Mann's discovery in exact detail after such a long interval of time. It was a reassurance of the continuity of both the natural world and the human mind.

As my companions and I proceeded across the Trinidad massif on our way to Mayarí, I encountered another ant, *Macromischa squamifer*, whose workers glistened golden in the sunlight. The color resembled the scintillations of tortoise beetles found in many parts of the world. This striking and unlikely color is most likely produced by microscopic ridges on the body that refract strong light. Bright colors are a widespread trait among West Indian species of *Macromischa* (the genus has since been reclassified as a group with the genus *Leptothorax*), and it is a fair guess that the ants use their raiment to warn predators of strong stings at the tips of their abdomens or poisonous chemicals held within the glands of their bodies. In the natural world, beautiful usually means deadly. Beautiful plus a casual demeanor *always* means deadly.

On this special day the old Cuban animals and plants continued to reveal themselves, like surviving spirits in a sacred ruin. On a tree fern near Naranjo, at 1,000 meters altitude, I found a species of anole lizard new to science, light brown with a greenish tinge, overlaid by cream rectangles along the back. While trying to escape me, it hopped like a frog instead of running like most of the other members of its genus.

The botanists brought me another kind of anole, a giant by the standards of its group of lizards, nearly a foot in length. Its eyelids were partly fused, giving it a permanently sleepy look, and it bore a strange crescent-shaped ridge along the back of its skull. The creature was very slow-moving for an anole and had the unique ability to rotate its eyes in different directions independently. I later found that my little monster was a known species, *Chamaeleolis chamaeleontides*, the sole member of an endemic Cuban genus. As the nineteenth-century zoologist who named it was aware, the species resembles the true chameleons of Africa and Madagascar in the traits I have just cited. Its superficially similar anatomy is not due to kinship with these lizards, however: it did not descend from an African species that rafted from Africa across the Atlantic to the West Indies. Rather, its peculiarities are the product of convergent evolution, a true all-Cuban creation.

I named the lizard Methuselah for its craggy features and gray wrinkled skin, and kept it as a pet for the rest of my summer's travels. I was fond of Methuselah but also recognized an unusual opportunity for original research. No one had previously studied a live *Chamaeleolis*. Was the species convergent with the true chameleons in behavior as well as in anatomy? In the fall I brought Methuselah back to Harvard, continued to study it daily, and found that its behavior was indeed convergent with that of the chameleons, as I had guessed. It stalked flies and other insects with extremely slow movements of its body, following its targets by a covert rotation of its eyes and then seizing them with startling speed by a forward lash of tongue and snap of jaws. Methuselah's manner was strikingly different from that of other anoles, which dash forward from their resting place to catch prey, then back again, like flycatchers. It diverged even though the species is related to them by common ancestry. I thus held in my possession an important bit of Cuban natural history never before reported. I subsequently published an article on my findings. Only later did I come to appreciate that *Chamaeleolis chamaeleontides* is probably a threatened species; as a consequence, having removed an individual even for scientific study is not something of which I can be proud.

In late July, accompanied by Robert Dressler, Quentin Jones, and Methuselah, I flew from Havana to Mérida, on Mexico's Yucatán Peninsula. We departed immediately for a week's collecting in the thorn forest along the Progreso–Campeche Road, with a side trip to the ruins at Uxmal. We found the great temples and courtyards of the Mayan city only partly cleared of vegetation. No tourists or guides were present, and we enjoyed a free run of the grounds. Ants abounded on and among the crumbling edifices, as no doubt they had done 1,400 years previously when the first stones were laid. I climbed the stairs of the Temple of the Magician to a fig tree growing on its apex, and from the branches of the tree collected workers of *Cephalotes atratus*, a large, shiny black ant with compound spines. Resting briefly by the tree, I reflected on this triumph of the ever-abounding life of insects over the works of man.

We next flew out of Mérida to Mexico City, where I left Dressler and Jones and began a solitary all-entomology expedition. I took a bus eastward, through the pine-dotted uplands of the Mexican Plateau and down the winding road that drops thousands of feet to the coastal plain and city of Veracruz. I arrived for the first time in what I like to call the *serious* tropics: not the island habitats of the West Indies, with their eccentric and interesting but limited fauna and flora; not the mangrove fringes of the Florida Keys and Caribbean coasts, however verdant; but the inland continental lowland tropics, the true Neotropics, with its vast biota deployed in endless combinations of species from Tampico in Mexico through Central and South America to Misiones Province in northern Argentina. Here in almost any patch of moist forest I could find more species of ants in an hour than would be possible in a month's travel through Cuba.

I searched for residues of the vanishing rain forest along the coast, finding them in the vicinity of El Palmar, Pueblo Nuevo, and San Andrés Tuxtla. All were under heavy siege, already cut back along the edges and high-graded in the interior. Off the highway other such refugia could be seen on distant hilltops and the slopes of steep ravines. Such was and remains the pattern of access left to visitors everywhere in the tropical world. It can be expressed in the form of a standard route: leave the road, climb through a barbed-wire fence, hike across a pasture, and slide down a slope to the edge of a stream. Cross the stream—if it is shallow enough—and start up the other side to the edge of the forest. Cut through fringing second growth until you reach the shade of trees. At this point you have arrived at your destination but are likely to be on an incline so steep that it is necessary to hold on to the trunks and exposed roots of bushes and small trees to avoid tumbling head over heels back down to the bottom.

How much longer will these precarious refuges last until they too are cut away? It was frustrating and heartbreaking to travel in Mexico with such thoughts in mind. When at last I made it into the rain forests of Veracruz State I operated like a vacuum cleaner, taking samples of every kind of ant I could find. At night I identified species, labeled my vials, and wrote natural history notes. I had remarkably quick success by entomological standards: I captured colonies of two genera, *Belonopelta* and *Hylomyrma*, that had never been studied before, and recorded my observations on their social organization and predatory behavior for later publication.

As I prepared to leave the Veracruz coast two weeks later, my attention was drawn to Pico de Orizaba, the great volcanic mountain just north of the city of Orizaba. Its beautiful symmetric cone rises 5,747 meters—18,855 feet—above sea level to a permanently snow-covered peak. Orizaba is not just a prominence atop an already towering mountain range or plateau like Popocatepetl and mighty Aconcagua, but a mountain of more solitary and mystic qualities, a lone giant born of Mexico's ring of fire, standing sentinel over the southern approaches of the central plateau.

I was drawn not just by the amazing sight but also by the very concept of Orizaba. I thought of the mountain as an island. It was isolated from the plateau, yet I believed that a lone climber could travel in one relatively short straight pass from tropical forest to cold temperate forest and finally into the treeless arctic scree just below the summit. The cooler habitats constituted the island. The surrounding tropical and subtropical lowlands were the sea. Orizaba's uplands were close enough to the plateau to receive immigrant plants and animals adapted to the middle and upper slopes, yet isolated enough for unique races and species to have evolved and dwell only there.

So what might I hope to discover if I climbed Orizaba? No one had toiled up the slopes of the mountain to study ants, generally the most abundant of small terrestrial animals, with the possible exception of the much smaller mites and springtails. For every bird there might be a hundred thousand or million ants, and I could reasonably expect to sample the species effectively during a single fast traverse. I knew that the change in fauna and flora from tropical to temperate was likely to be dramatic. The southeastern face of the Mexican escarpment, where Orizaba sits, is the site of the most abrupt changeover of biogeographic realms found anywhere in the world, except perhaps in the Indian and Bhutanese Himalayas. On the plateau live large numbers of plants and animals typical of the Nearctic Region, a realm extending northward to encompass all of North America. While descending earlier the tortuous road from Puebla over the plateau to the Veracruz plain, I had left this world of beech, oak, sweetgum, and pine and entered the Neotropical Region, where aroids and orchids cling in masses to arrow-straight tree boles and lianas hang like ropes from the lofty horizontal branches.

I expected to find all this and more if I climbed Pico de Orizaba. Let me put it more strongly: I was foreordained to try it. I would start at La Perla, at 3,000 feet, and follow a donkey trail I had heard about to the hamlet of Rancho Somecla, at 11,000 feet. I would simply ask for the hospitality of the people there, who were rumored to be friendly to strangers, and proceed the next day on up to the snow line, at about 16,000 feet. I would collect ants and make notes on the environment all along the way.

I was a fool of course, traveling alone on foot up a high mountain without a map and no more than phrasebook Spanish. But I did make it most of the way. Early in the morning of a beautiful late August day, I took a bus from the city of Orizaba to La Perla and started walking. The mountain's south slope was mostly uninhabited; I en-countered no one on the trail until I reached Rancho Somecla, my destination, late that afternoon.

My journey began in subtropical vegetation. At 5,500 feet I en-tered a forest dominated by hornbeam and sweetgum, both temperate-zone trees, with tree ferns abundant in the understory. Scattered through the habitat at lower elevations were dense, wet patches of tropical hardwoods. The ants in this transition belt, which composed nothing less than the passage from the Neotropical to the Nearctic regions, were a mix of tropical and temperate species: army ants and fire ants mingled with species of the typical north temperate genus *Formica*. Two of the *Formica* species later proved new to sci-ence. At 8,000 feet I found a mixture of pines, making their first ap-pearance along the ridges, and broadleafed trees dominated by horn-beam on the slopes. The woodland was tessellated by pastures and stump-filled glades recently cleared by woodcutters.

When I arrived at Rancho Somecla, which turned out to be a col-lection of about a dozen houses, I was close to exhaustion. To the people who came out to meet me, I explained as best as I could why I was there. I doubt that they really understood my words or gestures, but one family promptly offered me lodging. I rested while they pre-pared a chicken dinner. Then, as the light failed, I headed out for one more try at ant collecting in the surrounding pine forest, this time ac-companied by several young men who listened gravely as I explained why I was tearing up the bark of rotting logs and putting insects in bottles. One of my companions agreed to guide me to the snow line the next day.

That night I slept not at all. My bed was a table, and the single blan-ket given me offered little warmth when the temperature fell into the forties Fahrenheit. Occasionally I rose to look through the door at the brilliant full moon in a cloudless sky. It would be a wonderful place to live, I thought, if you brought a lot of blankets.

At dawn the next morning, after pressing some pesos on my

hosts, I headed on up the mountain with my guide. When we reached an elevation of between 12,000 and 13,000 feet, we entered open cloud forest, where the pine trunks were gnarled and the branches draped with epiphytes. My excitement was growing, but I could go no further. The air was too thin for someone who had been living at sea level, and I was gasping for breath. I estimate that I had come to within 400 feet of timberline and perhaps 3,000 to 4,000 feet below the snowcap. Of course I was at my physical limit. I had been entirely naive to suppose that anyone could walk three miles from the low-lands straight up into the air in thirty-six hours and keep on going.

In any case ants had become very scarce, even in the clearings warmed by the morning sun. I searched for an hour before finding one colony nesting beneath a wood chip. Then I turned around and started walking back down. At Rancho Somecla I shook hands with my guide and headed alone down the trail to La Perla, moving rapidly now, then to my hotel in Orizaba, where, the sated adventurer, I slept for twelve hours.

PART 2
STORYTELLER

If you're a storyteller, find a good story and tell it.
HOWARD HAWKS, FILMMAKER

chapter ten

THE SOUTH
PACIFIC

ON A COLD MARCH DAY IN 1954, IN THE SEASON WHEN CAM-
bridge is its least lovable, Philip Darlington called me to his office.
How would you like, he said, to go to New Guinea? The Society of
Fellows and Museum of Comparative Zoology had agreed to cover
my expenses for an extended visit. No specialist had collected ants in
that fabulously rich and still mostly unexplored fauna. Other islands
such as New Caledonia might be visited en route. I could work hands
on in the very arena where a hundred years before young Alfred Russel Wallace had begun to turn zoogeography, the study of animal dis-

tribution, into a scientific discipline. Who knows how the experience might transform my own thinking as a zoogeographer? And if I picked up some ground beetles, Darlington's favorite group, that would be all right too.

Here was the brass ring for a young field biologist. Many years were to pass before another generation of well-funded researchers were to descend in teams on New Guinea and other South Pacific islands and set up field stations. I could be a pioneer. Darlington said, Go, while you're still footloose and fancy-free.

I was not footloose and fancy-free. I was in love. The previous fall I had met a beautiful young woman, Renee Kelley, from Boston's Back Bay, and we were engaged to be married. She was a fellow introvert, pleasured by long hours of quiet conversation, a budding poet, deeply interested in literature, a scholar by temperament, and thus, though not a scientist, able to understand my dreams of pursuits in faraway places. Our marriage was to be happy and enduring.

We were young then, in 1954, and a parting seemed almost unbearable at the start of our engagement. But we agreed I should go to New Guinea. I would be away ten months, much of the time in remote areas. No jetliners existed then to shuttle me back and forth, and the great distance and high costs of transportation by other means made interim visits improbable. Telephone calls were difficult and expensive, to be used only for emergencies.

On the morning of November 24 the Eastern Airlines carrier to San Francisco taxied from the gate at Boston's Logan Airport and out onto the runway. I could see Renee pressed to the visitors' observation window, her right hand waving slowly. Around her neck she wore a long woolen scarf striped in Harvard maroon and white, its tasseled ends nearly touching the floor. We were both weeping. Divided by two passions, the tropics and romantic love, I was a young seafarer venturing into another age on a long and uncertain voyage. Until I came home we would write to each other daily and at length, accumulating a total of some six hundred diarylike letters.

I had decided on a tour of the outer Melanesian archipelagoes, then Australia, and finally New Guinea. From San Francisco I took a propeller-driven Pan American Super Constellation across the Pacific. It touched down for refueling at Honolulu and Canton Island— a dry, cheerless atoll in the Phoenix group—before proceeding to Fiji. As it descended toward Nandi Airport in Viti Levu the next morning, I looked down upon a passage of white and green atolls in a turquoise sea. Never before or afterward in my life have I felt such a surge of high expectation—of pure exhilaration—as in those few minutes. I know now that it was an era in biology closing out, a time when a young scientist could travel to a distant part of the world and be an explorer entirely on his own. No team of specialists accompanied me and none waited at my destination, whatever I decided that was to be. Which was exactly as I wished it. I carried no high-technology instruments, only a hand lens, forceps, specimen vials, notebooks, quinine, sulfanilamide, youth, desire, and unbounded hope.

The South Pacific is a galaxy of thousands of islands, spread out in configurations that have served many of the key advances in evolutionary biology. Darwin conceived of evolution by natural selection from what he learned about birds in the Galápagos Islands, and Wallace had the same idea after studying butterflies and other organisms in the old Malay Archipelago, now modern Malaysia, Brunei, and Indonesia.

A true, biogeographic island, I knew as I stepped off the plane at Viti Levu and looked around, is a world that holds most of its organisms tight within its borders. It is the ideal unit for the study of evolution. Enough immigrants fly, swim, or drift ashore to colonize the island, yet not so many in each generation to form the commanding elements of its populations. If the island is large and old and distant enough, the descendants of the immigrants evolve into new races peculiar to the new home. Given enough time the races diverge still further from their sister populations on the continent and on neighboring islands to deserve the taxonomic rank of species. We speak of such local races and species as endemic: they are native to the island and nowhere else in the world. The Hawaiian hawk is a good example of an endemic, as well as the Jamaican giant swallowtail and the Norfolk Island pine. By factoring in the age of the island and the origin of the immigrants, biologists can reconstruct the evolution of the plants and animals there more easily than on continents. The simplicity of islands makes them the best of all natural laboratories.

The experiments are conducted in opposite manner from those in conventional laboratories. They are retroactive rather than anticipatory. Whereas most biologists vary a few factors under controlled conditions and observe the effects of each deviation, the evolutionary biologist observes the results already obtained, as learned from studies of natural history, and tries to infer the factors that operated in the past. Where the experimental biologist predicts the outcome of experiments, the evolutionary biologist retrodicts the experiment already performed by Nature; he teases science out of history. And because so many factors may have operated in the guidance of evolution and the creation of wild species, the best result of the retrodictive method can be obtained if the ecosystems are relatively small and simple. Hence islands.

Unlike experimental biologists, evolutionary biologists well versed in natural history already have an abundance of answers from which to pick and choose. What they most need are the right questions. The most important evolutionary biologists are those who invent the most important questions. They look for the best stories Nature has to tell us, because they are above all storytellers. If they are also naturalists—and a great majority of the best evolutionary biologists are naturalists—they go into the field with open eyes and minds, complete opportunists looking in all directions for the big questions, for the main chance.

To go this far the naturalist must know one or two groups of plants or animals well enough to identify specimens to genus or species. These favored organisms are actors in the theater of his vision. The naturalist lacking such information will find himself lost in a green fog, unable to tell one organism from another, handicapped by his inability to distinguish new phenomena from those already well known. But if well equipped, he can gather information swiftly while continuously thinking, every working hour, What patterns do the data form? What is the meaning of the patterns? What is the question they answer? What is the story I can tell?

This is the strategy I brought with me to the ant fauna of the Pacific

Islands. I would collect samples of every species I found and write notes on all the aspects of ecology and behavior I observed, all the while watching for patterns in the form of geographic trends and adaptation of species to the environment. I was well aware of existing theory and the conventional wisdom of my discipline, but I would hold my mind open to any phenomena congenial enough to enter it.

Nadala, Viti Levu, December 1954. Fiji in one dreadful sense was Cuba and Mexico all over again: the native biota had already been driven back to scattered and nearly inaccessible enclaves. At Nandi I hired a driver and traveled along the north coast road of Viti Levu through villages, domestic groves, and pastureland. Virtually no natural forest survived along this thoroughfare, crowded as it was by the dense settlements of immigrant East Indians. We turned south at Tavua toward the central hills to search for patches of native forest, all on the land of the aboriginal Fijian population. One elderly man I met remembered another ant collector who had visited nearby Nandarivatu forty years back. He could not recall the name, but I knew it was William Mann, also my predecessor in Cuba, sent by Harvard to the islands in 1915–16 to collect for the Museum of Comparative Zoology. The forest I could reach in one day was similar to what he had known except that it had been disturbed by high-grade lumbering and perforated by slash-and-burn clearings. At Nadala I crawled up a steep slope over scattered pumice rocks to a well-shaded pocket of native trees, densely hung with lianas, where I found elements of the endemic ant fauna. One of them shot adrenaline into my veins: *Poecilomyrma*, a genus known solely from Fiji and collected only one time previously—of course by William Mann.

The next day, working south off the coastal road near Korovou, I learned another melancholy fact about conservation. In a small patch of what appeared to be natural forest I found only exotic ant species. I realized that on islands harboring native species of limited diversity, the ecosystems are vulnerable to invasion by aliens even if left physically intact. Much of the Pacific fauna has gone under in the path of pigs, goats, rats, Argentine ants, beard grass, and other highly competitive forms introduced by human commerce. Strangers have savaged the islands of the world.

I did not linger in Fiji. The ant fauna was already reasonably well known, thanks to Mann's lengthy residence. The next day I caught the Qantas flying boat from Suva to Noumea, the French colonial center of New Caledonia.

Mount Mou, New Caledonia, December 1954. With my arrival in New Caledonia, I had reached what I would thereafter consider my favorite island, a large, pencil-shaped land 1,200 kilometers off the east coast of Australia, the southernmost reach of Melanesia. The very name of the place meant, and still means, "alien" and "distant" to me. I knew from the work of previous naturalists that plants and animals had come to its shores during millions of years, for the most part eastward from Australia and southward from the Solomon Islands through the New Hebrides. They had mingled and evolved to form unique ecosystems. Among the native species were archaic trees and other plants, a few of ultimate Gondwanaland origin, whose ancestors had lived as far afield as Antarctica, when warmer climates prevailed. Also present were stocks of animals and plants that have evolved into extreme forms found nowhere else, including the famous kagu, representing an entire family of birds, the Rhynchochetidae. This flightless endemic, its shrill call piercing the night, had been reduced to near extinction since the French colonized the island in the 1860s. Early records indicated that the same broad biogeographic pattern of mixed origin and endemicity, with extreme rarity for some species, held for ants. I intended to find out.

On one hot day in this austral midsummer I caught the northbound bus from Noumea and got off at the little village of Païta. I hiked six kilometers up a small dirt road to the estate of a family named Bourdinet and dropped my gear at the gazebo, where I set up camp. The Bourdinets were not home that week and could offer no other accommodation. No matter; I was happy to concentrate entirely on my work. I walked another kilometer to the house of the Pentecost family, their nearest neighbors, climbing in the process to 300 meters elevation. My goal was the summit ridge forest of Mount Mou rising beyond, to 1,220 meters. To get there I pushed my way through a broad thicket of dense, dry bracken. When I reached the western crest of the ridge, I found myself still in the midst of bracken. But at least I had broken out onto the summit trail. The going grew easier, and the forested mountaintop was in full view only a kilometer away.

Because I was completely alone and had seen no one since Païta, it occurred to me that if I were crippled in an accident it would be three or four days before my contacts in Noumea became aware that anything was wrong. I stepped more carefully for the rest of the climb. As newly gathering mountaintop mist closed around me, I entered the forest. There I encountered first low shrubs and scattered trees, then continuous stands of *Araucaria* and *Podocarpus* conifers, their trunks and branches laden with mosses and other epiphytes. A little farther on, near the summit, I entered the true cloud forest. Here the trees were gnarled and stunted, and their canopies closed overhead at only ten meters. Their trunks and the surface of the soil in which the trees grew were coated with an unbroken blanket of wet moss.

I had arrived on an island within an island, a world of my own. The warm proprietary feeling of my boyhood flooded back. My imagination drifted back across epochs. The conifers there were ancient members of the Antarctic realm, still distributed across southern Australia, New Zealand, temperate South America, and here, the uplands of New Caledonia. Some of the species of plants and animals dated back to the Mesozoic Era, when they were surely browsed by dinosaurs, and when parts of the Antarctic continent itself were still habitable by all. As I began hunting ants, a little green parrot with a red cap landed on a branch close by and stayed there. At intervals he squawked at me in some mysterious psittacine language. We were perfect companions in the mossy forest, native and exotic joined in momentary harmony. I would do no harm, I told the parrot, and leave soon, but this place would live forever in my memory.

Not just the ants but everything I saw, every species of plant and animal, was new to me. These creatures were a fully alien biota, and it is time to confess: I am a neophile, an inordinate lover of the new, of diversity for its own sake. In such a place everything is a surprise, and I could make a discovery of scientific value anytime I wished. My archetypal dream came clear:

Take me, Lord, to an unexplored planet teeming with new life forms. Put me at the edge of virgin swampland dotted with hummocks of high ground, let me saunter at my own pace across it and up the nearest mountain ridge, in due course to cross over to the far slope in search of more distant swamps, grasslands, and ranges. Let me be the Carolus Linnaeus of this world, bearing no more than specimen boxes, botanical canister, hand lens, notebooks, but allowed not years but centuries of time. And should I somehow tire of the land, let me embark on the sea in search of new islands and archipelagoes. Let me go alone, at least for a while, and I will report to You and loved ones at intervals and I will publish reports on my discoveries for colleagues. For if it was You who gave me this spirit, then devise the appropriate reward for its virtuous use.

Ciu, near Mount Canala, New Caledonia, December 1954. I had to go to what seemed the edge of nowhere in order to sample ants on the northern coast, in moist lowland and foothills forest. The insects were likely to belong to different species from those around Noumea and might include at least two rare endemic genera taken by earlier collectors. I had risen at 3:45 in the morning to catch the daily bus to Canala. The antique vehicle followed a route that wound 170 kilometers across the central massif of the island. The driver made countless detours and stops to pick up and drop off native New Caledonians. We arrived at Canala at 10:30 in a driving rain that continued for the rest of the day. I lunched at the Hôtel de Canala, tumbled into bed, and dreamed of blue skies as I fell asleep.

Canala in 1954 was a collection of twenty rundown houses, the hotel, and a Catholic mission. The marquee social activity of the village was cricket played by men and women on the same teams, supported by cheerleaders who beat bamboo sticks together. The glamor ended there. The Hôtel de Canala contained a kitchen, a dining room, and a row of six square cubicles, each three meters on a side and furnished with a bed, table, and water basin. Lodging was U.S. $4.80 a night. The cubicle next to mine was the entertainment parlor of a prostitute who practiced her trade very noisily. All the guests used the same shower and evil-smelling outhouse. Meals were of uncertain provenance and often inexplicably cold, but I didn't care. Dinner was only $1.60 with wine, and all I wanted anyway was enough nourishment to fuel me to the nearby forests and back free of dysentery.

The next morning, packing a sandwich and a bottle of diluted red wine, I walked the one-lane dirt road seven kilometers south to Ciu, an aggregate of farms on the edge of the inland forest. For part of this distance the road passed through a marsh, from which clouds of striped *Aedes* mosquitoes poured through the hot sunlight like sniper bullets. In the manner of *Aedes* in other parts of the world, they commenced biting as soon as they landed on a patch of bare skin. The repellant I splashed on myself meant little to them. I named this stretch of the road Mosquito Alley, and started to jog-walk its length, head down and arms folded like a man running a gauntlet.

My destination was the Fèré farm, bordered by a small river of the size we call a creek in Alabama. I followed once again the universal formula for gaining access to tropical forest: crawl through a barbed-wire fence, walk across a cow pasture, wade a shallow part of the river (in this case adorned by an upstream waterfall), and climb a hillside into the forest. The effort proved worth the trouble. I soon entered the shade of native timber, a prehistoric New Caledonian world. I had passed no one on the Canala–Ciu road, and as I worked back into the forest I could see no sign of recent human disturbance. The solitude, as usual, felt right. Human beings mean comfort, but they also mean a loss of time for a field biologist, a break in concentration and, for strangers in an unknown land, always a certain amount of personal risk.

The Fèré tract was not a true rain forest in the familiar, Amazonian sense. It comprised only two stories of trees, with the upper canopy twenty meters high and broken in enough places to let sunshine fall in large, radiant patches on the forest floor. The habitat was ideal for ants. It abounded with pure New Caledonian species, many new to science. I was struck by the prevalence of red-and-black coloration among the workers foraging above ground. At Chapeau Gendarme near Noumea the same species were predominantly yellow. What was the meaning of this local color code? Perhaps it was just coincidence. But I suspected mimicry. My guess was that one to several of the species were poisonous, as I had supposed to be true of the metallescent ants of Cuba. The bright and distinctive color says to potential visual predators such as birds and lizards: Don't even try to eat me, you'll be sorry. In theory it pays for all the local poisonous species to evolve the same color, forming a consortium among the advertisers. It also pays for harmless, tasty species to acquire the same appearance and enjoy a free ride on the repellant forms they imitate. I had neither the means nor the time, however, to test either hypothesis.

My attention soon shifted to a phenomenon that was more tractable to immediate study and would later prove important in tracing certain aspects of ant evolution. Near Noumea I had collected the first ants of the genera *Cerapachys* and *Sphinctomyrmex* and hence of the entire ant tribe Cerapachyini ever recorded from New Caledonia. Here at Ciu they were so abundant I could observe them within the first hours of my arrival. I discovered that the peculiarly cylindrical, hard-bodied workers feed on other ants. To overcome their formidable prey, they hunt in packs much like the army ants of the mainland tropics. Their sorties, I saw, are much smaller and less well organized yet also effective in breaking down the defenses of the

NATURALIST

target colonies. "Real" army ants, the kind that march in thick columns in Asia and Australia, never managed to cross the Coral Sea and colonize New Caledonia. The less spectacular cerapachyines somehow succeeded, and even though they are less formidable huntresses they have the army ant niche to themselves. That is why, I conjectured, they are so abundant on New Caledonia and so rare on most continents. The concept was ill-formed in my mind then. I recorded the habits of the cerapachyine ants only because they are interesting in their own right. But three years later I would use the field notes as a key piece in my reconstruction of the evolutionary origin of army ants.

Ratard Plantation, Luganville, Espiritu Santo, New Hebrides, January 1955. Curiosity and opportunism brought me to this most remote and least-known large island of all the South Pacific. Still mostly covered by undisturbed rain forest, the northern New Hebrides had never been collected for ants, so every record I put in my notebook would be new. Even a brief glimpse of the fauna as a whole might allow me to place the New Hebrides (now the republic of Vanuatu) in the larger biogeographic picture. The archipelago is a potential stepping-stone to the more distant islands of the western Pacific. It can receive both Asian elements from the fully tropical Solomon Islands, to the north, and Australian elements from subtropical New Caledonia, to the south.

On this day, however, my exploration had been cut short. I was in bed with a high fever; the opening strains of *Swan Lake* ran inexplicably through my head, over and over, scrambling my thoughts into chaos. To add to my distress, I was occasionally bounced by aftershocks of an earthquake that had struck from an epicenter near Malekula three days earlier. Several large circular bruises were spaced at regular intervals across my chest. They had been inflicted by a doctor—he *claimed* he was a doctor—in Luganville in an attempt to draw the fever out with powerful suction cups. Surely I was one of the last patients in the Western world to endure this archaic and useless remedy.

My hosts were Aubert Ratard, his wife, Suzanne, and their two teenage sons. The Ratards were among the wealthiest of the two hundred French families who owned copra plantations on Espiritu Santo. Down the road from their coastline property were an airstrip and Quonset huts, remnants of an American base from the Second World War. The American forces and the people of the New Hebrides were the inspiration for James Michener's *Tales of the South Pacific*. Michener had also been a houseguest of the Ratards a decade earlier, and Ratard himself was the inspiration for the French planter in the book and musical. At dinner Aubert told me about the real Bloody Mary, who still lived in the central administrative town of Vila, on the island of Éfaté. From the shore of his property he pointed to Bali-ha'i across the Segond Channel, in real life the island of Malo.

Literary history was forgotten when I turned my attention to the wilderness that surrounded us. Soon after arriving and before falling ill, I walked into lush rain forest that reached all the way to the sandy beach, a rarity in the overpopulated tropics. It was home to undisturbed flocks of parrots and crowing jungle fowl, the wild ancestral species of the domestic chicken. Flying foxes, giant fruit-eating bats, flapped leisurely above the treetops. I soon fixed the affinities of the ant species I found there: Melanesian, as expected, Solomon Islands most likely, hence ultimately Asian. I made a general observation on the ecology of these insects that would find a place in my later synthesis of island evolution. It is as follows. Relatively few species of ants inhabit Espiritu Santo; the island is just too distant and geologically young to have received many immigrants. Freed from heavy competition, some of the colonists have dramatically increased their niche; they occur in dense populations across a wide range of local environments and nest sites. I would later call this phenomenon "ecological release," and help to establish it as an important early step in the proliferation of biodiversity.

Esperance to Mount Ragged, Western Australia, January–February 1955. I disliked leaving Espiritu Santo just when I had begun to study its fauna, but now I had to go to Australia for a potentially even more important excursion scheduled some months earlier. I took the weekly Qantas flying boat back to Noumea, then to Sydney and, after a brief stay in the city and a collecting excursion into the surrounding countryside, flew on to Kalgoorlie. From this inland center of Western Australia's sheep country, I proceeded south by rail to Norseman for a round of ant collecting. At a local bar I fell in with a group of construction workers, who invited me to collect ants out at their workplace in the nearby eucalyptus scrub. A full day in the bush completely dehydrated me; two months in the humid tropics had rendered my system unable to handle evaporation in such a hot, semidesert environment. When we arrived back at the bar late that afternoon, I chugalugged four beers in a row. My hosts, themselves heavy consumers in a country known for Olympic-class beer drinking, were impressed. So was I: I am normally a one-beer-maximum occasional drinker.

I then went farther south to Esperance, an isolated coastal town just west of the Great Australian Bight. Here I was joined by Caryl Haskins, a fellow entomologist and the newly appointed president of the Carnegie Institution of Washington. This outpost was our point of departure on a quest for the grail of ant studies. A hundred kilometers to the east, out across the sandplain heath, lived the grail: *Nothomyrmecia macrops*, the most primitive known ant, a lost species since its discovery twenty-three years before, and quite possibly the key to the origin of social life in ants. We meant to rediscover the species and be the first to study it in life.

Before departing, we decided to look for ants around Esperance. We walked out of the small town to the top of nearby Telegraph Hill, a low granitic rise covered by woody shrubs and patches of open gravelly soil ideal for ant nests. We stood quietly for a while admiring the long sweep of bush-covered land down to Esperance Bay, where huge combers thundered in from Antarctica. Out on the horizon were scattered islands of the uninhabited Recherche Archipelago.

We had been told they were home to dense populations of poisonous elapine snakes. Great white sharks were known to be common in the blue-black waters. We were a long way from home, as far as it was possible to be from Boston, and Renee, and remain on land.

Telegraph Hill and its environs were strange and beautiful to behold, but not comfortable. January is the hottest month of the year. Just four days previously the temperature in Esperance had reached 41° Celsius (106°F). On the day of our excursion, the sun beat down from a nearly cloudless sky, and a hard dry wind blew in from the mainland semidesert behind us. Bush flies, aggressive relatives of house flies, swarmed around our heads, ran about on our ears and faces, and attempted to feed on the moisture of our eyes, nostrils, and mouths. We responded by continuously performing the "Australian salute," a wave of the hand around the head to chase bush flies away.

Caryl set out at once to collect colonies of bulldog ants, his favorite insects. This was no casual undertaking. The workers, measuring up to three centimeters in length, possess large bulging eyes with excellent vision, long saw-toothed mandibles, and painful stings. They are among the most belligerent insects in the world. Imagine a crater nest one to two meters across, with an opening in the center several centimeters wide, from which come and go dozens of surly red-and-black ants the size of hornets. Disturb them in the slightest and they charge you fearlessly. A few will follow your retreat for as much as ten meters from the nest. These ants, in short, are not the furtive picnic and kitchen raiders of America.

Caryl showed me how to gather entire bulldog ant colonies without risking one's life in the process. One needs a bit of courage and a willingness to endure pain. He went straight at the nest, snatching up each attacking ant closest to him and popping it into a large bottle— quickly, before it had a chance to curl its abdomen around and sting him. Usually the method worked, but occasionally a charging worker climbed onto his ankle or forearm and nailed him before he could brush it away. When all the outside guards had been cleared off, he started to dig into the entrance hole. More angry workers poured out, only to join their nestmates in the bottle. Caryl continued until he had excavated a shaft a meter or so below the surface where, in every case, he found the mother queen hiding in one of the deepest nest chambers. He walked away with each colony clean and healthy, ready for transport back to the United States and laboratory study.

The next day our thoughts turned entirely to *Nothomyrmecia macrops*. The idea of the "missing link" ant is about as romantic a concept as is possible for an entomologist. The whole story began on December 7, 1931, when a holiday party set out by truck and horseback from Balladonia, a sheep ranch and beer stop on the cross-Australia highway northeast of Esperance. They traveled leisurely for 175 kilometers southward across the vast, uninhabited eucalyptus scrub forest and sandplain heath. In this first leg they passed close to Mount Ragged, a forbidding treeless granitic hill. Then they stopped for a few days at the abandoned Thomas River station on the coast before turning west to Esperance, where they took rail and automobile transportation back home. The habitat they traversed is botanically one of the richest in the world, harboring large numbers of shrubs and herbaceous plants found nowhere else. A naturalist and artist resident at Balladonia, Mrs. A. E. Crocker, had asked members of the party to collect insects along the way. These they placed in jars of alcohol tied to the saddles of their horses. The specimens, including two large, oddly shaped yellow ants, were turned over to the National Museum of Victoria in Melbourne. There the ants were described by the entomologist John Clark in 1934 as a new genus and species, *Nothomyrmecia macrops*.

Our hopes were high as we left Esperance the next day, retracing the 1931 party's route in reverse. We were accompanied by the Australian naturalist Vincent Serventy and Bob Douglas, an Esperance native who served as camp manager and cook. We rode on the flatbed of a huge hand-cranked truck that had seen service on the Burma Road during the war. On the nearly invisible rutted dirt road to the

Thomas River farm, we encountered not a single person. The sun bore down from the blue summer sky, from which bush flies descended in relentless swarms. When we stopped the only sound we heard was the wind whispering through sandheath shrubs.

We found the Thomas River to be a dry bed—an arroyo—in a basin depressed twenty-five to thirty meters below the level of the sandplain. Its floor had once been shaded by tall yate trees and carpeted by grass. Not long after their arrival in the 1890s, the first settlers had thinned the yate forest, and their flocks of sheep had destroyed the grass. Now, a half-century later, the groves were composed of a mix of yate, paperback, and wattle, and the forage had been replaced by patches of succulent salt-tolerant herbs. Huge nests of meat ants, five to ten meters across and seething with hundreds of thousands of big red-and-black workers, dominated the more disturbed swaths of open terrain.

Nothomyrmecia could have been anywhere in such a varied environment. I was excited and tense, knowing that we might find scientific gold with a single glance to the ground. Haskins and I set to work immediately, each hoping to be the lucky discoverer. We searched back and forth through the basin grove, turning logs, scanning the tree trunks, inspecting every moving light-colored ant remotely resembling a Nothomyrmecia, but found nothing. We hiked up onto the sandplain heath and swept the low bushes back and forth with a net to capture foraging ants, again without success. That night, armed with flashlights and net, we walked back out onto the sandplain, and this time lost our way. Rather than risk wandering farther from camp in a dangerous desert-like environment, we settled down to wait for daybreak. To my surprise Caryl found a football-sized rock, pulled and rocked it as though positioning a pillow, lay on his back on the ground, and fell asleep. I was too keyed up to attempt the same feat and spent the rest of the night searching for the ant in the immediate vicinity. How marvelous it would be, I thought, if I could hand Caryl a specimen when he awoke!

But again, no luck. The four days we spent at the Thomas River station, broken by a side trip north to Mount Ragged, were a textbook introduction to wild Australia. Dingoes, the feral dogs of Australia, whined unseen around our camp at night. Kangaroos and emus could be seen moving across the sandplain at a distance during the day. One morning, while absorbed in close inspection of insects on the sandplain, we were startled by the sound of an animal snorting behind us. We turned to find a white stallion standing ten meters away, gazing placidly at us as though waiting to be saddled up. In a few moments he turned and trotted away. Returning to our work, we looked up now and then to locate him again until he passed out of sight in the distant gray-green heath.

Research progress was rapid and satisfying around the Thomas River, at least by ordinary standards of field biology. We discovered new species, in the course of which we also defined an entire ecological guild of sandplain ants specialized for foraging on the low vegetation at night. Large-eyed and light-colored, they represent members of the genera *Camponotus*, *Colobostruma*, and *Iridomyrmex* that have evidently converged in evolution to fill this arid niche. Because *Nothomyrmecia* is also large-eyed and pale, we reasoned that it was a member of the guild, and so we concentrated our efforts on the sandplain.

We never found *Nothomyrmecia*, but we made it famous. In the years to follow, other teams of Americans and Australians scoured the area with equal lack of success. The ant acquired a near-legendary status in natural history circles. The break finally came in 1977 when Robert Taylor, a former Ph.D. student of mine at Harvard and at that time chief curator of the Australian National Insect Collection, stumbled upon *Nothomyrmecia* in eucalyptus scrub forest near the little town of Poochera, in South Australia, a full thousand miles east of the Thomas River. It was a totally unanticipated discovery. Taylor came running into camp shouting (his exact words) in pure Australianese, "The bloody bastard's here! I've got the *Notho*-bloody-*myrmecia*!"

A small industry then grew up among ant specialists, who studied every aspect of the ant's biology. Many visited the Poochera site. The details supported a theory, originally promoted by William Morton Wheeler while professor of entomology at Harvard and furthered by Haskins, that social life in ants began when subordinate daughters remained in the nest to assist their mother in rearing more sisters. At that point in distant geological time, according to this now strengthened scenario, solitary wasps evolved into ants.

Brown River Camp, Papua, March 1955. After taking the train back to Kalgoorlie I flew to Perth, then to Sydney, and on to New Guinea. The great island was to be the "ultimate" tropics and the climax of my odyssey. Immediately after my arrival in Port Moresby in a Qantas DC-3, I contacted Joseph Szent-Ivany, a Hungarian refugee from the postwar communist takeover and the Mandated Territory's only resident entomologist. We called on G. A. V. Stanley, a longtime resident and planter known as "bush pig" by the natives for his exploits as a civilian scout for the Allied forces during the war. Both men were expert field travelers in New Guinea. After filling me with advice and a couple of good dinners, they accompanied me while I set up a camp near the Brown River, a tributary of the Laloki near Port Moresby. Thanks to their selfless assistance, I was able within five days to commence work in primary rain forest. My little expedition was supported by a native cook, a driver, and a personal assistant. I had no trouble supporting this crew, despite my own impecunious state as a mere postdoctoral fellow far from home. Each man's salary was thirty-three cents U.S. a day plus rations; this rate was the going standard, and Szent-Ivany and Stanley cautioned me not to exceed it.

Our tents stood in a small clearing ringed by giant trees whose fin-like plank buttresses gave their trunks the appearance of rockets poised for flight. More than thirty meters above us, the dense canopy, festooned with lianas and epiphytes, closed out most of the sunlight. Only a few shafts cut to the floor through scattered breaks caused by naturally falling trees and branches.

NATURALIST

I was immersed in a pandemonium of life. The racket made by parrots and other birds, frogs, and singing insects beat incessantly upon my ears—a cacophony but one of great eloquence so long as I listened to the separate instruments and not the orchestra all at once. Less congenial were the mosquitoes, gnats, and stingless bees that hummed around my head in merciless attendance. The body fluids paid these pests are the expected tariff for tropical field work. But I was where I most wanted to be in all the world; I had no complaint.

Tree trunks, lianas, and rotting logs teemed with thousands of species of insects. I scurried about continuously through the days and on into the nights, closely followed by my assistant, who rapidly turned into an enthusiastic amateur entomologist. Together we gathered more than fifty species of ants, many of them new to science. During all that time my eyes were fixed on the ground and lower vegetation. Rarely did I look upward, and then only to watch giant birdwing butterflies churning the air, or flocks of parrots rushing back and forth through the canopy, a riot of different species, first one brown in plumage, then another green, then another yellow. I heard a bird of paradise calling once, but stared skyward too late to find it. I never saw one during my four-month visit to New Guinea, although I must have passed close to a variety of species many times. My eyes were locked to the ground, head bent and shoulders hunched in the lifetime posture I had already acquired by my late teens. At dusk we dined on wallaby, wild pigeon, and, for appetizers, nut-flavored grubs of long-horned beetles dug from nearby decaying logs and roasted like marshmallows on sticks over the fire.

In New Guinea I felt like a real explorer. I *was* an explorer, at least in the world of entomology. Shortly after returning from the Brown River and then a second, week-long trip to the foothills rain forest of the Sogeri Plateau (where I discovered an extraordinary new kind of ant living as a social parasite in the nest of another species), I drove with Joe Szent-Ivany to the Port Moresby airport to meet Linsley Gressitt. The great entomologist was soon to turn Hawaii's Bishop Museum into a world center for research on Pacific insects. He was rightly to be known as the pioneering expert on insect biodiversity in this region. He arrived on that day for his first visit to New Guinea. I had beaten him there by two weeks, and I think back now with pride on the advice I gave him on local collecting.

The Huon Peninsula, Northeast New Guinea, April 1955. The Huon Peninsula is the horn of New Guinea, a mountainous extension of the northeastern corner of the island that projects into the Solomon Sea. Its spine is the Sarawaget Range, which runs most of the length of the peninsula before dividing eastward into the Rawlinson and

NATURALIST

Cromwell Mountains. At its tip, below the foothills of these satellite spurs, is the little coastal town of Finschhafen, where I arrived on April 3 to begin the greatest physical adventure of my life.

I had been invited there by Bob Curtis, an Australian patrol officer, to accompany him on a government-sponsored tour into the mountainous interior. His mission was an official visit to villages in the Hube country as far west as the Sarawaget highlands. He would consult with the village chiefs, settle disputes within and between villages, offer advice on agriculture, and if possible capture and return two suspected murderers for trial in Finschhafen. He anticipated no special risks, the murderers notwithstanding, but a great many unknowns did lie ahead. Although messages were carried regularly by natives back and forth between the coast and mountains, the villages of the region were visited by patrol officers at intervals of only one to two years. Some had not been contacted since 1952.

The most remarkable aspect of the patrol may have been Bob Curtis' age. He was twenty-three, and would turn twenty-four on April 19, near the end of the trip. As he reviewed the itinerary with me, he seemed as self-possessed and competent as a man twice his age. Curtis was blond, powerfully muscled, and possessed of movie-star good looks. I was reminded that a quarter-century earlier, Errol Flynn, up from Tasmania, had also started his career as a New Guinea patrol officer. Prior to his employment on the Huon Peninsula Bob had played semiprofessional rugby in Australia, the distinctive Australian rough-and-tumble kind, and had lost his upper front teeth in the process. He now wore a bridge. Any concern he may have felt about the patrol he kept to himself.

He seemed above all delighted to have my company. I was even happier. I had nothing to do but tag along, collecting and studying ants in a remote mountainous region that had never been visited by an entomologist. Curtis proposed as a bonus that we also climb to 3,600 meters on the central range, where the summits and passes rise in near-freezing cold to a treeless grassland. Natives had died there trying to cross from one side to another, and rumor had it that Japanese soldiers had also perished in the cold after being driven inland from Finschhafen by Australian forces in 1944. Were there mummified bodies still here, we wondered, preserved like the fabled leopard atop Mount Kilimanjaro? I didn't expect to find any ants so high, but looked forward to the climb with enthusiasm. It would be a difficult and possibly risky trek. Looking back later, I wondered whether Bob and I were bold nineteenth-century adventurers or just a pair of excited kids having fun. Almost certainly, both.

We left Finschhafen at the head of forty-seven bearers, three camp assistants, and a uniformed police boy with rifle. Boy: that is what a native policeman was still called in the days of waning colonial rule. Other men were assigned their various tasks as cook boy, hunt boy, and so on. Aside from Curtis' platoon-sergeant manner, however, we all treated one another with courtesy, and once on the trail we were effectively close to being equals. Perhaps it would have been dangerous to act otherwise. These people still belonged to a culture whose recent hallmark was war and the collecting of blood debts.

The carriers changed at successive villages along the way, and each man was paid between twenty-five and fifty cents U.S. for a day's work. On one leg of the trip, when too few adult males were available, Curtis recruited women and children to fill the gap.

The land that we entered, as we pushed north across the Mape River and then westward into Hube country, was sparsely populated. Most of the terrain was covered by rain forest, with little evidence of disturbance except for cultivated fields close to the settlements. The villages were four to seven hours' walk apart. Each settlement contained several hundred men, women, and children.

Because the villages were invariably set on mountain ridges, we almost never walked on level ground. On a typical day we set out at around nine in the morning on narrow trails that descended tortuously through as much as 1,000 meters of elevation. At the bottom we crossed white-water rivers on a suspension bridge, in some cases no wider than the span of a hand with a bamboo railing added above for balance. From there we zigzagged uphill for a similar distance to the next village. The paths were muddy and slick, often widening into almost impassable traps of deep black mire resembling pig wallows. Their steep, slippery banks were surmounted by dense undergrowth that made off-trail travel nearly impossible. Most of the time we were forced to walk in single file.

These treks were a great deal harder on the bearers than on Curtis and me, or on the native policeman, who was responsible only for his rifle and a few personal belongings. Each man handled twenty kilograms or more of cargo. Most of the neatly packed pieces were supported by a headband and slung over the back or else suspended from a bamboo pole carried in tandem by two of the porters. But the men were almost invariably cheerful. Hard climbing with heavy loads is a part of daily life for mountain Papuans. Even though I was in excellent physical condition at this time, they were far tougher, especially at the higher elevations. I came to suspect that they were also genetically better adapted to the harsh physical conditions in which they lived. I wondered: Would they make good marathoners?

The men were also serenely indifferent to the land leeches that attacked their bare feet and legs during the long walks. At intervals they stopped to pull the engorged worms off with about the same casualness one reties loosened shoe laces. After passing through heavily infested woodland their skin was often streaked with drying rivulets of blood. I never saw evidence that any suffered illness from these attacks.

In researching the trip for this memoir, I pored over the most detailed and updated maps I could find of the region, principally official topographic charts drawn from patrol reports and 1973 stereoscopic aerial photographs. I was able to locate only about half of the villages we visited in 1955, whose names I recorded in my notebooks: Mararuo, Boingbongen, Nanduo (or Nganduo), Yunzain, Homohang, Joangen, Zinzingu, Buru, Gemeheng, Zengaru, Tumnang, Ebabaang, Wamuki, Sambeang, and Butala. Had some of the settlements already been abandoned? In 1955 I took photographs of some of them for future archives.

The deeper we penetrated into the Hube country, the more excited and pleased the people were to see us. At Zinzingu we were honored by a sing-sing, an intricately choreographed program of dances and songs, lasting a large part of the day. At Gemeheng the *luluai* (chief) organized an archery contest, with meter-long bamboo arrows fired from black palm bows at banana-stalk targets ten paces away. I took one shot that passed a meter to the side, and braced myself for laughter. Instead, I heard the man next to me grunt, "Him all right," which probably meant, Not bad for someone who doesn't have to work for a living.

To the Hube people, Curtis and I were curiosities of the first order. In several of the remotest villages women and children ran and hid until we had settled in the thatched guest house, then quietly filtered back home. Throughout the day crowds of people stood outside our lodging, watching our every move with open curiosity. Curtis remained at ease with all of them, conversing smoothly in pidgin English. Once, at Joangen, we put on the brief equivalent of a magic show, mostly for the children. Standing in front of the house entrance, Curtis pulled out the bridge of his front teeth and held them up. I turned around, put my glasses on the back of my head and pointed backward at the crowd as though I could see them from behind. We were both met with gasps of amazement. One child broke out crying, and I decided not to try the trick again. I felt more like a fraud than an entertainer. And who knows what taboos we broke, or ghosts summoned?

At every opportunity I collected ants. I would rush ahead a few hundred meters, work for a few minutes, and fall in again as the others came by, or linger behind the bearers to work promising patches of forests and clearings, then walk fast or jog to catch up. I ventured from the villages at trail's end to work nearby habitats in the fading afternoon light. When we stayed in one place for two or three days, as at Gemeheng and Ebabaang, I left on more distant excursions. My worst problem was the weather: on most days afternoon mist and sporadic light rain settled throughout the mountain country. Most of the time, day and night, the temperature swung between a chilly 10° and barely comfortable 20°C. Only near midday in open sunny ground did it rise to the upper twenties, and it was under these conditions that ants were most numerous and active.

I was also hampered by the oppressively curious and helpful Hube people. Because I spent so much time in the forest, they called me "bush man." In the early days I was accompanied by mobs of boys of all ages and a few men, who pressed in so closely to see what I was doing that I could barely work. When they understood my purpose, they began to hunt for me, with the result that all the nearby logs and stumps were quickly torn to pieces with little result. I started telling them, as politely as I could, to stay away. But on several occasions I asked my retinue to collect spiders, frogs, and lizards and to ignore the ants and other smaller insects I was picking up myself. They scattered in all directions and in short order filled all the spare bottles I carried. I remember especially one boy, about twelve years old, who ran up to me clutching a giant silk spider in one hand, its fangs gnawing at a callused pad on his thumb. Grinning widely, he held it up for me to take. I am a bit of an arachnophobe, and for an instant I panicked. Then I grinned widely myself and held out my open lunch bag to receive the monster.

To my relief, we never caught the murderers. We also failed to make it to the high Sarawaget. At Buru a runner from Finschhafen brought Curtis a message: he was to report to Port Moresby as soon as possible to be interviewed for another, better-paying position. The next day we turned southward along the Bulum River, away from the Sarawaget and toward Butala on the coast, where a truck had been reserved to carry us the rest of the way to Finschhafen. As I walked homeward one day during this final leg I experienced an in-

sight about the diversity of tropical ants. All through my stay in New Guinea I had studied long stretches of relatively undisturbed rain forest, first at the Brown River, then at the Busu River near Lae, and now partly along the length of the Huon Peninsula. I had paid close attention to the identity and relative abundance of all the ants I could find, writing notes on every colony. I noticed that although the forest seemed to change very little in outward appearance from one kilometer to the next at the same elevation, the composition of the ant fauna usually shifted in a striking manner. It was possible to find, say, fifty species in one hectare, and another fifty species in a second hectare a short distance away, but at most only thirty or forty of the same species occurred in both places. Some of this variation was due to a local change in the physical properties of the habitat: the second hectare, for example, might contain a small sago palm slough or a clearing caused by a falling tree. That is the kind of easily understood change ecologists now call beta diversity—variety in species based on local differences in habitat. But much of the shift could not be so easily explained. It represented what is today called gamma diversity, the changeover in species with growing geographic distance.

The pattern I observed was very different from that in temperate forests, where gamma diversity occurs to the same extent only over tens or hundreds of kilometers. I had discovered something new about the structure of ant faunas in the tropics, and perhaps about the origin of the fabulous diversity of rain forest faunas and floras as well. In 1958 I concluded a formal article on the subject as follows:

> In any appraisal of comparative ecology, the New Guinea ant fauna is first of all to be characterized by the exceptional richness of its species and the great size of its biomass . . . In addition to sheer size, an additional factor adds greatly to the total faunal complexity. This is the discordant patchy distribution of individual species . . . As a result of discordant patchiness, no two localities harbor exactly the same fauna. Considering that several hundreds of species are thus involved, it is clear that the spatiotemporal structure of the entire New Guinea fauna must present the appearance of a great kaleidoscope. The effects of such a structure on the evolution of individual species of ants, as well as of other kinds of animals, must be considerable. It very possibly hastens the genetic divergence of local populations and plays an important role in the "exuberance" and amplitude that characterize evolution in the tropics. ★

★"Patchy Distributions of Ant Species in New Guinea Rain Forests," *Psyche* 65(1) (1958): 26–38.

I later learned that André Aubreville and Reginald Ernest Moreau had earlier and independently noted similar patchiness in African rain forest trees and birds. So patchiness is a general phenomenon, as I had hoped in 1955. My own insight was to be an early step in the development of my theory of the taxon cycle and, later, in collaboration with Robert MacArthur, the theory of island biogeography. Most important, it fixed my attention on biological diversity as a subject worthy of study in its own right.

I felt gratified—indeed, exuberant—that I had discerned what appeared to be a broad ecological pattern from my undisciplined collections and journals. But this was the way it is supposed to be. Nature first, then theory. Or, better, Nature and theory closely intertwined while you throw all your intellectual capital at the subject. Love the organisms for themselves first, then strain for general explanations, and, with good fortune, discoveries will follow. If they don't, the love and the pleasure will have been enough.

This insight came to me at Wamuki, which faces southward on the mountain ridge separating the Bulum Valley on the west from the Mongi Valley on the east. A day's walk farther south, the two rivers converge to form the greater Mongi, which runs on to the sea at Butala. As I strolled back at dusk one day at the end of one of my final excursions, I watched the clouds clear over the entire Bulum Valley below me. I could then see unbroken forest rolling down to the river and beyond for fifteen kilometers to the lower slopes of the Rawlinson Range. All that domain was bathed in an aquamarine haze, whose filtered light turned the valley into what seemed to be a vast ocean pool. At the river's edge 300 meters below, a flock of sulfur-crested cockatoos circled in lazy flight over the treetops like brilliant white fish following bottom currents. Their cries and the faint roar of the distant river were the only sounds I could hear. My tenuous thoughts on evolution, about which I had felt such enthusiasm, were diminished in the presence of sublimity. I could remember the command on the fourth day of Creation, "Let the waters teem with countless living creatures, and let birds fly above the earth across the vault of heaven."

Central summit ridge, Sarawaget Mountains, May 1955. When I returned to Lae, the administrative center of northeastern New Guinea, at the coastal base of the Huon Peninsula, my mind stayed on the Sarawaget Mountains. Standing in the main street on a clear morning, I could look north all the way to the blue-gray ridge of the center of the range. I learned that no European had ever climbed to the top of this main part of the mountain crest, which thrust up in such plain sight. Eight men, including the ornithologist Ernst Mayr, had independently reached the eastern end of the Sarawaget out of Finschhafen along the route partly traveled by Bob Curtis and me, but none had pushed on west toward the center ridge. In 1955 this lack of exploration did not seem very surprising: the Lae area had been settled only in the 1920s, and when I was there the population of planters, lumbermen, and colonial officials was still small; clearly, they had other things to do.

I hungered to get to the top of the Sarawaget. I was excited by the possibility of being the first white to visit the center of the crest. The problem was how to get there. Hearing that there was a Lutheran mission at Boana, halfway up the Bunbok Valley between Lae and the summit ridge, I inquired about Boana at the Agricultural Service office and soon received word that the resident minister, Reverend G. Bergmann, would be glad to have me as a guest and provide native help if I decided to attempt the climb. Bergmann was one of the eight Europeans to have climbed to the eastern end. He believed that it would not be too difficult to reach the middle as well.

On May 3 I walked into the office of Crowley Airways, the main transportation link to the Bunbok Valley. The president and sole full-time employee, Mr. L. Crowley, was seated behind a battered wooden desk. He rose, we shook hands, he shuffled some papers, and I paid the round-trip fare to Boana, four pounds and ten shillings Australian. A few days later Crowley and I walked across the tarmac to his 1929 biplane for the weekly flight to Boana. He stepped into the forward cockpit and I into the rear passenger cockpit, and we took off for the Bunbok Valley. I enjoyed the open-air, low-altitude view while peering over the edge of the cockpit. I also noticed that the double wings on each side waved up and down slightly throughout the flight. I supposed—hoped may be the better word—that the birdlike movement was a normal part of the airplane's aerodynamics.

The approach to the Boana was tricky. The mission was perched on a mountain spur to the east of the valley, and the airstrip could be reached only from the tributary valley by a southward approach. So we flew north along the river, mountains rising on both sides, turned right at the tributary, then immediately turned right again, now pointed south, and there, coming up fast, were the mountain ridge and, plastered on its side, the airstrip. As we glided in for a landing on the grassy surface, I saw the second aircraft of the Crowley fleet, also a 1929 biplane, this one recently crashed and still nose down on the edge of the airstrip.

In the late morning the Sarawaget crest, blue-gray against a lowering cloud bank, seemed close to Boana, a day's walk perhaps, and I ached to get started. It was in fact five days' walk away. I departed two days later, accompanied by a half-dozen young Papuan men hired as guides and carriers. The trip proved to be the physically most demanding of my life. It beggared even the hardest parts of the just-finished Sarawaget patrol. We reached the village of Bandang the first day, then proceeded up into virtually untracked country in daily marches lasting five to seven hours. Seldom were we able to travel for more than a hundred meters in a straight line on level ground. We wove, stumbled, waded, climbed, and sometimes just crawled our way, following stream banks, tracing animal trails up and along the crests of ridges, down into stream valleys and then up again. To my dismay my guides occasionally became lost, and we had to wait while one or two left to reconnoiter higher terrain and reestablish our position.

Our little party was almost constantly wet from intermittent rain, which set in predictably by early afternoon and continued into the early evening. Our clothing was stained by the soaked and puddled moss-grown earth over which we struggled. Beyond 2,100 meters, the temperature dropped to below 15°C at night and never rose as high as 20° during the day. Land leeches were everywhere—big, aggressive, and black, quickly swelling to half the size of a thumb with fresh blood—and periodically we stopped to take them off our legs and feet. To sit on a muddy stream bank in near exhaustion, pull off boots and peel down socks, and burn free a half-dozen engorged leeches, then watch blood trickle down from the bite wounds: that is an experience best savored after a few years have passed.

I was afraid, at times, of a crippling accident, of the possible unreliability of my assistants, with whom I could communicate very little, but most of all of the inexpressible unknown. Would I fail from physical incapacity or lack of will? Would I have to turn back as I did in Mexico, short of the Orizaba snowfield? Why had I come here anyway, except to be able to say I was the first white man to climb the central Sarawaget? That prideful goal was part of the truth, but I was looking for something more. I wanted the unique experience of being the first naturalist to walk on the alpine savanna of this part of the Sarawaget crest and collect animals there. And I wanted release from the mountain-peak compulsion that gripped me. I decided to keep going, even if I crawled or had to be carried.

Slogging on, we began to pass from the midmountain rain forest into mossy forest at about 2,000 meters. Here ferns, orchids, and other epiphytes thickly encrusted the branches and trunks of low gnarled trees. By 3,000 meters moss flowed like a continuous carpet from the trunks onto the forest floor. The canopy was also low here, only five meters above the ground, so in places progress was re-

stricted to wide tree-tunnels with mossy floors, walls, and roofs. Then at 3,200 meters, as we worked up at last onto the central ridge, the moss forest began to give way to scattered patches of *Eugenia* shrubs and alpine grasses.

Early on the fifth day, before the inevitable clouds descended and cold rain began to fall, we walked the final two hours to the summit. Here, at 3,600 meters, we were in a savanna composed of tall grass sprinkled with cycads, squat gymnospermous plants that resemble palm trees and date from the Mesozoic Era; a very similar scene might have existed here 100 million years before. The ground was mostly a mountaintop bog difficult to navigate. I made it on up to the nearest high point, sat down, wrote my name and the date on a scrap of journal paper, put the memento in a tightly capped bottle, then buried the bottle beneath a cairn of small rocks. From that position I could look south all the way down to the grasslands of the Markham Valley and the more distant Herzog Mountains, and north to the Bismarck Sea. Zigzagging back down the savanna, I collected every insect I could find, as well as small frogs that turned out to be a new species, while my companions hunted alpine wallabies with bows and arrows and dogs.

Then we turned back and began the two-day return trip to Boana, a far easier trek than the climb up. As we fast-walked and slid our way down the ridges and into the upper Bunbok Valley, something resistant and troubling finally broke and receded inside me. The Sarawaget, cold and daunting, had proved a test of my will severe enough to be satisfying. I had reached the edge of the world I wanted, and knew myself better as a result. By passing from the sea to its peaks I had finally encompassed the serious tropics of my dreams, and I could go home.

chapter eleven

THE FORMS
OF THINGS
UNKNOWN

_____

_____

_____

FROM NEW GUINEA I CONTINUED MY JOURNEY WESTWARD
on around the world. After pausing for a week of field work in the
rain forests of Queensland, I boarded an Italian liner in Sydney that
carried me south around the Victoria coast and then west along the
Bight to Perth. From this most distant city on Earth from my home,
the ship churned slowly north across the Indian Ocean toward its
eventual destination of Europe. I got off at Ceylon, now the republic
of Sri Lanka—in any case the island "Pearl of Asia" that hangs like a
teardrop from the tip of India.

NATURALIST

I traveled inland from the port of Colombo to search for one of the rarest ants in the world. *Aneuretus simoni* is the apparent evolutionary link between two of the great worldwide groups of ants, the Myrmicinae and Dolichoderinae. Fifty million years ago the group to which it belongs, the Aneuretinae, abounded throughout the northern half of the world. Now only one species remains, the endangered *Aneuretus simoni*. I began my quest in the Botanic Gardens at Peradeniya, where the only specimens in museums had been collected around 1890.

I hoped to find *Aneuretus* at the original find site, near the center of the island. No luck; the place had been shorn of native vegetation. For three more days I worked without result in the forest of the neighboring Udawaddatekele Sanctuary, close to Dalada Maligava, the temple holding a giant tooth said to be that of Buddha. Unrewarded by His blessed aura, I took a bus south to the gem center of Ratnapura. There, somewhere in the remnants of rain forest scattered along the road to Adam's Peak, Sri Lanka's highest elevation, the prize might be found. I checked into the government rest house, eager to get started. Dropped my Army-issue duffel bag in my room. Swung my stained canvas collector's bag over my shoulder. Walked down the stairs and out the back entrance a hundred meters to a line of trees fringing the town reservoir. Looked around. Picked up a dead twig lying on the ground, broke it open, and stared as a colony of small, yellow ants ran out over my hand. *Aneuretus*! I could not have been happier if I had discovered a priceless Ratnapura sapphire lying unclaimed on the ground. Settled back in my room, I turned the vial of specimens slowly over and over in my hand, looking at the first queen, larvae, and soldiers of the living aneuretine ever seen (the 1890 specimens had all belonged to the worker caste). This was one of the great thrills of my life. Dinner tasted fit for a gourmet that evening, and afterward, sleep came easily.

In the days that followed, I ventured into forest closer to Adam's

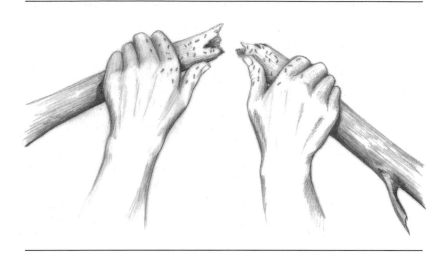

Peak. Though sometimes delayed for hours by monsoon down-pours, the kind called gully-washers or frog-stranglers back home, I easily secured more colonies, finding the *Aneuretus* in one locality to be among the most common ants. In a short while I was able to put together a picture of the social life of the last surviving aneuretine. Twenty years later one of my undergraduate students, Anula Jaya-suriya, a native Sri Lankan, found the species rare or absent in the same localities. I recommended placement of *Aneuretus simoni* in the Red Data Book of the International Union for Conservation of Na-ture and Natural Resources, and in time it became one of the first of several ants to be officially classified as a threatened or endangered species.

My field adventure was now finished. I continued on by a second Italian liner (cheap fare) to Genoa, where I worked on the ant collec-tion of Carlo Emery at the Museo Civico di Storia Naturale. Then I proceeded by train across Switzerland and France and finally to Lon-don, visiting other ant collections in museums along the way. That was my European tour as a young academic: the great ant collections of the world. When others at Harvard spoke of their experiences at Hagia Sophia and the Prado, I reminisced about the wondrous ants I examined in Geneva and Paris.

On September 5, 1955, I flew to New York. The last four hours up to Boston by train, eased only slightly by an anesthetic reading and rereading of a copy of that week's *Life* magazine, were the longest of my life. Finally, clad in khaki and heavy boots, crew-cut, twenty pounds underweight, and tinted faint yellow from the antimalarial drug quinacrine, I fell into Renee's arms. I came home innocent of hula hoops, Davy Crockett, Tommy Manville's ninth divorce, and other Western Hemispheric events of 1955. I had not heard Vice President Richard Nixon say, "Sincerity is the quality that comes through on television." I was ignorant of the latest in men's leisure clothing, which, should you wish to learn or be reminded, consisted of cotton jersey pullovers, bateau necklines, and moccasin slip-ons worn in chaste combinations to create a European effect. American culture had begun to fade for me around the edges in the ten months of my absence. I began quickly to recover, however, with the help of ten-cent hamburgers at the White Tower and hours of serious television watching.

Six weeks later Renee and I were married in Boston's St. Cecilia Church. We moved to Holden Green, university housing on the Cambridge-Somerville line that seemed to be the starting point of most young Harvard couples. There were young Holden Greeners on their way up and out and older Holden Greeners who apparently wanted to stay there and at Harvard forever.

The following winter I was offered an assistant professorship in Harvard's Department of Biology. My main function would be to assist William H. ("Cap") Weston, an elderly professor and fungus expert, in the creation of a new beginning biology course for non-science students. The department chairman, Frank Carpenter, who had previously served as my doctoral adviser, cautioned me that the appointment would be for five years only. After that I had a distant chance of further employment, but the position was not tenure track. Would I be interested just the same? I had already sent letters of inquiry to thirty other prospective employers and gleaned offers from the University of Florida and the University of Michigan, both tenure track. Then, as now for most colleges and universities, this meant that all I had to do was perform well for the first few years to be guaranteed a lifetime position.

The impermanence of the Harvard position did not faze me. I was young, only twenty-six, and wanted the added time there to settle in a world-class collection and library and to expand my research program. I accepted Harvard's offer and set out to plan my first lectures.

Partway into the first year, however, my nerve began to fail. Like all assistant professors at the great university, I felt disposable. And obviously, I *was* disposable. With Renee's assistance, I made plans to find a new position long before the end of my five-year term put me on the street. Then providentially, in the spring of 1958, with more than three years to go, Stanford University offered me an associate professorship with lifetime tenure as part of the package. The invitation came out of the blue in a letter from Victor Twitty, chairman of the Department of Biology, flat and definitive, prefaced by no tentative inquiry, and conditional upon no visit and seminar. Twitty said in effect: Here it is; will you join us?

Soon afterward Frederick Terman, dean of the Stanford faculty, came to visit me in my office in the Biological Laboratories. He was accompanied by an older gentleman whom he introduced as Wallace Sterling.

When the two were seated, I turned to Sterling. "Are you with Stanford, too?"

Terman answered for him: "Yes, he's the president."

Leaving me time to regain my composure, the two men went on smoothly to explain that the biology faculty hoped that I would come to Palo Alto to build a new program in entomology. The incumbent professor, a specialist on scale insects, was retiring. I listened with intense excitement. Stanford was the Harvard of the West, and California was the golden state of the 1950s. Come to this land of opportunity, they said, and help us to grow. I knew that others were responding to the call. Earlier that year *Time* had reported a westward surge of scientists and other academics from the older eastern universities.

Renee and I were thrilled by Stanford's commitment. I was really wanted for my special skills in entomology and for my myrmecophilia, the love of ants! The salary was also good for the times, $7,500 a year, and Stanford would assist us in buying a house, a policy unheard of at Harvard. The next morning I told Carpenter that I was going to Stanford. Thank you, I said, for all you have done. He said, Wait a few weeks before making a firm commitment. Let's see what Harvard can do. Over the next two months the biology faculty and McGeorge Bundy, dean of the Faculty of Arts and Sciences, moved to review my status and decide whether to match the offer from Stanford. As I waited I tossed the matter around in my mind. To the present day this is how Harvard makes most offers of tenure to its own young faculty. It reacts to outside threat, and even then turns down a majority of the hopefuls. The process seems more ponderous than anything west of the Vatican, usually taking a year or more to complete. But I was favored by an accelerated schedule. I received the offer from Mac Bundy, and I decided.

Nowadays on freezing January mornings in Cambridge, as I pick my way across Kandinsky landscapes of snow painted with automobile smudge and dog urine, I remind myself that the New England winter is a hard but fair price to pay to work closely with the best collection of ants in the world. Thirty-five years after accepting Harvard's tenure offer, having reached the same age as Cap Weston when he walked with me into the lecture room of Allston Burr Hall that first September morning, I still teach a large class in beginning biology for nonmajors. My contentment with this repetitive schedule does not rise from the comfortable stagnation of the tenured academic. Rather, it exists because I find Harvard undergraduates wonderfully talented, and because each year's contact with them renews me. Most share my own restlessness and optimistic rationalism. We work each other up into enthusiastic conversation. The nonscientists in particular are a prime investment. I know they will carry with them into great ventures, in law, government, business, and art, the commitments they first acquire in the university's hothouse environment, and a few (it has happened) will convert to biology. I speak to these students as intellectual equals, keeping in the back of my mind their prospective if not immediate attainment of that status. In 1992 the Committee on Undergraduate Education, consisting of undergraduate students, awarded me the Levenson Prize, as outstanding tenured teacher in the college. But I have another, more selfish reason for lecturing on biology to nonscientists. The bourgeois life of the college teacher, if one's schedule is not too crowded, frees the mind for creative work.

By 1958 I had temporarily forsaken field biology to press research in the laboratory and museum. My central aim was the classification and analysis of the ants of New Guinea and the surrounding regions of tropical Asia, Australia, and the South Pacific. I had embarked on a bread-and-butter task, of a largely descriptive nature. It was time-consuming, tedious, fact-centered, and, for this combination of reasons, virtuous in my own mind.

So let me digress for a moment to explain the special satisfaction of taxonomy. It is a craft and a body of knowledge that builds in the head of a biologist only through years of monkish labor. The taxonomist enjoys the status of mechanic and engineer among biologists. He knows that without the expert knowledge accumulated through his brand of specialized study, much of biological research would soon come to a halt. Only a specialist expert enough to recognize the species chosen for study ("Ah, that is a carabid beetle of the genus *Scarites*") can unlock all that is already known about it in the literature. From journal pages and museum specimens he is able to go promptly from the already discovered to the exhilarating unknown. If a biologist does not have the name of the species, he is lost. As the Chinese say, the first step to wisdom is getting the right name.

There is much more. A skilled taxonomist is not just a museum labeler. He is a world authority, often *the* world authority since there are so few taxonomists, on the group he has chosen. He is steward and spokesman for a hundred, or a thousand, species. Other scientists come to him to seek entry to his taxon—sharks, rotifers, soldier flies, weevils, conifers, dinoflagellates, cyanobacteria, and so on down the long roster comprising over a million species. He knows not only the classification but also the anatomy, physiology, behavior, biogeography, and evolutionary history of the group, in fine detail both published and unpublished. In conversation he will speak as follows: "Come to think of it, there *is* an enchytraeid I ran into in Honduras with a reddish color, and that just might be the invertebrate hemoglobin you're looking for." Or, "No, no, the main center of that particular moth family is the temperate forests of southern Chile. Those species haven't been worked on yet, but there is a big collection in the National Museum made by the Hensley expedition in 1923. Let's check it out." No CD-ROM, no encyclopedia can replace the taxonomic expert. Once, after receiving an award in Japan for such studies, I had the additional honor of spending an evening in conversation with Emperor Akihito, a noted specialist on the taxonomy of gobiid fishes. Soon I fell into a comfortable routine of listening to him speak about gobies and Japan's endangered fish species, while he and his family asked me questions about ants. It was like a Harvard seminar. At times I almost (but never completely) forgot with whom I was speaking.

In 1958, sitting in my office on the first floor of the Biological Laboratories, occasionally glancing out the window past the monumental bronze statues of the Indian white rhinoceros, I felt on temporarily safe professional ground returning to this kind of enterprise. It guaranteed a stream of tangible results, the kind for which grants-in-

aid and other professional emoluments are awarded. At the age of twenty-nine, I had fifty-five technical articles published or in press. Being thoroughly professional in attitude by that time, I knew that every young scientist needs such proof of productivity. Otherwise the National Science Foundation and J. S. Guggenheim Selection Committee will wave his grant applications aside. But if truly creative he does not always hug the coast. He gambles repeatedly on risky projects, stays alert and aggressive, ready to move whenever a long shot shows a hint of promise.

What, then, were my gambles? Highly diverse in nature, they came to me as unplanned products of pedestrian daily research. During my accumulation of facts about ant biology, vaporous notions—

constructs, definitions, inchoate patterns (the perfect phrase escapes me)—drifted in and out of my mind like Celtic fog. My daydreams were mostly about the origins of biological diversity. Most took coherent form, only to prove marginal or unattractive, then to fade and disappear. A few went on to gain robust life in the course of my daily reverie. They then turned into narratives, which I began to repeat to myself like stories. I prepared to speak about the matter to others. I imagined how the narrative would look in print, how it might sound in a lecture before a skeptical audience. I rehearsed, edited, and performed in silence. I was a storyteller, sorting and arranging pieces of nonfiction, dreaming in order to fill in the gaps. Then I tried the performance before a real audience.

One of my first constructions was a critique of subspecies, the formal category of race used universally in biological classifications. My coauthor in this endeavor was William L. Brown, seven years my senior, who had enticed me to come to Harvard as a graduate student. During 1952 we met almost daily at lunch to gossip and mull over issues in evolutionary biology. Brown, I soon learned from his pungent remarks, was a scientific curmudgeon. He seemed happiest when he could sprinkle doubt on the reputation of a reigning academic pooh-bah. He tended to divide all scientific ideas into two piles: those he embraced passionately and those he ridiculed. Passionate he was (and remains), but also thoroughly professional. And proletarian in spirit, a hater of pomposity and pretense. Grinning impishly, he would hold up an imaginary "phony meter" when certain faculty notables walked nearby, and take a reading: Red zone! Off the scale! In other lives he would have been the first sergeant who wisecracks about the foibles of the company commander, or the engineer, oil-streaked in the bowels of the plant, who makes up for and grumbles about the incompetence of management. He enjoyed having a beer, or two or three, with working-class stiffs at a nearby bar after a day in the Museum of Comparative Zoology. He was annoyed with me for not joining him. "Can't completely trust someone who doesn't like beer." It seems never to have occurred to him that he was himself a member of the ruling class. But no matter; his animadversions were usually on target. Management *was* incompetent, a lot of the time. This year, as we began collaborating, he had been roused by the subspecies.

It was a subject deserving close inspection. Everywhere taxonomists were treating the subspecies as an objective category and one of the key steps of evolution. Consider their logic: species are divided into subspecies, which we must assume to be real and objective because given enough time they evolve into species, which are real and objective. Subspecies were (and still are) given formal latinized names by taxonomists. The bald eagle *Haliaeetus leucocephalus*, for example, is a species divided by taxonomists into two such races, the southern bald eagle *Haliaeetus leucocephalus leucocephalus* and the northern bald eagle *Haliaeetus leucocephalus washingtoniensis*.

For reasons not immediately clear to Brown and me, subspecies seemed insubstantial and arbitrary. We set out to conduct a critical review of the premises behind their recognition, by looking at real cases. The foundations proved even weaker than we had imagined. We discovered that the geographic limits of subspecies are often hard or impossible to draw, because the traits used to define them vary in a discordant pattern. The nature of the discordance can be most immediately understood with an imaginary but typical example: color in a butterfly species varies east to west, size decreases from north to south, and an extra band appears on the hind wing in a few localities near the center. And so on for any number of traits the taxonomist might choose from an almost endless list available for classification. It follows that the identity of the subspecies into which the butterfly species is divided depends on the traits chosen to define them. Pick color, and you have two east–west races. Pick color plus size, and four races in a quadrant come into existence. Add the hind-wing band, and the number of races can double again. Hence the subspecies are arbitrary. In 1953 we published a report recommending that subspecies not be given formal names.★ We argued that the geographic variation is real all right but should instead be analyzed trait by trait. It is more informative to focus on the traits and not on the subspecies that might be concocted from them.

Our critique of the subspecies triggered a tempest of controversy in the journals of systematic biology. When the debate subsided several years later, opinion had shifted to our side. Fewer triple-name races were formally described thereafter, and emphasis was increasingly placed on the properties of independently varying traits. Nevertheless, I realize now that Brown and I overstated our case in 1953. Some populations can be defined clearly with sets of genetic traits that do change in a concordant, not a discordant manner. Furthermore, the subspecies category is often a convenient shorthand for alluding to important populations even when their genetic status is ambiguous. What, for example, is the Florida panther? It is a subspecies, a nearly vanished remnant of a series of populations once widespread across the United States, now further altered by hybridization with panthers of South American origin released to the wild in south Florida. Biologists rightly speak of the Florida population in a way that calls attention to its genetic distinctness, using one sharp phrase: the Florida subspecies (or race, meaning the same thing) of *Felis concolor*.

Soon afterward Brown and I made a second conceptual discovery, this one unfettered by controversy. We found a new phenomenon in biodiversity, which we came to call character displacement. The process is the exact opposite of hybridization. In hybridization, two species exchange genes where they meet, and as a result become overall more similar. In character displacement two species spring apart where they meet, like particles with the same charge. I first encountered the mysterious effect in the ant genus *Lasius*, which I had chosen as the subject of my Ph.D. dissertation. During our

★E. O. Wilson and W. L. Brown, "The Subspecies Concept and Its Taxonomic Application," *Systematic Zoology* 2(3) (1953): 97–111.

ABOVE: *Robert Trivers, William Brown, and Hope Hare (Trivers' assistant) on a field trip in Concord, Massachusetts, on May 15, 1975 (the day* Sociobiology *was featured in a front-page story of the* New York Times).
RIGHT: *Ed with his daughter Catherine in 1969.*

The author with his mother, Inez Huddleston, at the University of West Florida, Pensacola, in 1979.

ABOVE: *Ed, Renee, and Cathy Wilson attending a parents' dinner at Regis College, in September 1982.*
BELOW: *Kathleen Horton, Ed, and Bert Hölldobler with the newly finished manuscript of* The Ants, *June 29, 1989.*

ABOVE: *Founders of sociobiology, at the first meeting of the Human Behavior and Evolution Society, Evanston, Illinois, in August 1989.* LEFT TO RIGHT: *Irenäus Eibl-Eibesfeldt, George Williams, E. O. Wilson, Richard Dawkins, and William Hamilton.* BELOW: *Wilson and Hölldobler in 1990, at the time of publication of* The Ants.

Wilson receives the annual gold medal of the Worldwide Fund for Nature from Prince Philip in Sydney, Australia, on November 26, 1990.

ABOVE: *The author's home laboratory in Lexington, Massachusetts, in 1994.*
BELOW: *Paul Ehrlich and Wilson receive the 1990 Crafoord Prize of the Royal Swedish Academy of Sciences from H. M. Carl XVI Gustaf, in Stockholm, September 26. The award was established to recognize fields of science, including ecology, not covered by the Nobel Prize.*

ABOVE: *Thomas Eisner and Ed Wilson in the Ant Room of the Museum of Comparative Zoology, spring 1991.*
BELOW: *The author accepting the International Prize for Biology, with Emperor Akihito and Empress Michiko in attendance, Tokyo, November 29, 1993.*

E. O. Wilson in 1990, with "Dacie," the metallic sculpture of one of his favorite ant species, Daceton armigerum *of South America.*

lunchtime dialogues Brown and I explored the possible causes and searched the literature for a similar pattern in other kinds of organisms.

We learned that the British ornithologist David Lack had already delineated character displacement in his 1947 study of Darwin's finches on the Galápagos Islands. In the 1970s and 1980s Peter Grant of Princeton University, his wife, Rosemary, and their students were to work out displacement in exquisite detail through a lengthy field study of the same finches in the Galápagos. Thus this little group of birds has been favored by three of the best field studies in the history of evolutionary biology: those by Darwin, Lack, and the Grants, respectively. The principal contribution that Brown and I made in our 1956 report was to show that the repellant effect is widespread among animals and is caused, according to the species pair considered, by either competition or the active avoidance of hybridization.* We brought character displacement to prominence in biology and gave it the name now in general use.

Character displacement, we also realized, is one means by which species can be packed together more tightly in ecosystems. The evolution of greater differences between species reduces the chance that one of them will erase the other through competition or hybridization. The better the mutual adjustment that avoids competition and hybridization, the more species that can live together indefinitely; hence the richer will be the biodiversity, as an outcome of evolution in the community as a whole. In 1959 Evelyn Hutchinson of Yale University, the doyen of ecology, used our presentation of character displacement as a key point in his highly influential article, "Homage to Santa Rosalia, or Why Are There So Many Kinds of Animals?" The question he posed in this title became the entrée for ecologists who later tried to analyze the basis of biodiversity in more quantitative terms. They asked, Why are there a certain number of butterfly

*W. L. Brown and E. O. Wilson, "Character Displacement," *Systematic Zoology* 5(2) (1956): 49–64.

species in Florida, and not some other? of snakes in Trinidad, of marsupials in Australia? Just posing such questions presaged the effort to understand more deeply the causes of species formation and extinction, which by the 1980s was to become a prominent social issue in biology.

I had grown more interested in theory by the late 1950s, but down deep I was still possessed by an elemental self-image: hunter in the magical forest, searching not just for animals now but also for ideas to bring home as trophies. A naturalist, real and then more metaphorical, a civilized hunter, I was destined to be more of an opportunist than a problem solver. The boy inside still made my career decisions: I just wanted to be the first to find something, anything, the more important the better, but something as often as possible, to own it a little while before relinquishing it to others. I confess that to the degree I was insecure, I was also ambitious. I hungered for the recognition and support that discovery in science brings. To make this admission does not embarrass me now as it would have when I was young. All the scientists I know share a desire for fair recognition of their work. Acknowledgment is their silver and gold, and why they are usually very careful to grant deserved priority to others while so jealously guarding their own. New knowledge is not science until it is made social. The scientific culture can be defined as new verifiable knowledge secured and distributed with fair credit meticulously given.

Scientists, I believe, are divided into two categories: those who do science in order to be a success in life, and those who become a success in life in order to do science. It is the latter who stay active in research for a lifetime. I am one of them, and I suspect that all my fellow devotees in this category are also driven by a childhood dream of one kind or another, possibly closer to my own than I have guessed, for evolutionary biology has become the last refuge of the explorer naturalist.

So I hunted this time for abstract principles in one of the more poorly mapped domains of evolutionary biology. As a result of my experience in zoogeography, I was drawn by the idea of the fountainheads of evolution, places in which dominant groups rise and spread to the rest of the world. Serious discussion of the phenomenon had begun in 1915 with William Diller Matthew, curator in invertebrate paleontology at the American Museum of Natural History and later professor of paleontology at the University of California at Berkeley. In his monograph *Climate and Evolution* he constructed a picture of dominance in mammals and other vertebrate animals. Matthew instructed the reader to look at a north polar projection of the globe. Europe, Asia, and North America are so close together as to form a single supercontinent. Citing evidence from his own and previous studies of fossil mammals, he audaciously posited that the dominant groups arise on this supercontinent and spread outward, displacing formerly dominant groups southward to the peripheral regions of tropical Asia, Africa, and South America. In our own time, he noted, the winners include deer, camels, pigs, and the most familiar of the rats and mice, members of the family Muridae. Among the losers retreating to the edges of the world are horses, tapirs, and rhinoceroses. Like a true Aryan biologist, Matthew suggested that competitive superiority is the result of the adaptation of the dominant groups to the harsh, constantly changing environments of the northern latitudes.

Then along came Philip Darlington with a new twist, presented first in a 1948 article in the *Quarterly Review of Biology* and later in his 1957 full-dress treatise *Zoogeography: The Geographical Distribution of Animals*. Matthew, Darlington wrote, was only half right. The fossil remains he had studied were biased toward the Northern Hemisphere, where most collecting had been concentrated during the early years of paleontology. Thirty years after *Climate and Evolution*, Darlington argued, we have more data on fossils to examine, and these come from all over the world, including Matthew's "peripheral" areas. In addition we must examine more carefully the evidence

NATURALIST

from the distribution of living groups, especially fishes, frogs, and other cold-blooded vertebrates, animals for which most of the new evidence is available. When we put all the pieces together, we see that the evolutionary crucible is not the north temperate land mass, but the Old World tropics. For the past 50 million years or so, groups of vertebrates have arisen in the vast greenhouse region that comprises southern Asia, sub-Saharan Africa, and, until recent geological times, much of the Middle East. The most dominant of the animal groups pressed on northward to Europe and Siberia, across the Bering Sea, a barrier periodically breached by the rise of isthmuses, and into the New World. People living in North America or Europe today need only look around to see the current hegemonic groups: cervid deer, canid dogs, felid cats, murid rats and mice, ranid frogs, bufonid toads, and other pioneer groups familiar to every child. Their species are extending their ranges into, not out of, the harsher climates.

I was enchanted by the idea of dominant animals and the succession of dynasties. There was a main center of evolution on the land, and Darlington seemed closer than Matthew to pinning it down. Either way, there remained a second question of major importance: What is the *biological* nature of dominance? More precisely, What hereditary traits cause an assemblage of species to spread into new lands and overwhelm the old endemics? The surrender of any group is all the more puzzling because endemics have had thousands or millions of years to become adapted to the habitats they occupy before the invaders appear.

This problem of the biological cause of dominance was not clearly in my mind as I began my own biogeographic study, a monograph on the ants of New Guinea and surrounding regions. But Matthew and Darlington, who never asked the question directly themselves, had primed me to formulate it. All I needed, I realize in retrospect today, was a small set of data to fall into place in order for the question to form somewhere in my subconscious. Then, driven by the power of the mythic conqueror archetype evoked by Matthew and Darlington, I would put together a tentative scenario, a story, and a phrase to capture it all, in the manner of Shakespeare's muse,

> *And as imagination bodies forth*
> *The forms of things unknown, the poet's pen*
> *Turns them into shapes, and gives to airy nothing*
> *A local habitation and a name.*

I asked the question and got a persuasive and verifiable answer because in the course of my taxonomic drudge-work I had sketched out on paper the geographic ranges of the ant species one at a time and possessed a large body of quantitative information. I knew what I was talking about. Matthew and Darlington had developed their images in a coarser resolution, at the level of entire genera and families of animal species. I understood the ants of the western Pacific, not all larger groups of land vertebrates of the world, but in more detail than they had available. As part of my omnibus approach, I had collected a great many data on the places the ant species lived, their nest sites, their colony size, what they ate, and anything else that might find use—somehow, I hoped, somewhere, someday. Because I considered all the information valuable in its own right, I had swept up specimens like a vacuum cleaner in the field and continued close work on them in the museum. My ultimate aim was to find interesting patterns of evolution, but I would have continued on to the end of my descriptive work even if I had expected nothing of superordinate value.

A pattern did emerge, however. Evolutionary biology always yields patterns if you look hard enough, because there are a hundred parameters and a thousand patterns awaiting examination. It came clear this time as I mapped ranges of one species after another. I saw that some of the ants were in the early stages of invading New Guinea and the eastern Melanesian archipelagoes. Other species, apparently survivors from older invasions, were splitting off as forms limited to one island or another. Some had fragmented into many such endemic residents. And still other ensembles of species were clearly in retreat, their populations now scattered here and there in pockets of island terrain. Finally, a small percentage had begun to expand again, this time from New Guinea. It dawned on me that the whole cycle of evolution, from expansion and invasion to evolution into endemic status and finally into either retreat or renewed expansion, was a microcosm of the worldwide cycle envisioned by Matthew and Darlington.

To find the same biogeographic pattern in miniature was a surprise then, although in retrospect it seems almost self-evident. But for some reason I just didn't anticipate that particular sequence at the time. It came within a few minutes one January morning in 1959 as I sat in my first-floor office next to the entrance of the Biological Laboratories, sorting my newly sketched maps into different possible sequences—early evolution to late evolution. Which came first, which came late? I occasionally glanced up at the giant metallic rhinoceros outside the window and the intermittent stream of students and faculty walking into and out of the building. My mind drifted round and about, home, museum, field trips, lectures. I looked back down to the maps, and up again, and at some point the pattern became obvious, the only one possible.

Discovery of the cycle of advance and retreat was followed immediately by recognition of another ecological cycle. As I reflected on the expanding and retreating species, I drew on my memories of the long walks in New Guinea. I saw that the expanding, hence dominant, species are adapted for ecologically marginal habitats, in which relatively small numbers of ant species occur. Such places include the savannas, the monsoon forests, the sunny margins of lowland rain forest, and the salt-lashed beaches. They are marginal not just in having smaller numbers of ant species than the inland rain forests, but also in a purely geographic sense. Located near river banks and sea coast, they are staging areas from which it is easiest to disperse by wind and by floating vegetation from one island to another. The marginal species, I also realized, are most flexible in terms of the places in which they live. Because they face only a small number of competitors, they have been ecologically "released," able to live in more habitats and in denser populations than would otherwise be possible. It seemed likely that these ants not only could move more easily but also would tend to press older native species back into the inner rain forests, reducing their dispersal power and shattering their populations into fragments prone to evolve into endemic species.

I knew I had a candidate for a new principle of biogeography. Though far from definitive, and attributable to only one animal group—ants—the concept is at least rested on solid data. I gathered my maps, stepped next door to the office of my old companion in Cuba, Grady Webster, spread the papers out, and recited my scenario. What did he think? Reasonable, he said, looks good. Congratulations! (What did he really think? It didn't matter. I was too pleased with myself to worry.) Over the next few months I presented a full-dress review to the evolutionary biologists I considered most knowledgeable in zoogeography: Bill Brown, Phil Darlington, the geneticist Theodosius Dobzhansky, Ernst Mayr, and the senior entomologists Alfred Emerson, Carl Lindroth, and Elwood Zimmerman. This is the way it is done on the path to publication, especially by young scientists. And these luminaries all wrote back: Okay, they said, no obvious flaws that stand out.

I named the phenomenon the taxon cycle. Let me explain here that a taxon is any subspecies, species, or group of species, such as a genus, recognized in taxonomic classifications as being similar by virtue of common descent and labeled as such in taxonomic classifications. The grizzly bear, *Ursus horribilis*, being a species, is a taxon; so is the genus *Ursus*, containing the grizzly and all the other species of bear, including the black bear and brown bear, close enough to each other to be reasonably considered to share a recent common ancestor. I conjectured that if the principle held for species, it would hold for other taxa as well. In two articles, I refined my analysis.★ The expanding species, I reported, have certain characteristics associated with life in the marginal habitats. The colonies are more populous and tend to nest in the soil rather than in decaying logs and tree limbs on the ground. The workers possess more spines on the body, an armament used against enemies in the open spaces of the marginal habitats. They orient more frequently by odor trails laid by scouts over the ground.

These traits are not the source of the dominance, however. They are only adaptations to life in the marginal habitats. I had no basis to infer the existence of special "dominance genes," a powerful ichor flowing in the blood of warrior ants. All that mattered in the history of the fauna was a happenstance: the dominant species had become adapted to the marginal habitats, which served as potent dispersal centers. Like the people of some island civilizations, a few ant species achieve dominance simply by their ability to cross the sea.

The taxon cycle led me to reconsider a very old concept, that of the balance of Nature: when one species is established, eventually another species has to go. But the replacement is rarely so precise; in fact, nothing in evolution ever is. The principle is more correctly defined as a statistical generalization. If a hundred species invade a certain ecological guild, say night-flying fruit eaters or orchid-pollinating bees, roughly a hundred comparable species will disappear, with many exceptions accruing to special places and times. The rule was reinforced in my mind by the discovery of a simple relation between the area of each of the Melanesian islands and the number of ant species found in it. The greater the area, the larger the number of species. When I plotted the logarithms, the points formed an approximately straight line. I expressed the area-species curve simply as follows: $S = CA^z$, where S is the number of species found on the is-

★"Adaptive Shift and Dispersal in a Tropical Ant Fauna," *Evolution* 13(1) (1959): 122–144; "The Nature of the Taxon Cycle in the Melanesian Ant Fauna," *American Naturalist* 95 (1961): 169–193.

land, A is the area of the island, and C and z are fitted constants. In 1957 Darlington had expressed the same relation in the reptiles and amphibians of the West Indies not as an equation but as the following general rule: with each tenfold increase in island area, the number of species on the island doubles. There are, for example, approximately forty species of reptiles and amphibians on Jamaica, and eighty-five on the nearby island of Cuba, which has about ten times the area of Jamaica. His expression is more readily understood in the many cases in which it applies, but the logarithmic equation is the more precise and flexible expression and therefore more generally true.

I did not grasp its significance just then, but the area-species relation that Darlington and I had defined would soon lead to a deeper understanding of the balance of species diversity. In order to explain clearly and congenially how that next step was taken, however, I need first to describe certain developments that were unfolding in biology as a whole and in Harvard biology in particular during the 1950s and 1960s.

chapter twelve

THE MOLECULAR WARS

WITHOUT A TRACE OF IRONY I CAN SAY I HAVE BEEN BLESSED with brilliant enemies. They made me suffer (after all, they were enemies), but I owe them a great debt, because they redoubled my energies and drove me in new directions. We need such people in our creative lives. As John Stuart Mill once put it, both teachers and learners fall asleep at their posts when there is no enemy in the field.

James Dewey Watson, the codiscoverer of the structure of DNA, served as one such adverse hero for me. When he was a young man, in the 1950s and 1960s, I found him the most unpleasant human being I had ever met. He came to Harvard as an assistant professor in 1956, also my first year at the same rank. At twenty-eight, he was only a year older. He arrived with a conviction that biology must be transformed into a science directed at molecules and cells and rewritten in the language of physics and chemistry. What had gone before, "traditional" biology—*my* biology—was infested by stamp collectors who lacked the wit to transform their subject into a modern science. He treated most of the other twenty-four members of the Department of Biology with a revolutionary's fervent disrespect.

At department meetings Watson radiated contempt in all directions. He shunned ordinary courtesy and polite conversation, evidently in the belief that they would only encourage the traditionalists to stay around. His bad manners were tolerated because of the greatness of the discovery he had made, and because of its gathering aftermath. In the 1950s and 1960s the molecular revolution had begun to run through biology like a flash flood. Watson, having risen to historic fame at an early age, became the Caligula of biology. He was given license to say anything that came to his mind and expect to be taken seriously. And unfortunately, he did so, with a casual and brutal offhandedness. In his own mind apparently he was *Honest Jim*, as he later called himself in the manuscript title of his memoir of the discovery—before changing it to *The Double Helix*. Few dared call him openly to account.

Watson's attitude was particularly painful for me. One day at a department meeting I naively chose to argue that the department needed more young evolutionary biologists, for balance. At least we should double the number from one (me) to two. I informed the listening professors that Frederick Smith, an innovative and promising population ecologist, had recently been recruited from the University of Michigan by Harvard's Graduate School of Design. I outlined Smith's merits and stressed the importance of teaching environmental biology. I proposed, following standard departmental procedure, that Smith be offered joint membership in the Department of Biology.

Watson said softly, "Are they out of their minds?"

"What do you mean?" I was genuinely puzzled.

"Anyone who would hire an ecologist is out of his mind," responded the avatar of molecular biology.

For a few moments the room was silent. No one spoke to defend the nomination, but no one echoed Watson either. Then Paul Levine, the department chairman, jumped in to close the subject. This proposal, he said, is not one we are prepared to consider at this time. With documentation, we might examine the nomination at some future date. We never did, of course. Smith was elected a member only after the molecular biologists split off to form a department of their own.

After this meeting I walked across the Biological Laboratories quad on my way to the Museum of Comparative Zoology. Elso Barghoorn hurried to catch up with me. A senior professor of evolutionary biology, he was one of the world's foremost paleobotanists, the discoverer of Pre-Cambrian microscopic fossils, and an honest man. "Ed," he said, "I don't think we should use 'ecology' as an expression anymore. It's become a dirty word." And sure enough, for most of the following decade we largely stopped using the word "ecology." Only later did I sense the anthropological significance of the incident. When one culture sets out to erase another, the first thing its rulers banish is the official use of the native tongue.

The molecular wars were on. Watson was joined to varying degrees in attitude and philosophy by a small cadre of other biochemists and molecular biologists already in the department. They were George Wald, soon to receive a Nobel Prize for his work on the biochemical basis of vision; John Edsall, a pioneering protein chemist and a youngish elder statesman who smiled and nodded a lot but was hard to understand; Matthew Meselson, a brilliant young biophysicist newly recruited from the California Institute of Technology; and Paul Levine, the only other assistant professor besides Watson and myself promoted to tenure during the 1950s. Levine soon deserted population biology and began to promote the new doctrine aggressively on his own. Zeal of the convert, I thought to myself.

At faculty meetings we sat together in edgy formality, like Bedouin chieftains gathered around a disputed water well. We addressed one another in the old style: "As Professor Wetmore has just reminded us . . ." We used Robert's Rules of Order. Prestige, professorial appointments, and laboratory space were on the line. We all sensed that our disputes were not ordinary, of the academic kind that Robert Maynard Hutchins once said are so bitter because so little is at stake. Dizzying change and shifts of power were in the air throughout biology, and we were a microcosm. The traditionalists at Harvard at first supported the revolution. We agreed that more molecular and cellular biology was needed in the curriculum. The president and several successive deans of the Faculty of Arts and Sciences were also soon persuaded that a major shift in faculty representation was needed. The ranks of molecular and cellular biologists swelled rapidly. In one long drive, they secured seven of eight professorial appointments made. No one could doubt that their success was, at least in the abstract, deserved. The problem was that no one knew how to stop them from dominating the Department of Biology to the eventual extinction of other disciplines.

My own position was made more uncomfortable by the location of my office and laboratory in the Biological Laboratories, the bridgehead from physics and chemistry into which the richly funded molecular biologists were now pouring. I found the atmosphere there depressingly tense. Watson did not acknowledge my presence as we passed in the hall, even when no one else was near. I was undecided whether to respond in kind by pretending to be unaware of his own existence (impossible) or to humiliate myself by persisting with southern politesse (also impossible). I settled on a mumbled salutation. The demeanor of Watson's allies ranged from indifferent to chilly, except for George Wald, who acquired an Olympian attitude. He was friendly indeed, but supremely self-possessed and theatrically condescending. On the few occasions we spoke, I could not escape the feeling that he was actually addressing an audience of hundreds seated behind me. He would in fact adopt political and moral oratory before large audiences as a second calling during the late 1960s. At the height of the campus turmoil at Harvard and elsewhere, Wald was the speaker of choice before cheering crowds of student activists. He was the kind of elegant, unworldly intellectual who fires up the revolution and is the first to receive its executioner's bullet. And on the future of our science he agreed completely with Watson. There is only one biology, he once declared, and it is molecular biology.

My standing among the molecularists was not improved by my having been granted tenure several months before Watson, in 1958. Although it was an accident of timing—I had received an unsolicited offer from Stanford and Harvard counteroffered—and in any event I considered him to be far more deserving, I can imagine how Watson must have taken the news. Badly.

Actually, I cannot honestly say I knew Jim Watson at all. The skirmish over Smith's appointment was only one of a half-dozen times he and I spoke directly to each other during his twelve years at Harvard and in the period immediately following. On one occasion, in October 1962, I offered him my hand and said, "Congratulations, Jim, on the Nobel Prize. It's a wonderful event for the whole department." He replied, "Thank you." End of conversation. On another occasion, in May 1969, he extended his hand and said, "Congratulations, Ed, on your election to the National Academy of Sciences." I replied, "Thank you very much, Jim." I was delighted by this act of courtesy.

At least there was no guile in the man. Watson evidently felt, at one level, that he was working for the good of science, and a blunt tool was needed. Have to crack eggs to make an omelet, and so forth. What he dreamed at a deeper level I never knew. I am only sure that had his discovery been of lesser magnitude he would have been treated at Harvard as just one more gifted eccentric, and much of his honesty would have been publicly dismissed as poor judgment. But people listened carefully, and a few younger colleagues aped his manners, for the compelling reason that the deciphering of the DNA molecule with Francis Crick towered over all that the rest of us had achieved and could ever hope to achieve. It came like a lightning flash, like knowledge from the gods. The Prometheans of the drama were Jim Watson and Francis Crick, and not just by a stroke of good luck either. Watson-Crick possessed extraordinary brilliance and initiative. It is further a singular commentary on the conduct of science that (according to Watson in a later interview) no other qualified person was interested in devoting full time to the problem.

For those not studying biology at the time in the early 1950s, it is hard to imagine the impact the discovery of the structure of DNA had on our perception of how the world works. Reaching beyond the transformation of genetics, it injected into all of biology a new faith in reductionism. The most complex of processes, the discovery implied, might be simpler than we had thought. It whispered ambition and boldness to young biologists and counseled them: Try now; strike fast and deep at the secrets of life. When I arrived at Harvard as a graduate student in 1951, most outside the biochemical cognoscenti believed the gene to be an intractable assembly of proteins. Its chemical structure and the means by which it directs enzyme assembly would not, we assumed, be deciphered until well into the next century. The evidence nevertheless had grown strong that the hereditary substance is DNA, a far less complex macromolecule than most proteins. In 1953 Watson and Crick showed that pairing in the double helix exists and is consistent with Mendelian heredity. ("It has not escaped our notice," they wrote teasingly at the end of their 1953 letter to *Nature*, "that the specific pairing we have postulated immediately suggests a possible copying mechanism for the genetic material.") Soon it was learned that the nucleotide pairs form a code so simple that it can be read off by a child. The implication of these and other revelations rippled into organismic and evolutionary biology, at least among the younger and more entrepreneurial researchers. If heredity can be reduced to a chain of four molecular letters—granted, billions of such letters to prescribe a whole organism—would it not also be possible to reduce and accelerate the analysis of ecosystems and complex animal behavior? I was among the Harvard graduate students most excited by the early advances of molecular biology. Watson was a boy's hero of the natural sciences, the fast young gun who rode into town.

More's the pity that Watson himself and his fellow molecularists had no such foresights about the sector of biology in which I had comfortably settled. All I could sift from their pronouncements was the revolutionary's credo: Wipe the slate clean of this old-fashioned thinking and see what new order will emerge.

I was of course disappointed at this lack of vision. When Watson became director of the Cold Spring Harbor Laboratory in 1968 (he kept his Harvard professorship by joint appointment until 1976) I commented sourly to friends that I wouldn't put him in charge of a lemonade stand. He proved me wrong. In ten years he raised that noted institution to even greater heights by inspiration, fund-raising skills, and the ability to choose and attract the most gifted researchers.

A new Watson gradually emerged in my mind. In October 1982, at a reception celebrating the fiftieth anniversary of Harvard's Biological Laboratories, he pushed his way across a crowded room to compliment me on a throwaway remark I had made during a lecture earlier that afternoon. "The history of philosophy," I had said, "consists largely of failed models of the brain." Afterward I realized that my phrasing was the kind of preemptive dismissal he would have made twenty years earlier. Had I been corrupted in the meantime?

Yes, a little perhaps. I had never been able to suppress my admiration for the man. He had pulled off his achievement with courage and panache. He and other molecular biologists conveyed to his generation a new faith in the reductionist method of the natural sciences. A triumph of naturalism, it was part of the motivation for my own attempt in the 1970s to bring biology into the social sciences through a systematization of the new discipline of sociobiology.

The conflict set in motion another and ultimately positive effect of the molecular revolution. By the late 1950s the atmosphere in the department had become too stifling for members to plan the future of Harvard biology in ordinary meetings. So the professors in organismic and evolutionary biology prepared to exit. We formed a caucus and met informally to chart our own course. We began to think as never before about our future position in the biological sciences. I am reminded of another anthropological principle by this development. When savage tribes reach a certain size and density they split, and one group emigrates to a new territory. Among the Yanomamö of Brazil and Venezuela the moment of fission can be judged to be close at hand when there is a sharp increase in ax fighting. By the fall of 1960 our caucus had hardened to become the new Committee on Macrobiology.

Odd name that: macrobiology. In 1960 we realized that zoology, botany, entomology, and other disciplines centered on groups of organisms no longer reflected the reality of biology. The science was now being sliced crosswise, according to levels of biological organization, that is, oriented to the molecule, cell, organism, population, and ecosystem respectively. Biology spun through a ninety-degree rotation in its approaches to life. Specialists became less concerned with knowing everything about birds or nematode worms or fungi, including their diversity. They focused more on the search for general principles at one or two of the organizational levels. To do so many contracted their efforts to a small number of species. Colleges and universities throughout the country accordingly reconfigured their research and teaching programs into departments of molecular biology, cell biology, developmental biology, and population biology, or rough equivalents of these divisions.

During this transitional period, which continued throughout the 1960s and into the 1970s, the expression "evolutionary biology" gained wide currency. It was meant to combine the higher strata of biological organization with multilevel approaches to the environment, animal behavior, and evolution. Conceding a spotty memory and not having undertaken archival research to improve upon it, I nevertheless believe that "evolutionary biology" was launched from Harvard and probably originated there. I know that in the spring of 1958 I concocted the term on my own and entered it in the Harvard catalog as a course title for the following year. It was then spread at Harvard as follows.

One fall day in 1961, after teaching the subject for three years, I was seated in the main seminar room of Harvard's new herbarium building across the table from George Gaylord Simpson, waiting for other members of the Committee on Macrobiology to arrive for one of our regular meetings. Simpson, considered the greatest paleontologist of the day, was then in the last years of his professorship at Harvard. I struck up a conversation, a necessity if we were not to sit looking at each other in silence: G. G., as we called him, almost never spoke first. He was shy, self-disciplined to an extreme, and totally absorbed in his work. I suspect that he prized every minute saved from talking with other people, which could then be invested in the writing of articles and books. He avoided committee work with stony resolution, refused to take graduate students, and gave lectures sparingly even by the cavalier standards of the general Harvard faculty. That day I approached him with a challenge. I was fretting about the proper name for our embattled end of biology. Macrobiology, we agreed, was a terrible word. Classical biology was out; that was what our molecular adversaries were calling it. Just "plain biology"? What about *real* biology? No and no. Population biology?

Accurate but too restrictive. Well then, I said, what about evolutionary biology? That would cover the ground nicely. Given that evolution is the central organizing idea of biology outside the application of physics and chemistry, its use as part of the disciplinary name might serve as the talisman of intellectual independence. I tried the expression on others, and it was received very well. By the fall of 1962 we had a formal Committee on Evolutionary Biology.

As the time for a complete departmental split approached, our conflict with the molecular faction centered with increasing heat on new faculty appointments, taken up case by painful case. The Harvard faculty is a well-known pressure cooker in the sciences, in most subjects most of the time. Peer pressure among the tenured professors is superintended by vigilant deans and presidents determined to keep quality high. That combination of intent is responsible in large part for Harvard's lofty reputation. The explicit goal of all concerned is to select the best in the world in every discipline represented, or at least a workaholic journeyman toiling at the forefront. The probing questions invariably asked by both faculty and administration are, What has he discovered that is important? Does Harvard need someone in his discipline? Is he the best in that discipline? More than half the assistant professors either fail to make tenure or go elsewhere before being put to the test. Such was intensively the case in the Department of Biology in the late 1950s and early 1960s. Every appointment recommended by one of the two camps was scrutinized with open suspicion by the other.

The rising tension was due not just to the clash of megafaunistic egos. The fissure ran deeper, into the very definition of biology. The molecularists were confident that the future belonged to them. If evolutionary biology was to survive at all, they thought, it would have to be changed into something very different. They or their students would do it, working upward from the molecule through the cell to the organism. The message was clear: Let the stamp collectors return to their museums.

The evolutionary biologists were not about to step aside for a group of test-tube jockeys who could not tell a red-eyed vireo from a mole cricket. It was foolish, we argued, to ignore principles and methodologies distinctive to the organism, population, and ecosystem, while waiting for a still formless and unproved molecular future.

We were forced by the threat to rethink our intellectual legitimacy as never before. In corridor conversations and caucus meetings, we tried to reach agreement on an agenda of future research and teaching that would soar and present the best of organismic and evolutionary biology to the world. But in these first years of molecular triumphalism our position was weak. We were moreover sharply divided in our individual interests and aspirations. Most of the caucus members were too specialized, too fixed in their ways, or too weak to resist. They sat through department meetings numbly, preferring to seek common ground by dwelling on subjects of lesser import: Who will teach the elementary course? What is the status of the Arnold Arboretum? Shall we be active partners in the new Organization for Tropical Studies? For their part the molecular biologists made little effort to articulate a philosophy of biological research. To them the future had already been made clear by the heady pace of their own progress. Unspoken but heavily implied was the taunt: Count our Nobel Prizes. Ernst Mayr and George Simpson, giants of the Modern Synthesis, heroes of my youth, and incidentally denied Nobel Prizes because none are given in evolutionary biology, seemed oddly reluctant to broach these central issues openly in the meetings. Part of the reason, I suspect, was the narrow spectrum of attitudes shown by the molecularists, ranging from indifference to contempt. Why rile them, and make an unpleasant situation worse?

In the absence of strong statesmanship in evolutionary biology, our potential allies were falling away. One of the two most distinguished organismic biologists of the time, Donald Griffin, discov-

erer of animal sonar, was early on persuaded by the molecularist philosophy. We are all evolutionary biologists, he declaimed at one
meeting, are we not? Doesn't what we learn at every level contribute
to the understanding of evolution? The eminent insect physiologist
Carroll Williams remained amiably neutral. A courtly Virginian
who had spent his adult life at Harvard with tidewater accent intact,
he insisted on maintaining the manners that had prevailed in the old
department. More important than personality, however, was the
plain fact that the evolutionary biologists could point to no recent
great advances comparable to those in molecular and cellular biology
swelling the pages of *Nature, Science,* and the *Proceedings of the National Academy of Sciences.*

The mood of the era is caught in a personal letter I wrote to Lawrence Slobodkin, a young evolutionary biologist and newly acquired
friend, on November 20, 1962. He had bravely journeyed from the
University of Michigan to give a lecture on ecology.

> *You will be glad to know that the students, both undergraduate and grad-
> uate, are nearly unanimous in their praise. They found the subject matter
> and your particular style exciting. . . . The faculty were less impressed.
> While quick to state that you were disturbingly original, your argumen-
> tation and data were not convincing. The reasons for this feeling are com-
> plex. My impression is that they arise in large part from the ancient prej-
> udice against ecology, whose stereotype includes that it is not "solid" or
> rigorously experimental. Had a well-known biochemist, speaking on a
> more "solid" subject, given an exactly analogous lecture, he would have
> been cheered for his limber imagination and boldness.*

There is a final principle of social behavior to help keep these many
developments in perspective. When oppressed peoples have no other
remedy they resort to humor. In 1967 I composed a "Glossary of
Phrases in Molecular Biology" that was soon distributed in departments of biology throughout the country and praised—by evolu-

tionary biologists—for capturing the strut of the conquerors. My samizdat included the following expressions, which I have changed here from alphabetical order to create a logical progression of the concepts:

Classical Biology. That part of biology not yet explained in terms of physics and chemistry. Classical Biologists are fond of claiming that there is a great deal of Classical Biology that individual Molecular Biologists do not know about; but that is all right because it is probably mostly not worth knowing about anyway, we think. In any case, it doesn't matter, because eventually it will all be explained in terms of physics and chemistry; then it will be Molecular Biology and worth knowing about.

Brilliant Discovery. A publishable result in the Mainstream of Biology.

Mainstream of Biology. The set of all projects being worked on by me and my friends. Also known as Modern Biology and Twenty-first Century Biology.

Exceptional Young Man. A beginning Molecular Biologist who has made a Brilliant Discovery (*q.v.*).

First-rate. Pertaining to biologists working on projects in the Mainstream of Biology.

Molecular Biology. That part of biochemistry which has supplanted part of Classical Biology. A great deal of Molecular Biology is being conducted by First-rate Scientists who make Brilliant Discoveries.

Third-rate. Pertaining to Classical Biologists.

First-rate, Brilliant, Wave of the Future . . . believe me, this was the phrasing actually used. Today those once oft-heard mantras clink with antique brittleness. The passage of thirty years has done much to close the divide between molecular and evolutionary biology. As I write, systematists, the solitary experts on groups of organisms, have unfortunately been largely eliminated from academic departments by the encroachment of the new fields. That is the worst single damage caused by the molecular revolution. Ecologists, pushed to the margin for years, have begun a resurgence through the widespread recognition of the global environment crisis. Molecular biologists, as they promised, have taken up evolutionary studies, making important contributions whenever they can find systematists to tell them the names of organisms. The surviving evolutionary biologists routinely use molecular data to pursue their Darwinian agenda. The two sides sometimes speak warmly to each other. Indeed, teams from both domains increasingly collaborate to conduct First-rate Work in what may now safely and fairly be called part of the Mainstream of Biology. The corridor language one overhears from molecular biologists has grown more chaste and subtle. Only hard-shelled fundamentalists among them think that higher levels of biological organization, populations to ecosystems, can be explained by molecular biology.

I did not foresee this accommodation in the 1960s, caught as I was in the upheaval. Worse, I was physically trapped in the Biological Laboratories among the molecular and cellular biologists, who seemed to be multiplying like the *E. coli* and other microorganisms on which their finest work had come to be based. In buildings a hundred feet and a world of ideas away were the principalities and margravates of the senior evolutionary biologists. They were mostly curators and professors in charge of Harvard's "Associated Institutions," comprising the Museum of Comparative Zoology, the University herbaria, the Botanical Museum, the Arnold Arboretum, and the Harvard Forest. I envied them mightily. They could retreat to their collections and libraries and continue to be supported by venerable endowments bearing the names of nineteenth-century Anglo-Saxons.

What I desired most was to emigrate across the street to the Museum of Comparative Zoology, to become a curator of insects, to surround myself with students and like-minded colleagues in an environment congenial to evolutionary biology, and never have to pass another molecular biologist in the corridor. But I held off requesting such a move for ten years, while Ernst Mayr was director. Perhaps I was overly timid, but the great man seemed forbiddingly stiff and cool toward me personally. There was also the twenty-five-year difference in age, and the fact that I had felt filial awe ever since adopting his book *Systematics and the Origin of Species* as my bible when I was eighteen. We have since become good friends, and I speak to him frankly on all—well, most—matters (he is still fully active in his ninetieth year as I write), but at that time I felt it would be altogether too brash to ask for haven in his building. My self-esteem was fragile then to a degree that now seems beyond reason. I felt certain that Mayr thought little of me. I dared not risk the humiliation of a refusal. I figured the odds at no better than fifty-fifty he would give it. When a new director, A. W. ("Fuzz") Crompton, was installed and proved as approachable in personality as the nickname implies, I asked him for entry. Fuzz promptly invited me to the newly erected laboratory wing of the Museum ("You've made my day, Ed") and soon afterward had me appointed Curator in Entomology. I do not doubt that the molecular biologists were also pleased to see me leave. One day near the end, while I sat at my desk, Mark Ptashne, one of the younger shock troopers of this amazing group, walked into my quarters unannounced with a construction supervisor and began to measure it for installation of equipment.

By this time I had been radicalized in my views about the future of biology. I wanted more than just sanctuary across the street, complete with green eyeshades, Cornell drawers of pinned specimens, and round-trip air tickets for field work in Panama. I wanted a revolution in the ranks of the young evolutionary biologists. I felt driven to go beyond the old guard of Modern Synthesizers and help to start something new. That might be accomplished, I thought, by the best effort of men my age (men, I say, because women were still rare in the discipline) who were as able and ambitious as the best molecular biologists. I did not know how such an enterprise might be started, but clearly the first requirement was a fresh vision from the young and ambitious. I began to pay close attention to those in other universities who seemed like-minded.

A loose cadre in fact did form. In January 1960 I was approached by an editorial consultant of Holt, Rinehart and Winston, a leading publisher of scientific texts, who asked me to referee the manuscript of a short book by Larry Slobodkin. The title was *Growth and Regulation in Animal Populations*. As I flipped through the manuscript pages I was excited by Slobodkin's crisp style and deductive approach to ecology. He advanced simple mathematical models to describe the essential features of population dynamics, then expanded on the premises and terms of the equations to ask new questions. He argued that such complex phenomena as growth, age structure, and competition could be broken apart with minimalist reasoning, leading to experiments devised in the postulational-deductive method of traditional science. He went further: the hypotheses and experimental results could be greatly enriched by explanations from evolution by natural selection.

Slobodkin was not the first scientist to advance this prospectus for the invigoration of ecology, but the clarity of his style and the authority implied by a textbook format rendered the ideas persuasive. It dawned on me that ecology had never before been incorporated into evolutionary theory; now Slobodkin was showing a way to do it. He also posed, or so I read into his text, the means by which ecology could be linked to genetics and biogeography. Genetics, I say, because evolution is a change in the heredity of populations. And biogeography, because the geographic ranges of genetically adapted populations determine the coexistence of species. Communities of species are assembled by genetic change and the environmentally mediated interaction of the species. Genetic change and interaction determine which species will survive and which will disappear. In order to understand evolution, then, it is necessary to include the dynamics of populations.

233

NATURALIST

With this conception in mind, and my hopes kindled that Slobodkin would emerge as a leader in evolutionary biology, I wrote an enthusiastic report to the editor. A short time later I approached Slobodkin himself, suggesting that the time had come to produce a more comprehensive textbook on population biology. Would he be interested in writing one with me? In such a collaboration, he might introduce population dynamics and community ecology, while I added genetics, biogeography, and social behavior. The material would serve as an intermediate-level textbook. It would also promote a new approach to evolutionary biology founded on ecology and mathematical modeling.

Slobodkin said he was interested. He would talk the matter over with me. Soon afterward we met in Cambridge to outline our prospective work. We went so far as to draw up individual assignments in the form of chapter headings.

Slobodkin was then an assistant professor at the University of Michigan. A rising star in the admittedly still depauperate field of American ecology, he was later to move to the Stony Brook campus of the State University of New York, where he founded a new program in evolutionary biology. His reputation as a researcher has been securely based on a series of eclectic studies conducted before I met him and in the years immediately following. He studied the red tide phenomenon, the periodic population bloom of toxic dinoflagellate protozoans that poison fish and other marine life. He pioneered the measurement of energy transfer across trophic levels in ecosystems by the use of the bomb calorimeter. In the realm of theory, he elaborated the concept of a balancing relationship between the "prudent predator" and "efficient prey."

During the years to follow, I never failed to find Slobodkin's physical appearance arresting: red-haired, alternately clean-shaven and dramatically mustachioed, an ursine body relaxed in scholar's informality. Not given to easy laughter, he preferred ironic maxims over funny stories. His conversational tone was preoccupied and self-protective, and to a degree unusual in a young man tended toward generalizations about science and the human condition. It was leavened in the company of friends with discursive sentences and fragments of crude humor, seemingly contrived to throw the listener off balance, especially when combined with Delphic remarks of the kind philosophers use to stop conversations. These latter asides implied: There is more to the subject of our banter, much more; see if you can figure it out. Slobodkin in fact was a philosopher. I came to think of him as progressing through a scientific career to a destiny somewhere in the philosophy of science, where he would become a guru, a rabbi, and an interpreter of the scripture of natural history. Some of our friends complained that his persona was a pose, and perhaps it was to some degree, but I enjoyed Slobodkin's subtle and penetrating mind, and his company. Not least, we were opposites in cultural origin, which made him all the more interesting to me. He was a New York intellectual, a Jew, as far in every dimension of temperament and style as it is possible to get from the sweat-soaked field entomologist I still fancied myself to be, then, in the early 1960s.

Slobodkin was heavily influenced by his Ph.D. adviser at Yale, G. Evelyn Hutchinson, himself as different from Slobodkin and me as Larry and I were from each other: our relationship formed an equilateral triangle. Born in 1903, the son of Arthur Hutchinson, the Master of Pembroke College at Cambridge University, Evelyn—"Hutch" to those who dared call him an intimate—was a creation of British high-table science. True to the Oxbridge prize Fellow tradition, he never bothered to earn the doctorate, but instead trained himself into a polymath of formidable powers. He was a free spirit, an eclecticist who proved brilliant at fitting pieces together into large concepts. He never seemed to have met a fact he didn't like or couldn't use, somewhere, to start an essay or at least place in a footnote. He began his career as a field entomologist studying aquatic "true bugs" as experts call them—members of the order Hemiptera—and especially notonectid backswimmers. He worked as far

235

from home as Tibet and South Africa. Then he turned to pioneering research on algae and other phytoplankton of lakes and ponds. He broadened his scope to include the cycles and stratification of nutrients on which life in these bodies of water depends. He was among the first students of biogeochemistry, a complex discipline combining analyses of land, water, and life. Still later, after becoming professor of zoology at Yale in 1945, he turned to the evolution of population dynamics, which also became Slobodkin's forte.

Hutchinson's insights were deep and original, and, notwithstanding that such tropes have been worn to banality through overuse, he deserves to be called the father of evolutionary ecology. Among his notions that proved most influential was the "Hutchinsonian niche." Like most successful ideas in science, it is also a simple one: the life of a species can be usefully described as the range of temperatures in which it is able to live and reproduce, the range of prey items it consumes, the season in which it is active, the hours of the day during which it feeds, and so on down a list as long as the biologist wishes to make it. The species is viewed as living within a space defined by the limits of these biological qualities each placed in turn on a separate scale. The niche, in short, is an n-dimensional hyperspace.

Hutchinson's independence was such that he remained unperturbed by molecular triumphalism; at least I never heard of his protesting in the manner of his colleagues in Harvard's overheated department. In his later years he metamorphosed gracefully from field biologist to guru, seated in his office with wispy white hair and basset eyes. Beside him presided a stuffed specimen of the giant Galápagos tortoise. In a teaching career spanning nearly three decades, he trained forty of the best ecologists and population biologists in the world to the doctoral level. They included Edward Deevey, Thomas Edmondson, Peter Klopfer, Egbert Leigh, Thomas Lovejoy, Robert MacArthur, Howard Odum, and, of course, Larry Slobodkin. They all seemed to admire and love the man, and to have drawn strength and momentum from his example. Fanning out across the country to represent the many growing fields of ecology, they exerted a crucial influence in American biology.

I asked several after they became my friends what "Hutch" did to inspire such enterprise in his disciples. The answer was always the same: nothing. He did nothing, except welcome into his office every graduate student who wished to see him, praise everything they did, and with insight and marginal scholarly digressions, find at least some merit in the most inchoate of research proposals. He soared above us sometimes, and at others he wandered alone in a distant terrain, lover of the surprising metaphor and the esoteric example. He resisted successfully the indignity of being completely understood. He encouraged his acolytes to launch their own voyages. It was pleasant, on the several occasions I lectured at Yale before Hutchinson's death in 1991, to encounter him and receive his benediction. Head bobbing slightly between hunched shoulders, a wise human Galápagos tortoise, he would murmur, Wonderful, Wilson, well done, very interesting. It would have been pleasant to stay near him, the kindly academic father I never knew. I came to realize that the overgenerous praise did not weaken the fiber of our character. Hutchinson's students criticized one another, and me as well, and that was enough to spare us from major folly most of the time.

Hutchinson and Slobodkin were then what today are called evolutionary ecologists. In my formative years they caused me to try to become one as well. Through them I came to appreciate how environmental science might be better meshed with biogeography and the study of evolution, and I gained more confidence in the intellectual independence of evolutionary biology. I was encouraged to draw closer to the central problem of the balance of species, which was to be my main preoccupation during the 1960s, as the molecular wars subsided to their ambiguous conclusion.

chapter thirteen

ISLANDS
ARE THE KEY

DURING A SEMINAR BREAK AT THE 1961 MEETING OF THE
American Association for the Advancement of Science, held in New
York's Biltmore Hotel, Larry Slobodkin told me that there was
someone I had to meet, someone we should ask to be another coauthor of the book on population biology. Two months had passed
since we had first met to discuss our joint venture. "It's Robert
MacArthur, and he's a real theoretician—very bright. I think we
need someone else closer to pure theory, with a better mathematical
background, to help with the book."

MacArthur, I learned, was a thirty-year-old assistant professor at the University of Pennsylvania. He had received his Ph.D. under Evelyn Hutchinson in 1957. After a year spent at Oxford studying with the British ornithologist David Lack, he had begun to move swiftly into a brilliant career. But neither Larry nor I could have guessed on that day we waited for him just how brilliant, that in one decade he would come to rival Hutchinson in influence. MacArthur was to bring population and community ecology closer to genetics. By reformulating some of the key parameters of ecology, biogeography, and genetics into a common framework of fundamental theory he set the stage, more than any other person during the decisive decade of the 1960s, for the unification of population biology. Then he was cut down by a fatal renal cancer, and became a legend. Today one of the most coveted honors for midcareer researchers in evolutionary biology is to be invited to give the MacArthur Lecture of the Ecological Society of America.

He joined Slobodkin and me, a thin, diffident young man who spoke with an American accent but in the British style of cautious understatement, perhaps acquired at Oxford. The book is an attractive idea, he said. We should explore it further. He had a headache. He wanted to go home. We shook hands, and he left.

Nothing more happened for nearly a year. That was my fault. I simply put the book project completely aside in order to return to field work. The tropics had reasserted their pull. A dream stirred deep within me that El Dorado was still there unattained. I had to go. In February 1961 Renee and I traveled to Trinidad, where we stayed as guests of an Icelandic native and widow named Asa Wright. Her property, Spring Hill Estate, was perched near the head of Arima Valley, in the North Range. It had become a popular stopover for naturalists and serious birders from around the world. Broken rain forest ran down the valley to Simla, the research station founded by William Beebe. The great naturalist was in the last year of his life, and I was grateful for the opportunity to meet him. Renee and I dined occasionally with him and his capable assistant Jocelyn Crane at Simla, admiring the silver candlesticks given to Beebe by his friend Rudyard Kipling and talking tropical natural history here in the place where so much of the best research on it had been conceived.

The tropics in those days nourished a strange collection of intellectuals. At Spring Hill we sat on the screened veranda listening to stories by another famous visitor, Colonel Richard Meinertzhagen, who had first served as an officer under Queen Victoria and fought with T. E. Lawrence in the Middle East during the First World War. I looked him up later in Lawrence's *Seven Pillars of Wisdom*, and sure enough, there was Meinertzhagen, reported in the same episodes he had described to Renee and me. Meinertzhagen was at Spring Hill to visit oil birds in a nearby cave and to collect the fruits of native forest trees. Given all this, and the aging Asa Wright's retrograde colonial attitude toward the Trinidadians of color, we felt we had been propelled backward in time fifty years.

There were adventures to savor, this time shared with Renee. Once a pet donkey wandered across the Spring Hill veranda into the open dining room, its hooves clopping loudly on the hardwood floor, and consumed a chocolate cake set out for afternoon tea. The maid quickly chased him back out. Soon afterward, as Renee sat in a corner of the veranda, waiting for my return from the field, she could not help overhearing Asa's reaction to the news: "Oh my god, Eutrice, do the Wilsons know?"

"No ma'am," Eutrice lied.

The donkey was tethered to a veranda post at night, and sometime during the evening it was usually visited by vampire bats that flew in from the neighboring forest. In the morning one or two dried rivulets of blood streaked some part or other of its flanks or legs. Such bloodletting was a common problem for livestock in the area, and the bats carried rabies. Seated on the veranda, armed with flashlights, Meinertzhagen and I watched eagerly for the arrival of the vampires

late into the night. We never saw one. That is the talent of vampires, evading detection.

Two months after arriving Renee and I departed for Suriname, to add field work on the South American mainland. We proceeded by freighter out of Port of Spain to the bauxite mining town of Moengo, then back to the capital of Paramaribo. We lived in a pension there while I explored the forests south as far as Zanderij. We then returned to Spring Hill for a while before proceeding to Tobago for the final three months, June through most of August, of our tour.

NATURALIST

I felt completely at home again in the heat and smell of rotting vegetation, although Renee did not, especially when she learned about the vampire bats. Discoveries came easily, as always for me in tropical forests. I acquired a colony of the giant, primitive dacetine ant *Daceton armigerum* from a nest high in a tree in Suriname and made the first study of its social organization. I rediscovered the apparently "true" cave ant *Spelaeomyrmex urichi* in a central Trinidad cavern, and proved that the species also lives in the open forest of Suriname—and thus is not an obligatory cave ant. I puttered here and there, in the opportunistic spirit that had always guided me.

But early on this field trip, while beginning work on Trinidad, I found the tropics less than paradise. To my dismay I slipped into a depression for the first time in my life. I began to worry again about the broader canvases of ecology and evolution, and the need to get on with the agenda of my young evolutionists' conceptual revolution. I hated the corresponding diminution of my naturalist's ardor. I was anxious about my own inadequacy in mathematics. I felt certain that the future principles of evolutionary biology would be written in equations, with the deepest insights expressed by quantitative models. I set out to remedy my deficiency by teaching myself calculus, probability theory, and statistics from textbooks I read on verandas and beach cupolas in Trinidad and Tobago. Progress was slow; I was not gifted; I worried even more. Here I was, thirty-two years old, time and the main chance about to slip away—or so it seemed. Would I miss out on the real action coming?

Soon after our return home in late August, Renee and I bought our first house, a small two-story cape in the suburban town of Lexington, ten miles west of Cambridge. It cost $19,000, about twice my gross annual salary at the time. By scrimping on expenses during our sabbatical trip, we had just managed to save the minimum $3,000 down payment for a first mortgage. Now five years into our marriage, we at last felt rooted and secure. I felt more confident in my

work and in the knowledge that I would probably stay at Harvard for the remainder of my career. My math anxiety faded.

Soon afterward MacArthur and Slobodkin joined me at Harvard for a one-day meeting to resume planning our book on population biology. We drew up an outline, divided chapter assignments, and went our separate ways. As much as I admired Slobodkin, I felt a stronger personal attraction to MacArthur. In subsequent correspondence and visits we discovered a surprising range of common interests, among which was a passion for biogeography—the geographic distribution of plants and animals. The traditional discipline, in which I had been steeped throughout my career, was in chaos. Grand chaos, in fact, since the subject matter is the largest in physical scale of all biology, and it spans the entire history of life.

In 1961, when MacArthur and I focused on it, biogeography was still largely descriptive. Its most interesting theory was the Matthew-Darlington cycle of dominance and replacement. Otherwise its main substance comprised such topics as the origin of the fauna and flora of the West Indies—whether by immigration across dry land bridges that once connected the islands to the mainland or by the chance arrival of organisms borne on water and in the air. Biogeography seemed ripe for the new thinking that was emerging in population biology. I showed MacArthur some of the curves in my files linking the area of individual islands to the numbers of resident species of ants and other organisms. I told him about my conception of the taxon cycle and the balance of species.

MacArthur's interest in these and related subjects grew rapidly. As our discussions deepened, and spread to include gossip and personal anecdotes, we became close friends. Our backgrounds proved similar in several respects that matter most in scientific collaboration. Although he had majored in mathematics at Marlboro College, and had a conspicuous talent for it, his heart was in the study of birds. He was a naturalist by calling, and seemed happiest when searching for patterns discovered directly in Nature with the aid of binoculars and field guides. It was his calling to scan the tangled bank of Nature and skeletonize it in his own and others' minds to its essential abstract features. As a mathematician-naturalist he was unique, approached only by his mentor, Evelyn Hutchinson. He was not as expansive in his interests as Hutchinson, but quicker and more deeply penetrating at strategic points. He shared the conviction of the great mathematician G. H. Hardy, whom he resembled in temperament and philosophy, "that a mathematician was a maker of patterns of ideas, and that beauty and seriousness were the criteria by which his patterns should be judged." He wished above all to discover beautiful true-life patterns.

In conversation, MacArthur would say that the best science comes to a great extent from the invention of new classifications of natural phenomena, the ones that suggest hypotheses and new rounds of data gathering. "Art"—he enjoyed quoting Picasso—"is the lie that helps us see the truth." His methodology bore testimony of the strength of an inherent naturalist: he knew what he was talking about, and he was concerned more with the tapestry of Nature and his power to see it independently than with what others thought of it, or of him.

MacArthur watched birds with the patience and skill of a professional ornithologist. He visited the tropics as often as he could, and delighted in relating endless facts of natural history. The store of random information thus accumulated and the play of its intersecting patterns were the inspiration of his theoretical work, by which he described the process of the origin of biological diversity.

When I first met him he was an assistant professor at the University of Pennsylvania, soon to be promoted to associate and then to full professor. He later moved to Princeton, where in a short time he was named Henry Fairfield Osborn Professor of Biology. His demeanor was subdued and pleasing. Of medium height, with a handsomely rectangular face, he met you with a disarming smile and widening of eyes. He spoke with a thin baritone voice in complete sentences and paragraphs, signaling his more important utterances by tilting his head slightly upward and swallowing. He had a calm, understated manner, which in intellectuals suggests tightly reined power. In contrast to the excessive loquacity of most professional academics, MacArthur's restraint gave his words an authority rarely intended. In fact he was basically shy and loathed being caught in a careless error. He was nevertheless conscious of his status among colleagues and felt secure about it. Although he was generous by instinct and capable of lavish, almost Hutchinsonian praise during private conversations for work he thought important, he did not hesitate to describe the foibles and weaknesses of others with pitiless accuracy. But he harbored no malice I could detect, only a taxonomic interest in other scientists and a frequent disappointment that tempered his enthusiasms.

He joined superior talent with an unusual creative drive and decent ambition. He placed his family, Betsy and the four children, above all else. After that came the natural world, birds, and science, in that order. One day as we strolled along a road in the Florida Keys, I told him of the effort I was making with several others to conserve Lignumvitae Key, one of the last islands of Florida with a relatively undisturbed Caribbean forest. He reacted with a warmth that surprised me—I had not even thought of mentioning it earlier. He declared that he would rather save an endangered habitat than create an important scientific theory.

MacArthur launched his scientific career with two articles that revealed his unusual powers. The first, in 1955, suggested a way to predict stability in a community of plants and animals by the use of information theory. It formalized a concept that until then could be expressed only through verbal description. Soon afterward, in 1957, came the famous "broken stick" model of relative abundance of bird species. To capture the essence of his approach, imagine that the combined numbers of a certain guild of birds, say warblers, found in a particular forest is represented by the length of a stick. Make the stick one meter long, representing 100,000 warblers, so that each bird is represented by a fraction of a millimeter somewhere on the stick. Have the guild consist of ten warbler species. Break the stick into ten pieces at random, with their lengths randomly distributed. Let the length of each piece represent the number of individuals of a particular species. One species, let us say, gets 200 millimeters, or 20 percent of the stick; it is therefore assigned 20,000 individual birds.

Another species gets 5 millimeters, or 5,000 birds. And so on for all ten pieces and the individual birds their lengths represent. Because the pieces and thence the species are not allowed to overlap, the array of numbers for the whole ensemble of ten warbler species will be the same as if real warblers divided up the resources of the forest among themselves competitively, so there is no sharing of resources, and the fraction each species has acquired is a random variable. The niche of each species is also unique. If real warblers were found to fit a numbers array like this array (more technically put, if its "species abundance distribution" fits the broken-stick model), we would be justified in supposing that the warblers are really segregated by competition for resources. At least we must keep that possibility open, subject to confirming studies of other kinds. What would be the alternative to the exclusion model? One proposed by MacArthur was that the species receive pieces of the stick with lengths being determined randomly, but that the pieces can be overlapping; in other words, the bird species do not exclude one another by competition. Because the exclusion model turned out to fit one set of bird data and MacArthur's first disposal more closely than did the alternatives he conceived, he concluded that competition is likely to be important in determining the abundance of birds.

The specific hypothesis of competition captured by the broken-stick distribution was later disputed by others, and MacArthur himself eventually dismissed his methodological approach—prematurely, I thought—as obsolete. Even while fading, however, the conception represented a breakthrough in ecological theory. In three pages, MacArthur confronted a central problem of community ecology with competing hypotheses expressed as numbers, in contrast to previous theorists, who had formulated the same general idea more vaguely by words. He characterized the issue in such a way as to allow logically possible alternatives to be tested and a choice made. By working out this example, he showed that the deepest remaining

mysteries of natural history might be solved by leaps of the imagination, so long as such efforts are disciplined by clear postulation
tested by data taken from the field.

The method of multiple working hypotheses was thereby introduced to the branch of ecology concerned with whole communities
of species. MacArthur's 1957 article set the tone of all his later work.
Inevitably, his entire approach, not just the broken-stick model, was
correctly criticized by some ecologists as oversimplification. That
defect matters little in the long haul of history. It was a step in the
right direction. Right or wrong in particular applications, it ener-
gized a generation of young population biologists and transformed a
large part of ecology. It helped us to think clearly.

As MacArthur and I extended our conversations, I expressed three
convictions of my own. First, that islands are the key to rapid progress in biogeography. The communities they contain are discrete
units that are isolated by the sea and can be studied in multiples. Second, that all biogeography, including even the histories of faunas and
floras, can be made a branch of population biology. And finally, that
species on islands are somehow in balance in a way that can be modeled quantitatively. MacArthur quickly agreed, and began to apply
his powers of abstraction to the data sets I showed him. In the following exchange I have telescoped our conversations and letters on the
subject in order to convey the crucial steps in the origin of species-
equilibrium theory.★

Wilson: I think biogeography can be made into a science. There are
striking regularities no one has explained. For example, the larger the
island, the more the species of birds or ants that live on it. Look at
what happens when you go from little islands, such as Bali and Lom-
bok, to big ones like Borneo and Sumatra. With every tenfold increase in area, there is roughly a doubling of the number of species

★This account was first presented in my essay collection *Biophilia* (Cambridge,
Mass.: Harvard University Press, 1984).

found on the island. That appears to be true for most other kinds of animals and plants for which we have good data. Here's another piece in the puzzle. I've found that as new ant species spread out from Asia and Australia onto the islands between them, such as New Guinea and Fiji, they eliminate other ones that settled there earlier. At the level of the species this pattern fits in pretty well with the views of Philip Darlington and George Simpson. They proved that in the past major groups of mammals, such as all the deer or all the pigs taken together, have tended to replace other major groups in South America and Asia, filling the same niches. So there seems to be a balance of Nature down to the level of the species, with waves of replacement spreading around the world.

MacArthur: Yes, a species equilibrium. It looks as though each island can hold just so many species, so if one species colonizes the island, an older resident has to go extinct. Let's treat the whole thing as if it were a physical process. Think of the island as filling up with species from an empty state up to the limit. That's just a metaphor, but it might get us somewhere. As more species establish themselves, the rate at which they go extinct will rise. Let me put it another way: The probability that any given species will go extinct increases as more species crowd onto the island. Now look at the species arriving. A few colonists of each are making it each year on the wind or on floating logs or, like birds, flying in on their own power. The more species that settle on the island, the fewer *new* ones that will be arriving each year, simply because there are fewer that aren't already there. Here's how a physicist or economist would represent the situation. As the island fills up, the rate of extinction goes up and the rate of immigration goes down, until the two processes reach the same level. So by definition you have a dynamic equilibrium. When extinction equals immigration, the *number* of species stays the same, even though there may be a steady change in the particular species making up the fauna.

Look what happens when you play around a little with the rising and falling curves. Let the islands get smaller. The extinction rates

UNIVERSITY *of* PENNSYLVANIA

PHILADELPHIA 4

The College
Division of Biology

ZOOLOGICAL LABORATORY
38th Street and Woodland Avenue

1262

27 april

Dear Ed,

I find I have far less time than I had expected and haven't finished the statistics on bird species vs. islands. (Although for Sunda group, no. of bird sp = 23.796 + .008535(elev.) − .021057 (Distance) + .006170 (√area))

R in sq. miles.

But I did want to tell you my ideas about a model of number of species so that you can improve it while I am away. Early in the fall I will get back to the analysis and we can compare notes.

Basically, unless immigration and local species extinctions are much rarer than I guess, they must about balance.

A

number of new species/year entering (some may be same as those dying out)

number of species dying out/year

equilibrium no. of species.

number of species present   n

B

new/year ?

loses ?

I think the mortality curve has the shape $np^{T/n}$ (approx.) where p is a probability of individual dying (about .5) and T is the total number of individuals (proportional to area) have to go up, since the populations are smaller and more liable to extinction. If there are only ten birds of a kind sitting in the trees, they are more likely to go to zero in a given year than if there are a hundred. But the rate at which new species are arriving won't be affected very much, because islands well away from the mainland can vary a lot in size without changing much in the amount of horizon they present to organisms traveling toward them. As a result, smaller islands will reach equilibrium sooner and end up with a smaller number of species at equilibrium. Now look at pure distance as a factor. The farther the island is from the source areas, say the way Hawaii is farther from Asia than New Guinea, the fewer new species that will be arriving each year. But the rate of extinction stays the same because, once a species of plant or animal is settled on an island, it doesn't matter whether the island is close or far. So you expect the number of species found on distant islands to be fewer. The whole thing is just a matter of geometry.

Weeks pass. We are sitting next to the fireplace in MacArthur's living room, with notes and graphs spread out on a coffee table.

Wilson: So far so good. The numbers of bird and ant species *do* go down as islands get smaller and farther from the mainland. We'll label the two trends the *area effect* and the *distance effect*. Let's take them both as given for the moment. How do we know that they prove the equilibrium model? I mean, other people are almost certainly going to come up with a rival theory to explain the area and distance effects. If we claim that the results prove the model that predicted them, we will commit what logicians call the Fallacy of Affirming the Consequent. The only way we can avoid that impasse is to get results that are uniquely predicted by our model and no one else's.

MacArthur: All right, we've gone this far with pure abstraction— let's go on. Try the following: line up the extinction and immigration curves so that where they cross and create the equilibrium, they are straight lines and tilted at approximately the same angle. As an exercise in elementary differential calculus, you can show that the number of years an island takes to fill up to 90 percent of its potential should just about equal the number of species at equilibrium divided by the number going extinct every year.

Wilson: Let's look at Krakatau.

Krakatau is the small island between Sumatra and Java that had been wiped clean of all life in the great volcanic explosion of August 27, 1883. Scientists from several nations, principally the Netherlands and Indonesia, then a Dutch colony, began to visit the reduced remnant of Krakatau within a year of the event. They managed to keep a spotty but serviceable record of the return of birds, plants, and a few other organisms to the bare volcanic slopes. The basic equilibrium model we developed predicted that the birds in particular, for which the best data of all were available, should reach equilibrium at about thirty species. Upon approaching that level, the fauna should be losing one established species by local extinction each year while acquiring one new species by immigration. The data gathered by the early researchers indicated that the bird fauna did indeed appear to be leveling off at approximately thirty species. But the turnover recorded was one species every five years, not one each year.

Was the model really off fivefold, or was the discrepancy due to sampling errors? There was no way to tell. At this point we saw the need of replicate data sets in order to advance equilibrium theory in a serious way. By 1965 I set out to devise such an experimental system in the Florida Keys, using the insects and other arthropods of the smallest islands. That is another story, an unusual, rather bizarre, adventure of field biology, to which I will return in the next chapter.

As MacArthur and I progressed on the island biogeography project, the loose confederation of young population biologists continued to grow. In late July 1964, five of us met at MacArthur's lakeside home at Marlboro, Vermont, to discuss our personal research agendas and how they might contribute to the future of population biology. Joining MacArthur and me were Egbert Leigh, a young mathematician with a special interest in the structure of plant and animal communities, later to join the Smithsonian Tropical Research Institute as research scientist; Richard Levins, a theoretical population biologist of contemporary renown who later joined the faculty of Harvard's School of Public Health; and Richard C. Lewontin, the rising star of theoretical and experimental genetics, who was to come to Harvard as Agassiz Professor of Zoology in 1973. In close touch with several of us but not present at the lakeside retreat were Slobodkin and Leigh Van Valen, a paleontologist and general evolutionary biologist at the University of Chicago.

For two days between walks in the quiet northern woodland, we expanded upon our common ambition to pull evolutionary biology onto a more solid base of theoretical population biology. Each in turn described his particular ongoing research. Then we talked together about the ways in which that subject might be extended toward the central theory and aligned with it. Besides island biogeography, in which MacArthur and I were now well advanced, I saw myself as adding the study of ants and other social animals to the enterprise. An animal society is a population, I argued, and it should be possible to analyze its structure and evolution as part of population biology. My student Stuart Altmann and I had already, early in 1956, discussed the idea of finding common principles to explain primates and insect societies. We had even used the term "sociobiology" to describe the effort. But we had had little intuition on how to proceed, and our collaboration had advanced no further. I hoped that the combined thinking of this new group, the "Marlboro Circle" as I have come to call it, would provide me with clues. The others were encouraging in their remarks, but few clues were forthcoming. William Hamilton's article on kin selection and altruism, which was to be a keystone of sociobiology, was published that year, but neither I nor the others had yet seen it.

How to proceed with the sociobiological and similar overlapping agendas? There emerged from our freewheeling talk the notion of pooling our work. We would produce a series of essays under the single pseudonym "George Maximin," in imitation of the French mathematicians who have been publishing since the 1930s under the name Nicolas Bourbaki. Maximin was named not in honor of the Roman soldier-emperor but after the point of greatest minimum in optimization theory; George was an arbitrary first name added. With Maximin we thought we could achieve the twin goals of anonymity, with its freedom from ego and authorial jealousy, while acquiring license to be as audacious and speculative as the group decided.

Maximin died an early death. He was an ill-conceived Frankenstein monster. By mid-August MacArthur was expressing serious doubts in letters to me. He argued that we should each take credit and responsibility for his own ideas. Slobodkin disliked the concept from the start. Maximin, he said, would look to others too much like a cabal. I had to admit that down deep I shared these misgivings. Personal idiosyncrasies doomed Maximin. MacArthur was particularly confident of his own powers and inclined to work unimpeded. He seemed to believe that he could generate ideas singly or in groups whenever the spirit moved him. Slobodkin for his part was turning against the idea of unifying theories and heavy dependence on mathematical modeling. I myself was temperamentally ill suited to Maximin, preferring to work alone or at most with a single partner. So the program faded, and for the most part the conspirators went their separate ways. We never met as a group again. But a lot was gained from Maximin's ghostly spirit. I cannot speak for the others, but I believe we all carried away a new confidence in the future of evolutionary biology, and in ourselves.

By the end of the year MacArthur and Slobodkin were growing apart. Slobodkin, Robert wrote me in a letter, "is in an antitheoretical mood." Nature defeats theory, Slobodkin was widely quoted as saying at the time. In August MacArthur pulled out of the biology textbook project we had planned three years earlier. Slobodkin by this time had produced little, and I had not done much better, having become distracted in the meantime by a half-dozen other projects. As a result the book soon followed Maximin into oblivion. We just stopped mentioning it. In 1966, when MacArthur published a short introductory text for freshman courses with Joseph Connell, Slobodkin condemned it with a slashing review. He opposed the very philosophy of science it represented. MacArthur in turn bridled at what he considered gratuitous hostility. He believed he had been misunderstood by retrograde thinkers. "I think I can tell why there are potatoes in the field and where they lie," he mused to me, "but these people say no good, they want to know the size and shape of the potatoes."

None of this had any effect on my collaboration with MacArthur. I believed deeply in the power of reductionism, followed by a reconstitution of detail by synthesis. In December 1964, I suggested that we write a full-scale book on island biogeography, with the aim of creating new models and extending our mode of reasoning into as many domains of ecology as we could manage. Robert agreed at once. He was enamored of the subject by this time, and had begun to call himself a biogeographer instead of an ecologist. In this domain existed in most readily definable state the patterns he wanted to discover. When he later brought out a book under his own sole authorship, in 1972, he titled it *Geographical Ecology*.

Off and on in the two years following the Marlboro meeting, MacArthur and I assembled the pieces of an expanded theory of island biogeography. We explored the implications of the balance of species in the colonization of islands, lakes, and other isolated habitats. From published data we traced the course of the recolonization of Krakatau and other devastated islands. We examined the general qualities of the niche and the forms of evolution by which species adapt to dispersal and competition. We considered from the bottom up, species by species, the means by which animals and plants are most efficiently packed together to create diverse communities.

255

NATURALIST

When our book, *The Theory of Island Biogeography*, was published in 1967, it met with almost unanimous approval in the scientific journals. Some of the reviewers declared it a major advance in biology. A quarter-century later, as I write, it remains one of the most frequently cited works of evolutionary biology. *The Theory of Island Biogeography* has also become influential in conservation biology, for the following practical reason. Around the world wild lands are being increasingly shattered by human action, the pieces steadily reduced in size and isolated from one another. Nature reserves are by definition islands. The theory serves as a useful tool in conceptualizing the impact of their size and isolation on the biodiversity they contain. Some parts of the formulation made in 1967 have been discarded by later authors, justifiably, and other parts greatly modified. Later researchers have added powerful new insights and definitive data sets unavailable to us at the time. I do not think it an exaggeration to say, however, that MacArthur and I accomplished most of what we set out to do. We unified, or at least began to unify, biogeography and ecology upon an internally consistent base of population biology.

In the 1960s and 1970s a new wave of population biologists trained in both ecology and mathematics passed through Ph.D. programs in the United States, Canada, and England. They gained the respect of the molecular and cellular biologists, and they were well funded for a while, before the academic recession of the late 1970s and 1980s. They shared the ambition and optimism of their immediate predecessors in the Marlboro Circle. I was able to play a role in this next step, more as a result of my residence at Harvard than of any special talent. My course "Evolutionary Biology," begun in 1958, was relabeled "Population Biology" in 1963 and focused more on basic theory. At first I thought that I had failed by pushing model construction too far at the expense of natural history. An undergraduate complained in the *Crimson Confidential Guide*, the uncensored and often scathing student review, that the course was a dull exercise in numerology. So it might have seemed to some, but I came to realize later that many of the students were greatly influenced by my presentation, and a few were drawn into population biology as a career. They include some of the current leaders in the field: William Bossert, Joel Cohen, Ross Kiester, Jonathan Roughgarden, Daniel Simberloff, and Thomas Schoener. In 1971 Bossert and I collaborated on a short, self-teaching textbook, *A Primer of Population Biology*, which remains popular more than twenty years later.

In the spring of 1971 Robert MacArthur experienced abdominal pains during a field trip to Arizona. Returning home to Princeton, he learned that he had renal cancer. The affected kidney was promptly removed, and he was placed on chemotherapy. Too late: the surgeon told him that he had only months or at most one or two years to live. Robert thereafter conducted his life with even greater intensity than before. He completed his final book, *Geographical Ecology*. He journeyed to Arizona, Hawaii, and Panama for more field work, and while at the university he continued to guide his students. He began a new round of theoretical research, this time with Robert M. May, a brilliant Australian physicist who soon thereafter joined the Princeton faculty. Under MacArthur's influence May converted to biology and developed into one of the world's most influential ecologists. He subsequently moved to Oxford University as a Royal Society Professor.

MacArthur was still reasonably strong as the fall term began at Princeton in 1972. He was coughing frequently as the cancer spread into his lungs, but he was still able to come to his office for short periods to talk to students and friends. In early October his health declined rapidly. By this time I had joined several senior American evolutionary biologists—James Crow, Darlington, Hutchinson, and Eugene Odum—to nominate him for the National Medal of Science. With news that he had only a very short time to live, we redoubled our efforts. Robert sent word through Hutchinson that the nomination was welcome, and he was "pleased that my friends think well of me." *Geographical Ecology* had also just been published, and he awaited the first reviews.

On a Monday afternoon, October 30, John Tyler Bonner, chairman of Princeton's Department of Biology, dropped by my office while visiting Harvard. He told me that MacArthur's condition had deteriorated badly and the end could come in hours or in weeks. The matters most on Robert's mind at this point beside his family were, he reported, the National Medal and the reviews of his book. I dropped everything and inquired about both matters. No progress in the committee office at the National Science Foundation on the medal. But two back-to-back reviews of *Geographical Ecology* had just appeared in *Science,* one by Thomas Schoener and the other by Scott Boorman, both important young population biologists. I called Katherine Livingston, the reviews editor, who said she would send copies directly to Robert.

They arrived too late. The next morning I tried to telephone Robert at his home. A nurse with an unidentifiable foreign accent said he was sleeping. I called again at two in the afternoon, and this time he came on. His voice was thin but level. He coughed frequently, and twice he had to stop to get his position changed in order to continue. I was relieved to find his mind clear and composed. I asked, Had he seen the *Science* reviews? Not yet. I fished out the manuscript of the one by Boorman (who was at that time studying under my direction) and read it. The text was long, detailed, and laudatory. Robert was fascinated, and stopped me several times to discuss technical points raised. Boorman is clearly bright, he said. Was the review by Schoener as good? I assured him it was. I'd seen the manuscript, which after exploring the general methodology of model building declared Robert's book to be the key synthesis in the field. He said, Good, it's better than I got from Slobodkin for my elementary biology textbook.

Had I heard more about the National Medal of Science? I had not, except that eighteen people had been nominated and the awards would be announced sometime after the November 7 presidential election. Robert was disappointed. I sensed that he was worried about his place in biology. We then moved on to gossip and miscellaneous news. Our conversation remained normal in content and tone, with no serious digression into his physical condition. We talked as though he had years to live. He grew tired and quiet. I began to do most of the talking, afraid to let him go. I nattered on about the arrival next term of my fellow entomologist Bert Hölldobler to assume a professorship at Harvard; the opening of the new laboratory wing of the Museum of Comparative Zoology; and Lewontin's political demonstration at the Chicago meetings of the American Association for the Advancement of Science and his widely publicized resignation from the National Academy of Sciences. We drifted on to a recent proposal to exterminate the kiskadee as a pest bird species on Bermuda. Robert mumbled assent as I went along.

At last Robert said we had talked enough and should stop now. We agreed to stay in touch. At dinner, Betsy later reported, he was calm and happy. He spoke with particular pleasure about the favorable *Science* reviews. In the early hours of the next morning he died without distress, in his sleep. Today I can imagine no more inspiriting intellect or steeper creative trajectory cut so short with such a loss to others. I wish he might have known in those final days that his place in the history of ecology was secure. I owe him an incalculable debt, that for at least once in my life I was permitted to participate in science of the first rank.

chapter fourteen

THE FLORIDA KEYS EXPERIMENT

WHERE COULD WE FIND MORE KRAKATAUS?

That question dominated my thought for months after Mac-Arthur and I published our first article on island biogeography in 1963. We had conjured a plausible image of the dynamic equilibrium of species, with new colonists balancing the old residents that become extinct, but we could offer very little direct evidence. There are few places in the world where biologists can study the approach to equilibrium on a large scale. Krakatau-sized events, the sterilization of islands the size of Manhattan or larger by volcanic explosions, occur at most once a century. Another hundred years might then be needed, once the smoking tephra cooled down, to observe the full course of recolonization. How might we get data more quickly, say within ten years?

I brooded over the problem, imagined scenarios of many kinds, and finally came up with the solution: a *laboratory* of island biogeography. We needed an archipelago where little Krakataus could be created at will and their recolonization watched at leisure.

My dream embraced more than the search for new experiments in biogeography. I was driven by a more general need to return to the field, to enjoy once again the hands-on kinesthetic pleasures of my youth. I wanted to remain an opportunist, moving among, seeing, and touching a myriad of plants and animals. I needed a place to which I could return for the rest of my life and possess as a naturalist and scientist.

It would have to be a different location and context from those previously enjoyed. I couldn't return to New Guinea to launch my endeavor. Work there would take me for months at a time away from Cambridge, where my duties at Harvard held me tightly. I had also begun experimental work on the social behavior of ants that required a well-equipped laboratory. They were proving too successful to abandon. Not least, I had a family now, Renee and our new daughter, Catherine.

How in the world could I explore an island wilderness while staying close to home? And if I found such a place, how could I turn it into a laboratory? There was only one way to solve the problem: *miniaturize* the system! Instead of relying on conventional islands the size of Krakatau, which are hundreds of square kilometers in area and usually have people living on them, why not use tiny ones, at most a few hundred square meters? Of course such places do not support resident populations of mammals, birds, or any other land vertebrates above the size of small lizards. Vertebrate biologists would not call them islands at all, even in a limited ecological sense. Yet they sustain large breeding populations of insects, spiders, and other arthropods. To an ant or spider one-millionth the size of a deer, a single tree is like a whole forest. The lifetime of such a creature can be spent in a microterritory the size of a dinner plate. Once I revised my scale of vision downward this way, I realized that there are thousands of such miniature islands in the United States, sprinkled along the coasts as well as inland in the midst of lakes and streams.

I thought I had the perfect solution. By exploring such places I would satisfy my emotional and intellectual needs. Working with insects, the organisms I knew best, I could conduct biogeographic research on an accelerated schedule. Succeed or fail, I would stay close to Harvard and my family.

In choosing the site of my laboratory, I preferred marine waters over lakes and rivers—strictly an aesthetic choice. I pored over maps of fringing islands all along the Atlantic and Gulf coasts, from Quoddy Head State Park in down-Easternmost Maine to the Padre Island National Seashore in southernmost Texas. I also studied charts of the small islands around Puerto Rico, still a relatively quick jet flight away. A decisive winner quickly emerged: the Florida Keys, if combined with the nearby northern islands of Florida Bay and the southwest mainland coast, seemed ideal. I turned to more detailed navigational charts and photographs for a closer look. The islands came in all sizes, from single trees to sizable expanses up to a square kilometer or more. They varied in degrees of isolation from a few meters to hundreds of meters from the nearest neighbor. The forests on them were simple, consisting in most cases entirely of red mangrove trees. And they were available in vast numbers. One sprawling miniature archipelago west of the Everglades bore the suggestive name Ten Thousand Islands. Almost all of them could be reached in a single day, if you started with an early four-hour flight from Boston to Miami, drove a rental car down U.S. 1 to the Keys, and finally took a short boat trip out to the island of choice.

In June 1965 I flew to Miami to enter my new island world. I was accompanied by Renee and Cathy—now twenty months old, walking, talking, and pulling down every movable object. For ten weeks I explored the small bayside mangrove keys from along Stock Island and Sugarloaf north to Key Largo. My spirits soared. I was back where I was meant to be! Each morning I pushed away from a marine dock in a rented fourteen-foot boat with outboard motor and moved out along the channels that had been cut through the mangrove swamps to the open waters of Florida Bay. I visited one islet after another, passing over turtle grass flats in water sometimes clear and sometimes, especially on windy days, milky white from the churned-up bottom marl. Once or twice a day I saw a distant fisherman or a powerboat moving to deeper water, but into the swampy archipelagoes of my choice few other people ventured. Less than a mile away U.S. 1, which runs the length of the keys to their southernmost point at Key West, was choked by traffic. It was lined by a noisome thicket of motels, trailer parks, amusement parks, marinas, fishing tackle shops, and fast-food restaurants. But beyond hearing range of the rumble and whine of traffic, the swamps and islets were pristine, a virgin wilderness. Mangrove wood has little commercial value. No one but a naturalist or escaped convict would choose to traverse the gluelike mud flats and climb through the tangled prop roots and trunks of the mangrove trees. So I had it all to myself: one more time, a world I knew so well, more complex and beautiful than anything contrived by human enterprise.

I pushed into the interiors of the islets to examine the arthropod inhabitants. Sometimes the little forests opened at the center into a slightly raised glade carpeted with aerial roots and algal mats. Sometimes I found myself beneath the massed nests of clamoring herons, egrets, and white-crowned pigeons. I drifted along from landfall to landfall, collecting specimens, studying charts, filling my notebook with impressions. Mine was anything but a world-class voyage, but I was as content as Darwin on the voyage of H.M.S. *Beagle*. I ate lunch in the boat while peering over the side at rich marine life along

263

the edge of the islets. Just beneath the reach of low tide, the mangrove prop roots were covered by masses of barnacles, sea squirts, anemones, clams, and green and red algae. Schools of mangrove snappers and young barracuda prowled in and out of the root interstices and alga-slimed cavities of the mudbanks. Should I have become a marine biologist? Too late to think about that now. I was at peace. The only sounds I heard were the call of birds and the slap of waves against the hull of my boat. An occasional jet droned high above, to remind me, you'll come back, dreamer, your life depends on those artifacts you've tried to escape.

I found what I had come for in the mangrove islets. The trees swarmed with scores of species of small creatures: ants, spiders, mites, centipedes, bark lice, crickets, moth caterpillars, and other arthropods. Many flourished in breeding populations, prerequisites for the establishment of an experimental biogeography. And from one mangrove clump to the next, the species changed. For ants the pattern was consistent with competitive exclusion. Below a certain island size, the colonization of some species appeared to preclude the establishment of others. I saw an opportunity in the study of these telescoped patterns. Instead of traveling great distances from one Pacific Island to another to study the distribution of birds, an effort requiring months or years, I could, by guiding a fourteen-footer among the islets, analyze the distribution of arthropods in a period of days or weeks.

How, then, might these mangrove dots be turned into little Krakataus? I saw no easy way, and cast about for some alternative approach. I made the following decision: continue with the mangrove studies, but in addition select other islands lacking trees in order to make sterilization easier. I had learned that treeless sandy islands in the nearby Dry Tortugas are occasionally flooded and swept clean of their low scrubby plant growth by hurricanes. If I could monitor them before and after a big storm, I might observe the recolonization process and establish whether it created an equilibrium. Let the Caribbean's stormy weather be the volcano. At least it was worth a try.

I called on William Robertson, official naturalist of the Everglades National Park, to explain my idea. Bill frequently visited the Dry Tortugas to study sooty terns, a far-ranging species that nests on this remotest of Florida's archipelagoes. He agreed that the procedure might work, and invited me to join his research party on the next boat trip out from the docks at the Everglades town of Flamingo to survey the area. Once settled in dungeonlike rooms at Fort Jefferson, the old Federal stronghold and prison on Garden Key, we took a smaller boat out to the other, smaller islands of the Dry Tortugas. I leaped into the surf and scrambled onto each of the little sandy keys in turn, making a record of the sparse vegetation and arthropods. My notebook was soon complete. All I had to do now was wait for a serious hurricane to pass over in order to begin a study of recolonization.

Providentially, from a biologist's possibly perverse point of view, two hurricanes struck the Dry Tortugas during the next ten months. Betsy, on September 8, 1965, threw gusts up to 125 miles per hour at Fort Jefferson. The milder Alma attained gale force winds on June 8, 1966. Between them they wiped the vegetation off the smallest sandy islands, as I had hoped. By that time, however, I had changed my plan and advanced to a bolder scheme. Why be confined to the haphazard distribution of a few remote keys? And why depend on the passing of hurricanes, which normally strike the Dry Tortugas only once or twice every ten years? The method was in any case not fully experimental. It could not be controlled. Instead, I thought, why not select ideally located mangrove keys from among the hundreds near U.S. 1, then fumigate them with pesticides? It should be possible to kill off all the insects and other arthropods. These islets could be chosen to represent different sizes as well as various distances away from the mainland. Other islets, left unfumigated but otherwise studied in identical fashion, might serve as controls.

At this point, the fall of 1965, Daniel Simberloff joined me as a collaborator. The added vision and inspired effort of this second-year graduate student made it possible to turn the mangrove keys into a laboratory. Dan was primed for an effort of this kind. While an undergraduate at Harvard he had majored in mathematics, graduating magna cum laude. He could have moved on easily to a successful career in mathematics or the physical sciences. But after taking Natural Sciences 5, the famous nonmajors course in biology given by George Wald, he decided this branch of science was more to his liking. During his senior year he interviewed Bill Bossert and me and asked: Is graduate study in biology feasible if one has a stout heart but thin undergraduate training in that subject? Indeed it was, we both responded, especially for a mathematician. If you enter population biology now, the new discipline will reward skills in model building and quantitative analysis. All you need to do is add an all-out effort in biological training.

Simberloff began his Ph.D. study under my sponsorship in the fall of 1964. I hesitate to use the usual expression "studied under me," because in the years to follow I learned as much from him as he did from me. We soon became partners.

Dan at least looked as though he could manage field biology. With somewhat hawkish features, a solid muscular body carried in a relaxed slouch, he might have passed for the kind of Ivy League quarterback who studies calculus or Chinese history too conscientiously to be an athletic star. Like many bright students of the day he was also a leftist radical, of the thinker rather than activist subspecies, suspicious of all authority and fierce enough to be a supporter of Eldridge Cleaver for President. This was quite all right with me. In 1965 the civil rights movement still meant idealism and courage tested on the dangerous back roads of Mississippi. The mere mention of Cuba, recently the site of history's only nuclear confrontation, chilled us both; and the war in Vietnam was slowly gathering momentum. The Florida Keys were bracketed by bases at Homestead and Key West, and the whole area hummed with military activity. That summer I saw my first Green Berets, a platoon riding through the streets of Key West in a troop carrier. My admiration for the military and my vaguely centrist political beliefs were yielding somewhat to uneasiness over the direction the country was headed. Soon Dan and I began to share acerbic jokes about Lyndon Johnson. We watched in resentment as helicopters flew overhead, bearing commanding officers from ships to their homes ashore. We perched on the branches of mangrove trees, collecting spiders and crickets, on a nearly invisible budget, trying to learn how ecosystems are assembled. A dozen helicopter rides would have paid for our entire project. But not one citizen in a hundred would have understood what we were trying to do. It was a time of massive imbalance in favor of military security over environmental security. We had no idea how or when the differential might be redressed, nor did we expect ever to see ecology given national priority as a science. We were just thankful for the opportunity provided us by modest funding from the National Science Foundation. And thankful just to be there, in this beautiful natural environment.

By joining the project, Dan took a career risk. Our endeavor had an uncertain future, because no one had previously tried or even conceived anything like it. If we were unable to eliminate the arthropods completely from the islets, we would be in trouble. If we failed to put scientific names on the myriad of species we found on the islands, our data would be far less valuable. If the colonization of the sterilized islands took ten or twenty years or longer to progress significantly, Dan would have to find other work to complete his Ph.D. thesis. Graduate students were expected to finish their degree requirements, including a complete and reasonably well polished research thesis, in no more than six or seven years. Most accepted low-risk projects, those new enough to generate significant results but close enough to preexisting knowledge and proven techniques to be practicable. Simberloff had none of these assurances. In September 1965 he nonetheless departed for the Florida Keys, with the initial task of selecting the experimental islets.

In the months that followed we divided the labor further. While Dan grew lean and acquired a deep tan laboring on the open waters of Florida Bay, I attended to the administration of the project. The details of my own role ranged from the unusual to the bizarre. For an effort of this kind we had first of all to engage the services of a professional exterminator. Fortunately, there was an abundance of companies in Miami. The executives of the first two I called answered with rich southern accents and clearly thought I was either joking or crazy. On the third try I got Steven Tendrich, vice president of National Exterminators, Inc. He had a northern accent, which gave me hope. Could he manage, I asked carefully, to spray clumps of mangrove in the Florida Bay with short-lived insecticides that would remove all the insects? We would ourselves eliminate by hand the tree snails and other larger animals that might be resistant to the chemical. Tendrich did not hesitate. He said yes, maybe he could do a job like that. Sure, give him some time to study the logistics. But even if it looked promising, he warned, he could not manage much in the field until the fall, when the heavy business of summertime Miami slacked off.

Progress in this sector having been achieved, I went with Simberloff to visit Jack Watson, the resident ranger of the National Park Service, to ask his permission to exterminate the whole faunas of islets. Most of the candidate islets were within the boundaries of the Everglades National Park and Great White Heron National Wildlife Refuge, over which he had partial jurisdiction. Obtaining permission to wipe out animal populations on federally protected land may sound like an impossible dream, but it proved relatively easy. Watson gave it without hesitation, asking only that we keep him briefed. Bill Robertson, our principal contact in the Park Service, was also in sympathy with the rationale and plan of the project. He knew that the targeted islets were no more than clumps of red mangrove among hundreds scattered through Florida Bay. They harbored species or races no different from those abounding elsewhere. We assured Watson and Robertson of our intent to protect the vegetation, and our expectation that the trees would be fully recolonized with insects and other arthropods following the "defaunation," as we now called it. The experiment, Simberloff and I argued, might provide information that would help guide future park management policy. Our earnestness proved persuasive, and we never faced opposition from government officials or the public.

Finally, I set out to contact specialists who could identify the species of insects and other arthropods living on the mangrove islets before fumigation and while the recolonization proceeded. This proved the most difficult task of all. There were at most several hundred entomologists in the United States able to identify insects from the Florida Keys. Their study would be complicated by the fact that many of the creatures we expected to find are immigrants from the West Indies, especially nearby Cuba and the Bahamas. Among our discoveries were to be the first specimens of the tropical spider family Hersiliidae recorded in the eastern United States and several large and striking long-horn beetles previously known only from the Bahamas. In the end we were able to persuade fifty-four specialists to assist us in the classification of our specimens. Most pitched in with enthusiasm. An expert on spiders, Joseph Beatty, went so far as to visit Simberloff in the field to assist with the on-site identification of the colonists.

During the spring of 1966 Simberloff reported in with his recommendation of islets that seemed well placed either for defaunation or to serve as controls. We began surveys prior to spraying by inspecting every square millimeter of trunk and leaf surface, digging into every crevice, prying beneath flakes of dead bark and into hollow twigs and decaying branches. We collected every species of arthropod we found. Later, after the defaunation, Dan took over the heavy duty of regular monitoring. To disturb the colonists as little as possible, he relied on photographs and his own growing familiarity with the mangrove fauna. It was hard and uncomfortable work, demanding the combined skills of insect systematist, roofer, and restaurant health inspector. Simberloff, the city-bred mathematician, did well. He endured the insect bites and lonely hours in the hot sun I had promised him. Once, after his outboard motor failed, he spent the night on one of the islets, managing to escape only when he hailed a passing fisherman the following morning. Exasperated with the gluelike mud through which we had to wade to reach several of our islands, he built a pair of plywood footpads shaped like snowshoes and drilled holes in them to reduce suction when they were lifted. When he tried them out he sank to his knees and had to be pulled out by me and another companion. I called the invention "Simberloffs" afterward. Dan was not noticeably amused.

I joined him at intervals to give assistance. On one memorable occasion—June 7, 1966—Dan met me at the Miami International Airport just as Hurricane Alma was churning up the central Caribbean in the general direction of Florida. A storm watch had been posted for Miami and the keys. When we awoke the next morning the sky had clouded over, wind was picking up from the south, and a light rain had begun to fall. The eye of the storm was expected to pass up the west Florida coast and sideswipe Miami. Here, I thought, was a rare opportunity to watch a hurricane disperse animals out of the mangrove swamps and across the water. Travel in high winds seemed a likely means of colonizing the little islands. I suggested that we stand inside a nearby mangrove swamp during the storm and watch for animals blown along by high winds. For some reason that escapes me now, I didn't think much about danger to ourselves. Simberloff agreed without hesitation. All right, he said, something interesting might happen. Good enough.

We were both a little crazy in those days. As stronger gusts of wind and rain blew in, and the streets began to empty of traffic, we drove to Key Biscayne and hiked into a patch of red mangrove swamp along the bay shore facing Miami. The eye of the hurricane was now passing up the west coast on its way toward landfall in northwest Florida. The gusts on Key Biscayne reached sixty miles an hour, gale but not hurricane force. I was disappointed. The wind was not strong enough to tear insects and other small creatures from the trees. They all stayed hunkered down safely on the branches and leaves as the rain-soaked winds roared through. We saw not a single animal blow by. Nor could we find animals struggling in the water at the edge of the swamp. I said, Well, let's see what would happen if an animal *were* blown free. Would the storm-tossed waves carry it out toward a distant shore? I caught an anole lizard and tossed it ten feet or so out into the water. To my dismay, it popped to the surface, swam expertly back to the shelter of the trees, and climbed up a mangrove trunk. Well, I continued, suppose a full hurricane blew an anole so far away on open water it couldn't get back. Our little experiment shows that it could swim to the nearest islet if it were not too far away. Dan, rainwater streaming from his hat, allowed that the notion was plausible. Our excursion was not a complete loss, but in later years we agreed we were lucky that Alma only brushed Miami. Otherwise we ourselves might have been washed to a distant shore, proving our own hypothesis *in extremis*.

A month later, I joined Steve Tendrich and a crew from National Exterminators on a trip into Florida Bay to spray the first two islets, "Experimental 1" and "Experimental 2," E1 and E2 for short. Simberloff was busy at another location preparing additional islets. We loaded a rented barge with equipment and set forth from a marina on Sugarloaf Key. Halfway out we came upon a stalled sports-fishing cruiser. Observing the law of the sea even in this relatively safe stretch of water, we took the captain and his two fisherman guests on board and back to Sugarloaf. Then we headed forth again. This time we reached E1 and sprayed the little island with parathion. The next morning we proceeded to E2. Here we spotted several nurse sharks, one nearly four feet in length, cruising the shallow waters around the islet. Trouble! The workmen refused to get off the barge. But I knew that nurse sharks never attack people unless hooked or seized by the tail and hauled from the water by the occasional reckless fisherman. They live on a diet of shellfish, crustaceans, and other small bottom-dwelling animals. So I volunteered to stand guard waist deep and drive the sharks away with an oar. Impressed by my specious bravery and with their male pride challenged, the crew got into the water and sprayed E2.

Several days later, after I had returned to Cambridge, Simberloff called with mixed news about E1 and E2. He had made a close inspection of the islets and found that the kill of the arthropods living on the surface of the vegetation had been total. But some beetle larvae living deep in the wood of dead branches survived. We realized we had no way of knowing what other creatures might still live in these

deeper spaces. So we quickly agreed that spraying with parathion or some other short-lived insecticide was not enough. In order to run a proper experiment, we had to start with islets scourged of all animal life, with no exception. It would be necessary to fumigate the islets with a poisonous gas, one that penetrates every crack and crevice.

I called Steve Tendrich: could National Exterminators fumigate an island? The ever-resourceful Tendrich responded in his usual positive manner: why not? It was common practice in Miami, he said, to cover entire houses with a rubberized nylon tent and fumigate the interior in order to remove all termites and other insect pests, no matter how deeply hidden in the woodwork. To transfer the method to a large object surrounded by water would be tricky, of course. The crew would need to erect a scaffolding around the islet as a frame for the tent. We couldn't just lay the cover on top of the fragile branches. And something else: the dosage of the gas must be set just right, high

273

enough to kill all the animals but low enough to leave the mangrove trees undamaged. To study a ghost island of dead wood and fallen leaves would have no meaning, I agreed. Not least, I had promised the National Park Service that we would preserve the live vegetation.

So it was to be poison gas. But what kind? We considered and quickly discarded hydrogen cyanide. It was too dangerous for the crew to use under these uncertain conditions, over water with possible stiff winds. Even if we could apply it safely, hydrogen cyanide is water-soluble and would probably kill the marine communities around the mangrove prop roots, an unacceptable side effect. Methyl bromide, Tendrich ventured, might fill the bill, if he could get the dosage just right. Tendrich immediately set up trials, using small mangrove trees in the swamps near Miami. Meanwhile Simberloff collected cockroach egg cases from mangrove swamps for Tendrich to test with various dosages. If these highly resistant insect life stages could be killed without damage to the vegetation, methyl bromide might work.

The window between insect kill and tree kill using methyl bromide was narrow, but Tendrich found it. On October 11, 1966, we all gathered for the first trial on an islet in the shallow waters of Harnes Sound, on the mainland side of Key Largo and a relatively short ride down U.S. 1 from Miami. As the men loaded the gear, we saw ospreys and pelicans flying nearby and herons spearing fish in the shade of the mangrove fringes along walls of barnacles and green algal mats stranded by a dropping tide. Somewhere close by, we had been told, was a nest of bald eagles. The men got the scaffolding up and closed the tent around it without mishap. They pumped the prescribed dose of methyl bromide through a flap-covered opening in the side, in the same manner used to fumigate a small house, then pulled the tent away, allowing the gas to dissipate quickly to harmless levels.

The next day we searched the islet thoroughly and found no trace of animal life. Even the deep-boring insects had been killed. Our colonization experiment was under way at last.

Tendrich, however, was not entirely satisfied with the procedure. It had worked all right at Harnes Sound a hundred yards from the highway, but the metal rods used to create the frame were heavy and clumsy and might be very difficult to transport to the more remote and less accessible mud-flat sites. He began to search for alternative techniques of scaffolding. One day as he drove through Miami he spotted a steeplejack working on a tower atop a hotel, and inspiration struck. Steve stopped the car, took an elevator to the hotel roof, and waited for the man to come down. He asked the steeplejack, whose name was Ralph Nevins, whether it might be possible to erect a small tower like that in the middle of a mangrove swamp, then drape a tent over the guy wires. Sure, Nevins replied—another optimist—why not? Would it be very difficult? Don't think so. Tendrich hired him on the spot. And so it was done thereafter. The rest of our islets were fumigated beneath tents wrapped around the guy wires of a tower raised by Ralph Nevins.

Simberloff continued to carry the main burden of monitoring. He was tied for months to a physically demanding routine of travel, search, and identification. When I found time I came down from Cambridge, and we worked together. Within weeks it was apparent that the project was going to be a success. The recolonization by arthropod species was already well under way. Moths, bark lice, and other flying insects appeared early, at first in small numbers but accumulating and reproducing as time passed. Winged ant queens, newly inseminated during their nuptial flights, landed, shed their wings, and started colonies. Spiders came early in abundance; some were wolf spiders the size of silver dollars. How were they crossing the water? Since there had been no major storms, we guessed that they used ballooning. Many kinds of spiders, when crowded or short of food, prepare to emigrate by standing in exposed places on leaves and twigs and letting out threads of silk into the wind. As the strands lengthen, the drag increases, until the spiders have difficulty holding themselves in place. Finally they let go, allowing the wind on the strands to pull them up and away. With luck they come down again on land, and best of all in some place like a distant mangrove island with few other spiders and an abundance of prey. Those that hit water instead soon become fish food.

Toward the end of the year following the defaunations, a pattern in the colonization began to emerge. With so much of our time invested, we now began to worry that a hurricane might strike, perturbing the new faunas and ruining the continuity of the experimental run. Fortunately, none came close to Florida. In fact no major storm struck the area again until Andrew devastated South Miami and the northern keys in 1992. After a while, we relaxed a bit and broadened our attention to include other aspects of local ecology.

Our first major project was to launch a survey of the arthropods of all the mangrove swamps, in order to gain a picture of the pool of all possible emigrants to the experimental islets. I hired Robert Silberglied, a graduate student working in entomology under my direction, to commence a general survey of the surrounding keys. Bob was a gifted naturalist and a polymath taxonomist who could on sight identify species from a wide array of animal groups. The challenge of a complete arthropod survey was made to order for his talents. He worked tirelessly from island to island, building a large reference collection of insects and other arthropods. His impressive potential was destined never to flower into a full career, however. On January 13, 1982, he died with others in the Potomac River crash of an Air Florida airliner on the outskirts of Washington, D.C. A winter storm was in progress, and the accident was later blamed on wing icing. The flight was to have been the first leg of a flight to Panama, where Bob had planned to continue research on tropical ecology.

Our interest in the Florida Keys, as our research moved onward into 1967, also extended to include conservation. Silberglied and

Simberloff heard rumors that Lignumvitae Key, a 280-acre island on the bay side close to Lower Matecumbe Key and its transecting segment of U.S. 1, was an unspoiled paradise covered by large hardwood trees. Undisturbed forest other than mangrove was a rarity in the Keys, and worth investigation. Few people had set foot on Lignumvitae to that time. One was Konrad Lorenz, who later opened his influential book *On Aggression* with a description of the coral reefs there and on nearby Key Largo.

When Silberglied and Simberloff put ashore, they were met by the caretakers, Russell and Charlotte Niedhauk, an elderly and reclusive couple who lived on the island alone. The Niedhauks were suspicious of all visitors, and rudely chased most away. But when Bob and Dan revealed that they were biologists interested in conservation of the island, they were given a warm welcome. As they walked inland from the caretakers' house, they confirmed the rumor: almost all the land was covered by a mature tropical hardwood forest. They were thrilled to find themselves in a near-primeval habitat that once predominated in the high islands of the Keys but had been almost completely obliterated by the 1960s. Huge mahogany and gumbo-limbo, including the largest individual of the latter species in the United States, towered over wild lime, torchwood, Jamaica dogwood, boxleaf stopper, strangler fig, and the only large stand of holywood lignum vitae in Florida. Sixty-five species of trees and woody shrubs, all tropical and subtropical, composed the woody flora. The fauna was also a remnant of the old Keys. Candy-striped tree snails hung like grapes from the trunks and branches. Large butterflies, including showy dagger wings, purple wings, and swallowtails, darted and floated back and forth above the shaded trails. Bald eagles, at that time nearly extinct in the eastern United States, were occasional visitors, and Bahama bananaquits were seen from time to time. Later, after he had visited the island, Archie Carr, the great expert on Caribbean natural history, reminded me that the Lignumvitae forest was a tropical West Indian lowland forest of a quality no

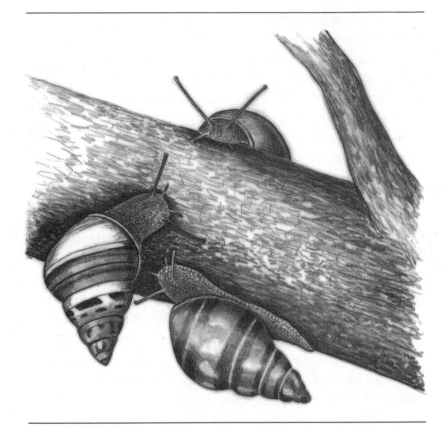

longer found in the West Indies themselves. The chances of finding stands of old mahogany and lignum vitae on the islands were close to zero.

The Niedhauks were almost paranoid about the future of Lignumvitae Key. It was owned, they explained, by a private consortium of wealthy Floridians who were planning to convert it into a community of expensive vacation residences. All the owners cared about, they said and I later confirmed, was a financial killing. Could the visitors help find a way to preserve the island in its natural state? Bob and Dan conveyed this information to me as soon as they returned to their base. Soon afterward, I visited the island and was similarly enchanted, and fearful. I invited Thomas Eisner, my old friend on the Cornell faculty, to join me on a second visit. Together we prepared an article for *Natural History* about Lignumvitae and its plight. While our effort was under way, I spoke at a meeting of the Florida Audubon Society in Miami on the subject, and to my delight an elderly couple living in Coral Gables pledged $100,000 toward the purchase of the island. It was a big first step toward saving Lignumvitae. But we needed more; the owners had set the tentative price at over $2 million. Their spokesman, a septuagenarian Miami dentist, was gleeful that conservationists had entered the bidding. He made it clear that the final price would be raised as high as the owners could make it. He would love to see his beautiful island saved in its natural state, he claimed, but if we did not act soon the land would go to developers. The Lignumvitae ecosystem, in short, had been placed in ransom.

I contacted Thomas Richards, president of The Nature Conservancy, in hopes of pressing the campaign to a successful conclusion. TNC was, as it remains today, famous for its policy of purchasing environmentally important land for preservation in the public domain. After a visit of his own, Richards committed his organization to the effort. He then approached Nathaniel Reed, an influential administrator in Florida's park system, for further assistance. In the end, after long negotiation, a reasonable price was agreed upon. The island was purchased with funds from The Nature Conservancy and the State of Florida, and Lignumvitae Key was turned into a fully protected State Botanical Site. Today visitors walk along trails where tree snails still decorate the gnarled old lignum vitae trees and dagger wings alight among their delicate blue flowers and petard-shaped yellow fruits. The public can in perpetuity, I trust, witness the Florida Keys as they were in prehistory.

Meanwhile, our experimental project continued to move swiftly

NATURALIST

forward. By the fall of 1967, a year after we fumigated the islets, the results were all but conclusive. In a formal article published two years later, Simberloff and I summarized the events of recolonization and the reattainment of equilibria:

> By 250 days after defaunation, the faunas of all the islands except the distant one ("E1") had regained species numbers and composition similar to those of untreated islands even though population densities were abnormally low . . . The colonization curves plus static observation on untreated islands indicate strongly that a dynamic equilibrium number of species exists for any island.★

At least the cruder predictions of the theory of island biogeography had been met. The closest island, as expected, had the largest number of species before fumigation, forty-three to be exact, and it regained approximately that number within the year. The most distant island, E1, had the smallest number, twenty-six, and climbed back close to that after defaunation. The other islands, at intermediate distances, had intermediate numbers before fumigation and also returned to their original levels afterward. Two years later, in 1968, these various levels still held.† The turnover in species was very rapid, also as expected from island biogeographic theory applied to small, swiftly occupied islands. In the course of our studies we added many observations on the dispersal and early colonization of various groups of arthropods, including spiders, mites, ants, earwigs, bark lice, crickets, and many others. Dan completed his Ph.D. thesis in the spring of 1968. It had taken us only three years to create miniature Krakataus, in replicate with controls, and follow their histories to an early form of equilibrium.

In 1971 Simberloff and I received the Mercer Award of the Ecological Society of America for our research, a welcome recognition.

★"Experimental Zoogeography of Islands: The Colonization of Empty Islands," *Ecology* 50(2) (1969): 278–295.
†"Experimental Zoogeography of Islands: A Two-Year Record of Colonization," *Ecology* 51(5) (1970): 934–937.

We had risked a new approach to biogeography, a subject still considered outside the mainstream of ecology, and succeeded. From many employment opportunities open to him, Dan accepted an assistant professorship at Florida State University, in order to be within easy distance of field sites. In time he became an ecologist of international stature. He conducted additional experiments with mangrove islets, varying their size and shape. He expanded his activities to include field studies on other ecosystems, and used his mathematical skills to conduct critiques of ecological theory and to develop new approaches in quantitative modeling. In time his university appointed him to the Robert O. Lawton Distinguished Professorship.

I did not return to the Florida Keys, and my dream of converting them into a natural laboratory languished. A new possibility—a different opening to the future—had seized my imagination. I wanted to make sociobiology into a single science, one that ranged from ants to chimpanzees.

chapter fifteen
ANTS

_____

_____

_____

THEY ARE EVERYWHERE, DARK AND RUDDY SPECKS THAT
zigzag across the ground and down holes, milligram-weight inhabitants of an alien civilization who hide their daily rounds from our
eyes. For over 50 million years ants have been overwhelmingly dominant insects everywhere on the land outside the polar and alpine ice
fields. By my estimate, between 1 and 10 million billion individuals
are alive at any moment, all of them together weighing, to the nearest order of magnitude, as much as the totality of human beings. But
a vital difference is concealed in this equivalence. While ants exist in

just the right numbers for the rest of the living world, humans have become too numerous. If we were to vanish today, the land environment would return to the fertile balance that existed before the human population explosion. Only a dozen or so species, among which are the crab louse and a mite that lives in the oil glands of our foreheads, depend on us entirely. But if ants were to disappear, tens of thousands of other plant and animal species would perish also, simplifying and weakening land ecosystems almost everywhere.

They are intertwined in our world, too, as illustrated by an incident that occurred in Harvard's Biological Laboratories in the late 1960s. At the risk of melodrama I will call it the Revenge of the Ants. The serious trouble began when an assistant in Mark Ptashne's laboratory, a humming center of research on gene repression, began the routine pipetting of sugar solution for the culture of bacteria. She could not draw the liquid through. Looking more closely, she saw that the narrow pipette channel was plugged with small yellow ants. Other, more subtle signs of a strange invasion had been noted in the building. Here and there yellow ants quickly covered food left out after lunch or afternoon tea. Portions of breeding colonies, with queens and immature stages surrounded by workers, appeared miraculously beneath glass vessels, in letter files, and between the pages of notebooks. But most alarming, researchers found the ants tracking faint traces of radioactive materials from culture dishes across the floors and walls. An inspection revealed that a giant unified colony was spreading in all directions through spaces in the walls of the large building.

I had reason to be concerned with the invasion. It had started by accident in my own quarters. The species was Pharaoh's ant, known to specialists by its formal name *Monomorium pharaonis*, a notorious pest of East Indian origin that infests buildings around the world. When a supercolony occupies hospitals, its workers feed on surgical waste and the wounds of immobilized patients, in the course of which they sometimes spread disease organisms. Portions of colonies transport themselves by moving into luggage, books, clothing, and any other objects with one or two inches of space. Arriving at a new accidental destination, which might equally well be an apartment house in Oslo, a florist shop in St. Louis, or a vacant lot in Caracas, they move out and commence to breed.

Harvard's propagule, as we reconstructed its history later, took passage in the airport at the Brazilian port city of Belém. Portions of a supercolony entered two wooden crates belonging to Robert Jeanne, a Ph.D. candidate studying under my direction. Now a professor of entomology at the University of Wisconsin, Jeanne in 1969 was homeward bound after a lengthy period of field research in the Amazon rain forest. By the time he opened the crates in the Biological Laboratories and discovered the hitchhikers, the ants had established themselves in the walls and were metastasizing.

To eliminate a large population of Pharaoh's ants by conventional means can be expensive and disruptive. An ingenious alternative solution was devised by Gary Alpert, a graduate student in entomology with a special interest in pest control. He was counseled and aided by Carroll Williams, Harvard's professor of insect physiology. Williams provided a chemical compound that mimics the action of the juvenile hormone of insects by sterilizing queens and preventing the full development of the larvae into the adult stage. By mixing this compound with peanut butter, Alpert fashioned baits that he hoped the foraging ants would carry back into the nests and thus spread its stultifying effect. The method was then in its earliest experimental stage, but it worked. Over a period of months the ant population steadily declined. After two years, it disappeared.

The saga of the Pharaoh's ants was, however, not quite over; it was to end on the pages of science fiction. The incident inspired the plot of the 1983 novel *Spirals*, by William Patrick, then the editor for biology and medicine at Harvard University Press. His imaginary ants were suspected of carrying around the laboratory a form of engineered DNA that induced progeria, a disease that fatally accelerates the process of aging. The daughter of a key bioengineer died from the condition, turning into a physiological old lady before she got past her childhood years. In the end the ants were exonerated, when the researcher himself proved at fault: he had cloned the daughter from cells of his dead wife, and her development had gone awry as a result.

One does not need to make ants protagonists of a novel to bring them deserved attention. I placed them at the center of my professional life, the focus of a near obsession, and I think I chose wisely. Yet I also confess that at the time their main appeal was not their environmental importance or the drama of their social evolution. It came from the discoveries they generously offered me. I built my career from easy revelation. The most important topic I addressed was their means of communication, which led me into a long period of productive research on animal behavior and organic chemistry.

My interest in chemical communication began in the fall of 1953, when Niko Tinbergen and Konrad Lorenz visited Harvard University to lecture on the new science of ethology. Twenty years later they shared the Nobel Prize for physiology or medicine, with Karl von Frisch as a third corecipient, for the years of work chronicled during their American tour. Tinbergen, a precise, carefully spoken Dutchman, arrived first. He gave an account of ethology that struck me with the resonance of important discovery. Because I was absorbed in systematics and biogeography, however, subjects remote from behavior, I took only a few notes and otherwise paid little attention. Then Lorenz came. He recounted his work begun in the 1930s, which he now was continuing at the Max Planck Institute in Buldern. He was a prophet of the dais, passionate, angry, and importunate. He hammered us with phrases soon to become famous in the behavioral sciences: imprinting, ritualization, aggressive drive, overflow; and the names of animals: graylag goose, jackdaw, stickleback. He had come to proclaim a new approach to the study of behavior. Instinct has been reinstated, he said; the role of learning was grossly overestimated by B. F. Skinner and other behaviorists; we must now press on in a new direction.

He had my complete attention. Still young and very impressionable, I was quick to answer his call to arms. Lorenz was challenging the comparative psychology establishment. He was telling us that most animal behavior is preordained. It is composed of fixed-action patterns, sequences of movements programmed in the brain by heredity, which unfold through the life of an animal in response to particular signals in the natural environment. When triggered at the right place and time, they lead the animal through a sequence of correct steps to find food, to avoid predators, and to reproduce. The animal does not require previous experience in order to survive. It has only to obey.

Obedience to instinct: that formula has the ring of an old and tiresome story. Operant conditioning sounds so much more modern. But Lorenz strengthened his case with the logic of evolutionary biology, which secured my allegiance. Each species has its own repertoire of fixed-action patterns. In the case of a particular bird species, for example, the individual spreads its plumes in a certain way to attract mates of its own species; it bonds at a certain time of the year; it builds a nest of the right shape at the right location. Fixed-action patterns are biological events; they are not "psychological." Having a genetic basis, they can be isolated and studied in the same manner as anatomical parts or biochemical reactions, species by species. They are prescribed by particular genes on particular chromosomes. They come into existence and change as one species evolves into another. They serve, no less than anatomy and physiology, as a basis for classification and the reconstruction of trees of evolutionary descent, which clarify the true relationships among species. Instinct, the great ethologist made clear to me, belongs in the Modern Synthesis of evolutionary biology. And that means you can take ethology out into the field and do something with it.

Lorenz's lecture and my supplementary reading in later months drew me in a new direction. The ethologists were giving shape to something I had tried to do earlier with the dacetine ants but for which I had lacked a theory and vocabulary. My thoughts now raced. *Lorenz has returned animal behavior to natural history. My domain. Naturalists, not psychologists with their oversimple white rats and mazes, are the best persons to study animal behavior.*

The fixed-action patterns are what count, I realized. They can be understood only as part of the adaptation of individual species to a particular part of the natural environment. One kind of bird compared to another. One kind of ant against another. If you watch a chimpanzee in a cage, even if you test all its supposed learning ability, you will never see more than a small part of the behavior with which the animal is programmed, and you will miss the full significance of even that part.

What made ethology even more beguiling was the principle that although fixed-action patterns are complex, the signals triggering them are simple. Take the European robin, an early subject of ethological analysis by the British ornithologist David Lack. The male, primed by springtime hormones, uses song and displays to chase other males out of his territory. If these warnings fail, he attacks the intruders with fluttering wings and stabbing beak. His aggression is not provoked by the whole image of a male robin as we see it. He vents his fury instead against a red breast on a tree limb. A stuffed immature male with an olive breast meets no response, but a simple tuft of red feathers mounted on a wire coil evokes the full response.

Lorenz ticked off other examples of the triggering stimuli, or releasers as ethologists call them. The great majority of case studies accumulated by 1953 were of birds and fishes, and he concentrated on them. But the choice of these animals imposes a great bias: their communication is mediated primarily by sight or sound. It occurred to me immediately that the fixed-action patterns of ants and other social insects are triggered by chemicals instead, substances these creatures can smell or taste. Earlier generations of entomologists had already suggested something along this line; after all, such creatures cannot see in the darkness of their nests, and little evidence existed that they could hear airborne sounds. Some earlier writers had also believed that ants communicate by tapping one another with their antennae and forelegs, using a kind of Morse code of the blind. But in 1953 we knew nothing about the anatomical source of the chemicals that evoke the smells and tastes, with one exception—a hindgut trail substance, passed through the anus, found by the British biologist J. D. Carthy in 1951. Still, no one had located the ultimate glandular source of the molecules or identified their chemical structure. The idea of fixed-action patterns and releasers suggested to me a way to enter this unexplored world of ant communication. The method should, I reasoned, consist of a set of straightforward steps: break ant social behavior into fixed-action patterns; then by trial and error determine which secretions contain the releasers; finally, separate and identify the active chemicals in the secretions.

As far as I knew I was the only person thinking along these lines. So I felt in no hurry to get started. In any case I had first to finish my Ph.D. thesis, a laborious exercise in anatomy and taxonomy of the ant genus *Lasius*. With that completed in the fall of 1954, I left for the South Pacific to launch my studies on ant ecology and island biogeography. Finally, four years later, back in Cambridge with a well-equipped laboratory, I began the search for the chemical releasers of ant communication. Even then the idea evidently still eluded others; I had plenty of sea room. It was to be a year before Adolf Butenandt, Peter Karlson, and Martin Lüscher introduced the word "pheromone" to replace "ectohormone" in the literature of animal behavior. They used the term "hormone" to designate a chemical messenger inside the body of the organism, "pheromone" for a chemical messenger passed between organisms.

I started with the imported fire ant, my favorite ant species since my college years and one of the easiest social insects to culture in the laboratory. I devised a new kind of artificial nest consisting of clear

Plexiglas chambers and galleries resting on broad glass platforms. The arrangement kept the entire colony in continuous view, allowing me to run experiments and record the responses of all the ants any time I chose. The ultrasimple environment did not distress the workers. After a while they habituated to the light and carried on their daily rounds in what appeared to be a normal manner. They flourished in an ant's equivalent of a fishbowl.

The most conspicuous form of communication in fire ants is the laying of odor trails to food. Scouts leave the nest singly to search outward in paths forming irregular loops. When they encounter a particle of food too big or awkward to carry home in one trip, most commonly a dead insect or a sprinkling of aphid honeydew, they head back to the nest in a more or less direct line while laying an odor trail. Some of their nestmates then follow this invisible path back to the food. As I watched from the side while the ants were foraging, I noticed that the returning scout touched the tip of her abdomen (the rearmost part of the body) to the ground and extruded and dragged her sting for short intervals along the surface. The chemical releaser apparently was being paid out through the sting like ink from a pen.

Now I had to locate the source of the chemical, which I presumed to be somewhere inside the abdomen of the worker ant. To take this next step I needed to identify the organ making the chemical and use it to lay artificial trails of my own; I needed to steal the ants' signal and use it to speak to them myself. The abdomen of a worker is the size of a grain of salt and packed with organs barely visible to the naked eye. Making the task more difficult was the fact that the anatomy of the fire ant had not yet been studied. I had to use diagrams drawn of other kinds of ants and add a bit of guesswork.

After placing the severed abdomens of fire ants under a dissecting microscope, I used the tips of fine needles and sharpened watchmaker's forceps to open them up and take out their internal organs one by one. I found myself close to the lower size limit of unaided dissection. Had the organs been only a fraction smaller, I would have been forced to use a micromanipulator, a difficult and expensive piece of equipment I hoped to bypass. If you buy instruments like that, and the experiment fails, you lose a lot of money. Although my hands were steady, I discovered that their natural muscle tremor, barely visible to the naked eye, was enlarged to a palsy under the microscope. Magnified twenty or thirty times, the tips of the needles and forceps spasmed uncontrollably as I brought them close to the abdomens. Then I found the solution: simply make the tremors part of the dissecting technique. Turn the needles and forceps into little jackhammers. Use the muscle spasms to tear open the abdomen and to push the separate organs out of the body cavity.

This much accomplished, I washed each organ in Ringer's solution, which is synthetic insect plasma with concentrations of various salts matching those in insects. Then I made artificial trails in the simplest, most direct way I could conceive, as follows. First I placed drops of sugar water on the glass foraging plate near the nest entrance and let mobs of feeding workers gather around them. With my experimental subjects in place, I crushed each organ in turn on the tip of a sharpened birch-wood applicator stick. Then I pressed the tip down on the surface of the glass and smeared the microscopic fleck of semiliquid matter in a line from the assembled workers outward in a direction away from the nest.

First I tried the hindgut, the poison gland, and the fat body, which together fill most of the abdominal cavity. Nothing happened. In the end I came to Dufour's gland, a tiny finger-shaped structure about which almost nothing was known. It empties into a channel at the base of the sting, the conduit known to carry venom to the outside. Might it contain the trail pheromone? Indeed it did. The response of the ants was explosive. I had expected a few workers to saunter away from the sugar-drop crowd to see what might lie at the end of the new trail. What I got was a rush of dozens of excited ants. They tumbled over one another in their haste to follow the path I had blazed for them. As they ran along they swept their antennae from side to side,

sampling the molecules evaporating and diffusing through the air. At the end of the trail they milled about in confusion, searching for the reward not there.

That night I could not sleep. After a delay of five years my idea had paid off with only a few hours' work: I had identified the first gland that contributes to ant communication. More than that, I had discovered what seemed to be a new phenomenon in chemical communication. The pheromone in the gland is not just a guidepost for workers who choose to search for food, but the signal itself—both the command and the instruction during the search for food. The chemical was everything. And the bioassay instantly became that much easier. It wasn't necessary, I realized happily, to arrange delicate social settings with a multiplicity of other stimuli to get the desired result. Biologists and their chemist partners should be able to proceed directly to the pheromone's molecular structure, provided they had an effective and easily measured behavioral test. If other pheromones— say, those inducing alarm and assembly—acted the same way as the trail substance, we might decipher a large part of the ant's chemical vocabulary within a short time.

Over the next few days I confirmed the efficiency of the trail pheromone assay over and over. In science there is nothing more pleasant than repeating an experiment that works. When I led my trails all the way back to the entrance of the nest, out poured the ants, even when they had been offered no food to stimulate them first. And when I let a concentrated vapor made from many ants waft down onto the nest, a large percentage of the worker force emerged and spread out in apparent search of food.

Next I enlisted a friend, the Harvard biochemist John Law, in an attempt to identify the structure of the trail substance molecule. We were joined by a gifted undergraduate student, Christopher Walsh, who in later years was to become a leading molecular biologist and president of the Dana Farber Cancer Institute. We were a capable team, but we encountered a technical snag: we learned that each ant carries less than a billionth of a gram of the critical substance in its Dufour's gland at any one time. The problem, however, was not insoluble. The late 1950s and early 1960s were the dawn of coupled gas chromatography and mass spectrometry, which allows the identification of organic substances down to millionths of a gram. That meant we needed tens of thousands or hundreds of thousands of ants, each with its vanishing trace of pheromone, to produce the minimum amount required for analysis.

How to gather such huge quantities? From my field experience, I knew of a relatively easy way. When fire ant nests are flooded in nature by rising stream waters, the workers float to the surface in tightly packed masses. Their bodies form a living raft within which the queen and brood are safely tucked. The colony floats downstream until it reaches solid ground, and there the workers proceed to excavate a new nest. After I had explained this phenomenon to Law and Walsh, we traveled to Jacksonville, Florida, one of the southern cities closest to Boston where fire ants are abundant. We took a rental car to the farm country west of the city, where we found two-foot-high fire ant mounds dotting pastures and grassy strips along the roads. There were as many as fifty to an acre, and within each mound lived 100,000 or more ants. Pulling the car over to the verge of the interstate highway, we shoveled entire nests into the water of a slow-moving stream passing through one of the culverts. The soil settled to the bottom, and large portions of each colony rose to the surface. We scooped up seething masses of ants in kitchen strainers and plopped them into bottles of solvent. Law and Walsh soon learned the source of the ants' common name: the sting of a worker feels like heat from a match brought too close to the skin. And every ant in the nest tries to sting you, ten times or more in succession if you don't squash it first. We took scores of stings on our hands, arms, and ankles, each of which produced an itching red welt. A day or two later, many of these sites erupted into white-tipped pustules. I suspect that my distinguished colleagues resolved then and there to stay with laboratory biology. Having paid the price, we returned home with enough material to proceed with the analysis of the trail pheromone.

Even with enough raw material, however, the structure of the molecule proved elusive. As Law and Walsh closed in on the active part of the spectrographic array, the peak most likely to be the pheromone diminished to levels too low to analyze further. Was the substance unstable during the separation procedure? Possibly, but now we were running out of extract. In the end the two chemists deduced that the material is a farnesene, a terpenoid with fifteen carbon atoms arranged in a basic structure previously found most commonly among the natural products of plants. They fell short of determining the exact structure, in which the location of every double bond is specified. That difficult feat was accomplished twenty years later by Robert Vander Meer and a team of researchers at the U.S. Department of Agriculture Laboratory in Gainesville, Florida. They discovered that the fire ant trail pheromone is actually a mixture of farnesenes, one of which is Z,E-α-farnesene, augmented by at least two other similar compounds. One gallon of the mixture would be sufficient, in theory at least, to summon forth the inhabitants of 10 million colonies.

For several years following my identification of the glandular source of the trail substance I pursued my goal of deciphering as much of the ants' chemical language as possible. As I looked more closely at the fire ant trail, I stumbled on a second phenomenon of social behavior, mass communication. The amount of food or the size of an enemy force cannot, I noticed, be transmitted by signals from a single scout. Such information can be conveyed only by groups of workers signaling to other groups. By laying trails on top of one another during a short interval of time, multiple workers, say a group of ten, can signal the existence of a larger target than one identifiable by only a single worker. A hundred workers acting together can raise the range of the smell volume still more. When the food site becomes crowded or the enemy subdued, fewer workers in the group lay trails, so that excess pheromone evaporates and the signal diminishes, and a smaller number of nestmates thus respond.

The information contained in the combined action of masses of individuals coming and going to a target is surprisingly precise. Later writers pointed to a parallel action in masses of brain cells, and the similarity that exists between the brain, the organ of thought, and the insect colony, the superorganism. The first to make the abstract comparison, I believe, was Douglas Hofstadter in *Gödel, Escher, Bach: An Eternal Golden Braid*, an ingenious disquisition on the nature of organization and creativity. The question then arose and has since been asked many times: Does the resemblance mean that an ant colony can somehow "think"? I believe not. There are too few ants, and those are too loosely organized to form a brain.

I moved on to pheromones that attract and alarm ants. The simplest such substance I found, almost certainly the most elementary pheromone ever discovered, was carbon dioxide. Fire ants use it to hunt subterranean prey and to locate one another in the soil. The most bizarre pheromone, if the generic term can even be used in this case, is the signal of the dead—the means by which a corpse "announces" its new status to nestmates. When an ant dies, and if it has not been crushed or torn apart, it simply crumples up and lies still. Although its posture and inactivity are abnormal, nestmates continue to walk by it as though nothing has happened. Two or three days pass before recognition dawns, and then it is through the smell of decomposition. Responding to the odor, a nestmate picks the corpse up, carries it out of the nest, and dumps it on a nearby refuse pile.

I thought: maybe with the right chemicals I could create an artificial corpse. It should be possible to transfer the odor from one object to another. When I soaked bits of paper with an extract of well-seasoned corpses, the ants carried them to the refuse piles. Thinking back to the basic idea of the chemical releaser I asked, will any decomposition substance trigger the removal instinct, or will the ants respond to just one or two? I found out that a quick answer was possible, because biochemists had already identified a large roster of compounds found in rotting insects. Don't ask me why such research had been conducted. The scientific literature is filled with such information, and however arcane it often proves useful in unexpected ways. Such was the case in my own (also arcane) study. With two newly recruited assistants I gathered an array of the putrid substances and offered them to my ants on bits of paper, one by one. They included skatole, a component of feces; trimethylamine, one of the essences of rotting fish; and several of the more pungent fatty acids that contribute to rancid human body odor. For weeks my laboratory smelled like the combined essences of sewer, garbage dump, and locker room. In contrast to the responses of my human nose and brain, however, the ants' responses to the chemicals were consistently narrow. They removed only the paper scraps treated with oleic acid or its ester.

The experiments proved that the ants are neither aesthetic nor me-

ticulously clean in any human sense. They are programmed to react to narrow cues that reliably identify a decaying body. By removing the source they unconsciously safeguard colony hygiene. To test this conclusion about the simplicity of ant behavior I asked, finally, what would happen if a corpse came to life? To find out, I daubed oleic acid on live workers. Their nestmates promptly picked them up, even though they were struggling to get free, and carried them to the refuse pile. There the "living dead" cleaned themselves for a few minutes, rubbing their legs against their body and washing the legs and antennae with their mouthparts, before venturing back to the nest. Some were hauled out again, and a few then yet again, until they became clean enough to be certifiably alive.

A new sensory world was opening to biologists. We came fully to appreciate the simple fact that most kinds of organisms communicate by taste and smell, not by sight and sound. Animals, plants, and microorganisms employ among their millions of species an astonishing diversity of devices for transmitting the chemicals. The pheromones are usually sparse enough in the bodies of the organisms to make detection difficult for human beings. Animals are unfailingly ingenious in the methods by which they manufacture and deploy these substances. In the late 1950s I was one of no more than a dozen researchers who studied them in ants and other social insects.

It was a bonanza that lay before us. We discovered new forms of chemical messages everywhere we looked, and with minimal effort.

In 1961 I invited William Bossert, a Harvard graduate student in applied mathematics, to join me in a project to synthesize all existing knowledge about chemical communication within a single evolutionary framework. Bill possessed in consummate degree the mathematical skills I so conspicuously lacked. At that time he was also pioneering the use of computers in the modeling of evolutionary change. One day he took me into the computer room in Harvard's Aiken Computation Laboratory, pointed to the spinning tape disks and futuristic control panels, and instructed me that here was housed the future of theoretical biology. Now was the time, he urged, to come aboard and master the powerful new technology. He failed to recruit this naturalist, however. I was just too overwhelmed by the alien culture, easing my way about like an eighteenth-century Pacific islander invited to inspect the armory and rigging of H.M.S. *Endeavour*. In the years thereafter, as hardware with the computing capacity of the Aiken room shrank to the size of a suitcase, Bossert continued his efforts, but I was never motivated to join him. I had no desire to struggle for years in a field in which I could never hope to become more than mediocre.

Instead, on this occasion, I gave Bossert everything I knew or could find about the chemistry and function of the known pheromones and let him devise the models of their dispersal and detection. He incorporated evaporation and diffusion rates of the known or likely candidate molecules, with estimates of the numbers disseminated and the densities required for animals to recognize them. Together we conceived a series of different forms of expanding gases and theorized on active spaces—the zones within which the molecular densities are high enough to trigger a response. Active spaces are hemispheric in shape when the pheromone is released from one spot in still air, and half-ellipsoidal when the material is released into a steady wind or streaked along the ground into still air. We factored in the size of the molecule as it affects the rates of evaporation and diffusion. We showed that the potential variety of signals dramatically increases—it goes up exponentially—as the size of the pheromone molecule is enlarged within a homologous series. We observed that the substance can either evoke an immediate response or else change the physiology of the animal and its propensity to respond over relatively long periods. When the theory was finally stitched together and all the evidence weighed, we concluded that animals have selected chemicals during their evolution that are well suited to particular meanings. For example, the molecules used as alarm pheromones are smaller in size and have higher response concentrations than those used for sexual attraction, allowing their active spaces to flash on and off more quickly. As a rule, the pheromones chosen are among the ones conceivably most effective in transmitting a particular message.*

Even though this theoretical study of the most general properties of pheromones was progressing well, I stayed close to ants and pushed my laboratory research. In time I estimated that the workers and queens of each colony use somewhere between ten and twenty kinds of pheromones to regulate their social organization. The number undoubtedly varies according to species. But this spread, ten to twenty, is only an educated guess, and remains no more than a guess as I write, thirty years later. The reason is that beyond a few of the most obvious classes, such as the trail and alarm pheromones, the bioassays and chemical analyses turned out to be increasingly difficult. I soon realized that to stay ahead in the field I would have to devote all my time to it and acquire advanced technical training in histology and chemistry. In the late 1960s, ten years after I performed my first crude experiments, the field of pheromone studies was

*W. H. Bossert and E. O. Wilson, "The Analysis of Olfactory Communication among Animals," *Journal of Theoretical Biology* 5 (1963):443–69; E. O. Wilson and W. H. Bossert, "Chemical Communication among Animals," *Recent Progress in Hormone Research* 19 (1963):673–716.

being flooded by a small army of gifted researchers prepared to make this commitment. So I pulled out, an outclassed elder at thirty-five, returning to experiments on chemical communication only when I saw the possibility of a quick result with low technology.

Now we have come to 1969. For some it is the easily remembered year when the Pharaoh's ants began to steal culture media from the molecular biologists, for others as the year student radicals stalked the campus and Harvard Square with raised fists and revolutionary slogans stamped on their T-shirts. For me it marked a significant change of another kind. My interest in pheromones and island biogeography, my two passions of the previous ten years, had begun to wane. But in September a young scientist with whom I had been corresponding, Bert Hölldobler, knocked at the door of my office in the Biological Laboratories. A lecturer in zoology from the University of Frankfurt, he had come to spend a year as a visiting scholar under my sponsorship. I was about to enter the most sustained and productive collaboration of my research career, built upon a close friendship and a common lifelong commitment to the study of ants.

Although we made no such lofty analysis at the time, we met as representatives of two national cultures in behavioral biology, whose melding would soon lead to a better understanding of ant colonies and other complex societies. One of the contributing disciplines was ethology, European in origin and Hölldobler's forte, the study of whole patterns of behavior under natural conditions. Though the product of many minds across two generations, in 1969 ethology had become associated in popular tradition with the leadership of Lorenz, Tinbergen, and von Frisch and was well on its way to cosmopolitan status. The other foundation discipline, the one in which I had been more intensively educated, was population biology. Mostly of American and British origin, it was radically different from ethology in its approach to behavior. It addressed entire ensembles of individuals, how they grow, how they spread over the landscape, and, inevitably, how they retreat and vanish. Modern population biology, now also cosmopolitan, attempts to span wide stretches of space and time, and consequently it relies as much on the disciplined imagination invested in mathematical models as it does on studies of live organisms. Its techniques are closely allied to those of demography, in the sense that it combines the births, deaths, and migrations of individual members to construct a statistical picture of the whole society.

The key to the second, higher-level approach is the perception that an insect colony is a population. Some colonies, like the queen and 20 million worker force of the African driver ant, have more inhabitants than entire countries. Like human populations, the only way to understand such ensembles fully is to trace the lives and deaths of their separate members. Both the population-level and the individual-level bodies of information, however, require ethology to create a complete science. This discipline alone addresses in concrete terms the heart of social organization, from communication and nest construction to caste and the division of labor. The final element in the mix is evolution. The behavioral descriptions and population analysis are the historical products of natural selection. Put together, population biology, ethology, and evolutionary theory form the content of the new discipline of sociobiology, which I was to define in 1975 as the systematic study of the biological basis of social behavior and of the organization of complex societies.

Bert Hölldobler and I were edging toward sociobiology. We were, however, first and foremost entomologists, committed to the study of insects. At the time we met he was thirty-three, seven years my junior, but had independently arrived at the conviction that ants are worthy of scientific study no matter how it is done, by ethology, sociobiology, or any other biological discipline. We nevertheless also foresaw, in our early occasional conversations, that ethology and population biology are complementary approaches to the study of social behavior, and potent in combination.

It could easily have ended there, as a declaration of common interests. At the end of his second year Hölldobler returned to Frankfurt to resume what he foresaw as a lifetime academic career in Germany. At just this time, however, John Dunlop, dean of Harvard's School of Arts and Sciences, decided to increase faculty representation in behavioral biology. He authorized the appointment of three new professors and placed me in charge of the search committee. In time, after sifting through many letters and evaluations from consultants, we identified this same Dr. Hölldobler as the most promising young scientist in the world working on the behavior of invertebrate animals. He was accordingly invited to come to Harvard as a full professor. He accepted, returning to Cambridge in 1972.

Thereafter we shared the fourth floor of the newly constructed laboratory wing of the Museum of Comparative Zoology. Our contact was close, and we collaborated with increasing frequency in projects in teaching and research. But it was not to be a lifetime arrangement. Sixteen years later, in 1989, Bert returned to Germany, this time to the University of Würzburg in Bavaria, where he had been asked to create a special department devoted to social insects in the newly founded Theodor Boveri Institute of Biological Science. By that time he had come to be greatly appreciated in his native country. Germany, like most other European countries, had a growing interest but weak representation in ecology and related subjects. Bert's hybrid experience in behavior and population biology uniquely qualified him for national leadership—and continues to do so as I write. In 1991 he received the Leibniz Prize, Germany's highest award in science.

Nearly two decades of residence in America had turned Bert Hölldobler into a lover of the Arizona mountains, where he spent summers with his family, and of country-western music. Underneath the new American, however, remained the Bavarian—practical, solid, warm-natured and humorous, flexible, altogether the antithesis of the stereotypical Prussian, a difference he was quick to point out whenever the German national character became the subject of conversation. The bluegrass songs of Doc Watson, he once noted in passing, reminded him of Bavarian folk music. Bert above all was rooted to the earth, a naturalist, perhaps, by hereditary predisposition. Fluent English came slowly during his stay in America, and he never lost a marked accent. But it was an asset at Harvard University, where students assumed, correctly, that they were receiving German science and philosophy straight from the source. They consistently gave his courses the highest ratings.

By strength of character alone no scientist more deserved recognition. Hölldobler was—and remains—the most honest scientist I have ever known. As we filled the hours around tedious replicate experiments with conversation ("Okay, that's—ah—sixty-three seconds, the forager just entered the nest, got it? Now, I want to go back and say just one more thing about Hennig and the original idea of cladism . . ."), he endeavored to make every datum in his notebook, every nuance of expression in his published reports, as straight and transparent as he could. If he had a fault worth mentioning it was one which I shared and which made us the more compatible, an obsessiveness of habit in work, expressed as a sometimes unreasonable need to bring one subject to closure before going on to the next.

In science, obsessiveness under psychological control can be a virtue. To a degree I have not encountered elsewhere Hölldobler extended this urge to the design of experiments and a weighing of evidence. Many successful researchers stop with a single well-conducted procedure, which they repeat often enough for the overall result to be statistically persuasive. Then they are prepared to say in print, "I think it likely that such and such is the case." Others hold back and ask, "What different experiment can I perform, using new kinds of measurements, that will test the conclusion more rigorously?" If they then perform the second procedure and find the second result consistent with the first, they conclude, "That pretty well proves it. Let's move on." Hölldobler is a member of the second group. But sometimes during our collaboration he would pause yet again and ask—to my consternation—"Is there a third way?" He did occasionally press on with yet another method. He was the only third-way researcher I have ever known.

He was a scientist's scientist. He simply loved science as a way of knowing. I believe he would have practiced it without an audience or financial reward. He played no political games. If new data did not fit, he quickly shifted to a new position. He was one of the few scientists I have known actually willing to abandon a hypothesis. He was meticulous about crediting others, quick to praise research when it was original and solid, harsh in his rejection when it was slovenly. The tone of his conversation was explicitly and uncompromisingly ethical, a posture born neither of arrogance nor of self-regard, but from the conviction of his humanistic philosophy that without self-imposed high standards, life loses its meaning.

But a somber picture of Bert Hölldobler would be misleading. He was fun to be with, the younger brother I never had. In periods of relaxation we confided in all things, both scientific and personal. His manner and even his physical appearance were reassuring. Bearded as he approached middle age, he had a burgher's pleasant countenance fitted upon the short muscular build of a gymnast, the latter a residue of his favorite sport as a youngster. He was deeply devoted to his family, somehow finding time to participate with his wife, Friederike, in every step of the rearing of their three sons. Science was not everything for Hölldobler. A gifted painter and photographer, a good musician, he enjoyed the arts as I never could, locked as I was into my unyielding workaholic's momentum. In darker moments I envied him that.

Though considerably the younger man, he made me a better scientist. During our work in the laboratory and field, I found myself anxious to meet his standards and to let him know I was trying. I am by nature a synthesizer of scientific knowledge, much better than Hölldobler at this activity, but I confess that in my effort to make sense of everything, to fit every piece into my schemes somewhere no matter how procrustean the result, I often overlooked detail. Hölldobler did not. By temperament and training, he belonged to the Karl von Frisch tradition, expressed to me succinctly one day by Martin Lindauer, Frisch's student and Hölldobler's mentor, while I was visiting Würzburg. Lindauer said, grinning as he typically did when speaking of serious matters, "Look for the little things."

That adjuration Bert and I followed many times during the Harvard years. In 1985 we made our first field trip together to Costa Rica. We drove north from San José to La Selva, the field station of the Organization for Tropical Studies. As we entered the rain forest, I used my more general knowledge of ants to find and identify colonies that might be of exceptional interest in behavioral work. I was looking for a quick and exciting payoff. One candidate was the primitive genus *Prionopelta*, which I found nesting in rotting logs. No colonies had ever previously been studied in life. I was eager to record the key facts of the social behavior of this ant, the kind of basic data that go comfortably into syntheses and evolutionary constructions. I plunged into the work with Bert's assistance. We took notes on colony size, the number of queens, division of labor, and the kinds of insects and other small animals captured by the workers. We found, for example, that they preferred silverfishlike creatures called campodeid diplurans. In the course of our work, Bert's attention fastened on fragments of old cocoon silk plastered on the walls of passageways of the *Prionopelta* nests. He asked, as much to himself as me, What does this mean? Nothing, just trash, I answered. When the new adults emerge from the cocoons, their nestmates throw out the silk fragments, and they don't bother to stack them in separate garbage dumps. No, no, he said, look: the pieces are lined up as a smooth layer on the gallery walls. He went on, with close study of his own and the aid of a scanning electron microscope back at Harvard, to show that the cocoon silk is employed as wallpaper. It keeps the chambers of the moist walls drier than would otherwise be the case, and thereby protects the growing brood. Wallpapering was a technique of climate control previously unknown in ants.

Hölldobler again said, Look, some of the foraging workers appear to be moving more slowly while they drag their hind legs. Again I was unimpressed. Individual ants, I responded, often move slowly or erratically for no particular good reason. Nor is there any cause to believe that these primitive ants lay odor trails in any case. But Hölldobler persevered. He found that not only do the workers lay odor trails—by which they recruit nestmates to new nest sites—but the attractive substance comes from a previously unsuspected gland located in the hind legs. The pheromones are smeared in a line as the ants drag their hind legs over the ground. The existence of the gland provided an important clue to the evolutionary relationships of *Prionopelta*.

From two weeks of data gathered in the La Selva forest we wrote five scientific articles. During our years of collaboration we made uncounted other discoveries while grubbing around and talking back and forth. First one took the lead, then the other. Our partnership in most respects ended when Bert, after being approached by several institutions in Europe, was offered the professorship at Würzburg. He needed the sophisticated new equipment and skilled assistants promised him at the Theodor Boveri Institute. He had a desire, almost an obsession, to get inside the muscles, glands, and brains of ants to learn how these organs mediate social behavior and organization. He wanted to understand a thousand "little things" to make a great whole. That kind of enterprise is expensive, too much so, it appeared, for the National Science Foundation and private U.S. organizations. Most of their support was either inadequate or unstable or both, contingent on appropriations made in three- to five-year cycles of renewal. Although Bert's applications to the NSF were consistently given the highest ratings and funded, the amounts provided fell short of sustaining the effort he envisioned.

NATURALIST

One day, as Hölldobler grew more serious about leaving, we decided to write a book recounting everything we knew about ants. And while we were at it, we asked ourselves, why not try for a book that has everything *everybody* ever knew about ants, throughout history? Such a project would take a great deal of effort and time, and it might fall short of the goal we set. But what a worthy conceit! Try for the impossible, as Floyd Patterson, the undersized heavyweight boxing champion of the world once said, in order to accomplish the unusual. The result was *The Ants*, published by Harvard University Press in 1990. It contained 732 double-columned pages, hundreds of textbook figures and color plates, and a bibliography of 3,000 entries. It weighed 7.5 pounds, fulfilling my criterion of a magnum opus—a book which when dropped from a three-story building is big enough to kill a man.

On Tuesday afternoon, the following April 9, the faculty and deans of the College of Arts and Sciences gathered for their monthly meeting in the portrait-encircled main room of University Hall. Just as the meeting was about to be called to order, a secretary entered and handed President Derek Bok a message. Bok announced its content: *The Ants* had been awarded the 1991 Pulitzer Prize in General Nonfiction. I stood and basked in the applause of the Harvard faculty. Bless my soul, the Harvard faculty. Where could I go from here but down?

I later learned that our book was only the fifth on science ever to receive a Pulitzer Prize, and it was the first with a primarily scientific content, written by specialists for fellow professionals. Soon after I left University Hall that day I called Bert and asked him how it felt to win America's most famous literary award. Note, I reminded him, not scientific, *literary*. Wonderful, he replied. They would celebrate in Würzburg. The accent was still there, of course. It made the occasion more special.

chapter sixteen

ATTAINING SOCIOBIOLOGY

ON AUGUST 1, 1977, SOCIOBIOLOGY WAS ON THE COVER OF *Time*. On November 22 I received the National Medal of Science from President Carter for my contributions to the new discipline. Two months later, at the annual meeting of the American Association for the Advancement of Science, held in Washington, demonstrators seized the stage as I was about to give a lecture, dumped a pitcher of ice water on my head, and chanted, "Wilson, you're all wet!" The ice-water episode may be the only occasion in recent American history on which a scientist was physically attacked, however mildly, simply for the expression of an idea. How could an entomologist with a penchant for solitude provoke a tumult of this proportion? Let me explain.

My interest in sociobiology was not the product of a revolutionary's dream. It began innocently as a specialized zoology project one January morning in 1956 when I visited Cayo Santiago, a small island off the east coast of Puerto Rico, to look at monkeys. I was accompanied by Stuart Altmann, who had just signed up as my first graduate student. Stuart was an academic anomaly, so much so that upon admittance to the Ph.D. program at Harvard the previous fall, he at first found himself without a sponsor. His problem was not his abilities, which were outstanding, but his proposed thesis research, which was too unusual. He had set his sight on the social behavior of free-living rhesus macaques, and particularly those maintained by the National Institutes of Health on Cayo Santiago, newly dubbed "monkey island." He came well prepared. He had recently worked on howler monkeys in the Panama rain forest. His command of the relevant literature was complete.

Unfortunately, no one at Harvard knew what he was talking about. The behavior of primates under natural conditions remained virtually unknown in 1955. C. Ray Carpenter, an American psychologist, had laid a foundation in the 1930s with field observations of howlers, rhesus, and gibbons. His published work was well respected by a small circle of biologists and anthropologists but had not spawned a school of research. It was not easy to journey to where wild primates live. Jane Goodall still lived in England, her first visit to the chimpanzees of the Gombe Reserve four years away. Several Japanese researchers, at the time Altmann began his own work, were observing macaques on Mount Takasoki, on the island of Kyushu, but they published reports in their native language, which was virtually unknown to American and European scientists.

No senior members of the Harvard biology faculty considered primate field studies to lie within their province. Some doubted that the subject even belonged in biology. Thus Stuart came to me. In the late fall of 1955 I had been offered an assistant professorship in biology, effective July 1 of the following year. Frank Carpenter, chairman of the department, asked me whether, given my interest in the social behavior of ants, I would sponsor Stuart even before my faculty term began. I accepted happily. I was hardly more than a graduate student myself, just a year older than Altmann, eager to learn the strange new subject he had chosen.

I had decided wisely. The two days Stuart and I lived among the rhesus monkeys of Cayo Santiago were a stunning revelation and an intellectual turning point. When I first stepped ashore I knew almost nothing about macaque societies. I had read Ray Carpenter but was unprepared for the spectacle unfolding. As Altmann guided me on walking tours through the rhesus troops, I was riveted by the sophisticated and often brutal world of dominance orders, alliances, kinship bonds, territorial disputes, threats and displays, and unnerving intrigues. I learned how to read the rank of a male from the way he walked, how to gauge magnitudes of fear, submission, and hostility from facial expression and body posture.

Altmann issued a warning: "Two things. Don't move too suddenly near an infant, as though you mean to harm it. You might be attacked by a male. And if you do happen to be threatened, don't look the male in the face. A stare is a threat and might provoke an attack. Just hang your head down and look away." Sure enough, in a careless moment on the second day, I twisted my body around suddenly while standing next to a very young monkey, and it let out a shriek. At once the number two male ran up to me and gave me a hard stare, with his mouth gaping—the rhesus elevated-threat expression. I froze, genuinely afraid. Before Cayo Santiago I had thought of macaques as harmless little monkeys. This individual, with his tensed, massive body rearing up before me, looked for the moment like a small gorilla. I needed no reminder. I lowered my head and looked away in my most studiously contrite manner, frantically sig-

309

naling the message "Sorry, didn't mean anything, sorry." After a few minutes my challenger left.

In the evenings Altmann talked primates and I talked ants, and we came to muse over the possibility of a synthesis of all the available information on social animals. A general theory, we agreed, might take form under the name of sociobiology. Stuart was already using that word to describe his studies; he had picked it up from the Section on Animal Behavior and Sociobiology, a working subgroup of the Ecological Society of America. A belief floated among zoologists even then that animal societies require a different kind of analysis, that they are properly the subject of a separate, minor discipline. But none could say what the general principles of this sociobiology might be, or how they would relate to the rest of biology. Under the guidance of senior zoologists such as Warder Clyde Allee, Alfred Emerson, and John P. Scott, sociobiology was taking form as a discipline but still consisted largely of descriptions of different kinds of social behavior. As Altmann and I talked over the subject during the pleasant Puerto Rico evenings, we could do no better. Primate troops and social insect colonies seemed to have almost nothing in common. Rhesus monkeys are organized strongly by dominance orders based on individual recognition. That much is also true of primitively social wasps but not of the rest of the social insects, whose colonies are composed of hundreds or thousands of anonymous and short-lived siblings living in harmony. Primates communicate by voice and visual gesture, social insects by chemical secretions. Primates fill temporary roles based on personal relationships; social insects have castes and a relatively rigid, lifelong division of labor.

We knew that no science worthy of the name is built wholly from a checklist of similarities and differences with an overlay of phenomena such as dominance and group action. In 1956 there existed no theory to explain diversity—why various traits have arisen in some groups and not others. Altmann had one good idea. He intended to devise probability transition matrices of behavioral acts, to provide a compendium of the following kinds of information: if a rhesus performs act *a*, then there is a certain probability that it will perform *a* again, another probability it will perform *b*, and so on. I agreed on the concept: a great deal of behavior and social interaction can be packed into transition matrices. It should then be possible to use the numbers to compare one kind of society more precisely with another. To quantify social interactions is an important step, but where would it lead? The result would still be a description, offering no explanation of how or why a particular species of monkey or ant arrived at one pattern in the course of its evolution as opposed to another. Neither

Altmann nor I had the conceptual tools in 1956 to advance sociobiology further, and we let the subject rest. Stuart pressed on to complete his thesis research.

A congenital synthesizer, I held on to the dream of a unifying theory. By the early 1960s I began to see promise in population biology
as a possible foundation discipline for sociobiology. I had entered
population biology not to serve sociobiology but to help fashion a
counterweight to molecular biology. I believed that populations follow at least some laws different from those operating at the molecular
level, laws that cannot be constructed by any logical progression upward from molecular biology. This view of the biological sciences
motivated me to collaborate with Lawrence Slobodkin, an alliance
that later led to the development of the theory of island biogeography with Robert MacArthur.

By the early 1960s population biology was gaining substantial independent strength, and my confidence in its canonical relation to
sociobiology rose. In late July of 1964, when I met with the "Marlboro Circle" in Vermont—Egbert Leigh, Richard Levins, Richard
Lewontin, and MacArthur were the others—I represented the idea
of sociobiology as a possible derivative of population biology. Societies are populations, I argued, and amenable to the same modes of
analysis.

I saw that the quickest way to make the point was to use population biology in a solid account of caste systems and division of labor
in the social insects. I was already well prepared for the task. In 1953
I had traced the evolution of caste in ants in a more descriptive manner, using measurements of scores of species from around the world.
I showed how the divergence in anatomy among queens, soldiers,
and ordinary ("minor") workers is the consequence of changes in allometry, the differential growth of different organs. Allometry, just
by increasing or diminishing one dimension of the body relative to
another, can produce larger or smaller heads, full-blown or shriveled
ovaries, and other divergent products in any part of the final adult

form. The idea was not new. It had been advanced earlier by Julian Huxley in his 1932 book, *Problems of Relative Growth*; he in turn had been inspired by D'Arcy Thompson's analysis of the evolution of morphological gradients, published in the 1917 classic *On Growth and Form*. I took the ants from there, following in plausible sequence the evolution of castes from one basic type in small steps all the way to multiple forms differing among themselves radically. Then I gave the subject a new twist. To allometry I added demography, the relative numbers of individuals of different castes within each colony. When allometry and demography are joined closely, the probable evolution of caste becomes much clearer. The anatomy of a particular caste member obviously determines the efficiency of its labor role; a soldier, for example, functions best with large, sharp mandibles and powerful muscles to close them. But the number of soldiers, I pointed out, is also crucial. If there are too few fighting specialists, the colony will be overwhelmed by enemies. If there are too many, on the other hand, the colony cannot gather enough food to care for the young. It follows that colonies must regulate the birth and death rates of the various caste members created by allometry. In later studies I came to call the phenomenon "adaptive demography." I interpreted it as a population-level trait of an advanced society.

Julian Huxley was intrigued by my employment of allometry and demography. When he visited Harvard in 1954, he asked to see me. My faculty advisers were impressed by the request, and I was thrilled to meet the great evolutionary scholar and humanist. Our common interest, we agreed, was a classic topic of general biology. The problem of ant castes had attracted the attention of Charles Darwin, who saw it as a threat to the theory of natural selection. Although Darwin had construed the idea of relative growth intuitively, Huxley and I knew that the ideas and data of our own studies had produced the first full and quantitative evolutionary explanation.

In 1968 I refined the idea of adaptive demography and developed several new principles of caste evolution with the aid of models in linear programming. In 1977 I was joined in a further, year-long study by George Oster, an exceptionally gifted and resourceful applied mathematician from the University of California, Berkeley. This time we explored the theory of caste evolution throughout the social insects. We were able to add other concepts from population biology to my earlier formulation. Oster led the modeling effort. His range of analytic techniques was awesome, affirming his generally held reputation as the mathematically most competent of all theoretical biologists. He often played with novel approaches, and he then had to lead me through the steps before we were able to continue the conversation. My role was the same as the one I had adopted with Bill Bossert in the synthesis of chemical communication fifteen years previously. At the beginning of each new avenue of exploration, I fed in all that I knew about caste and division of labor, information that often consisted of no more than doubtfully related fragments, along with the best intuitive conclusions I could draw. Oster then built formal models with what we could see—or guess—of the empirical relationships and trends, extending our reach in space and time. I responded with new evidence and guesses, he reasoned and modeled again, I responded, he modeled, I responded.* During breaks we gossiped and explored our other common interests. A magician of professional grade, he once dazzled me with sleights of hand I could not fathom even when he repeated them a foot or two from my concentrated gaze. I found my incapacity deeply disturbing. I was a proud scientific materialist, but I had to ask, How much else seemingly real in the world is an illusion? I learned a principle that others have established, often from painful experience: never trust a scientist to evaluate "evidence" of telekinesis and other feats of the paranormal; go instead to an honest magician.

Through the 1960s I searched for other ideas to add to the socio-

---

*E. O. Wilson, "The Ergonomics of Caste in the Social Insects," *American Naturalist* 102 (1968):41–66; George F. Oster and E. O. Wilson, *Caste and Ecology in the Social Insects* (Princeton: Princeton University Press, 1978).

biology armamentarium. One that I fashioned from population biology was the evolutionary origin of aggression. In his early writings, and again in his famous book *On Aggression* in 1966, Konrad Lorenz postulated aggression to be a widespread instinct that cannot be suppressed. It wells up in organisms and, like a crowded liquid, seeks release in one form or another. In human beings, Lorenz suggested, it is better released in organized sports than in war. In 1968, in the first of two Man and Beast symposia sponsored by the Smithsonian Institution, I showed that a more precise explanation consistent with the growing body of evidence from field studies is the role of aggressive behavior as a specialized density-dependent response.* As populations increase in density, those of many species are constrained by a growing resistance from one or more factors. Among these density-dependent responses are the rise in per capita mortality from predation and disease, the loss of fertility, a greater propensity to emigrate, and—aggression. Whether aggressive behavior originates at all during evolution depends on whether other density-dependent factors reliably intervene to control population growth. Even then the form it takes can vary, emerging as territorial defense, dominance hierarchies, or all-out physical attack and even cannibalism, depending on the circumstances in which population limits are attained. Thus aggression is a specialized response that evolves in some species and not others. Its occurrence can in principle be predicted from a knowledge of the environment and natural history of the species.

The elements of sociobiological theory came from many sources. But when the most important idea of all came along, I at first resisted it with all my ability. In 1964 William Hamilton published his seminal theory of kin selection in the *Journal of Theoretical Biology*, in a two-part article titled "The Genetical Evolution of Social Behav-

---

*"Competitive and aggressive behavior," in J. F. Eisenberg and W. Dillon, eds., *Man and Beast: Comparative Social Behavior* (Washington, D.C.: Smithsonian Institution Press, 1971), pp. 183–217.

iour." In the decades since, a sizable research industry has been built upon this single paper. Some of Hamilton's reasoning and conclusions have been challenged, then defended by enthusiasts, only to be challenged, and defended, again. The core of the theory has stood up well. Its essence, like that of all great ideas, is simple, of the kind that evokes the response, "Obviously that is true (but why didn't I think of it?)." Conventional Darwinism envisages natural selection as an event occurring directly between generations, from parent to offspring. Different lineages carry different genes, most of which prescribe traits that affect survival and reproduction. How an organism grows in body form, how it searches for food, how it avoids predators: these are among the traits affected by genes. The genes therefore determine survival and reproduction. Because by definition lineages that survive and reproduce better create more offspring in each generation, their hereditary material comes to predominate in the population over many generations. The increase of one set of genes at the expense of another is (again by definition) evolution by natural selection. The history of life has been guided by the appearance of new genes and the rearrangement of chromosomes bearing the genes through random mutations. These ensembles are winnowed by natural selection, which is the increase or decrease of particular combinations of genes and chromosomes through the differential survival and reproduction of the organisms carrying them.

In one important respect this traditional process of natural selection can be called just one type of kin selection. Parents and offspring are, after all, close kin. But Hamilton observed that brothers, sisters, uncles, aunts, cousins, and so forth are also kin; and he thought about what this truism means for evolution. The other kin share genes by common descent no less than parents and offspring. So if there is any interaction among them that is influenced by genes, say, a hereditary tendency toward altruism, or cooperation, or sibling rivalry, the interaction will result in a change in survival and reproduction and should equally well cause evolution by natural selection. Perhaps the ancillary forms of kin selection drive most forms of social evolution.

What made Hamilton's idea immediately attractive was that it helped to resolve the classic problem in evolutionary theory of how self-sacrifice can become a genetically fixed trait. It might seem on first thought—without considering kin selection—that selfishness must reign complete in the living world, and that cooperation can never appear except to enhance selfish ends. But no, if an altruistic act helps relatives, it increases the survival of genes that are identical with those of the altruist, just as the case in parents and offspring. The genes are identical because the altruist and its relative share a common ancestor. True, the corporeal self may die because of a selfless action, but the shared genes, including those that prescribe altruism, are actually benefited. The body may die, but the genes will flourish. In the enduring phrase of Richard Dawkins, social behavior rides upon the "selfish gene."

Hamilton had traveled that high road of science once described by the great biochemist Albert Szent-Györgyi, "to see what everyone has seen and think what no one has thought." But I am reasonably sure that had Hamilton expressed kin selection in merely abstract terms, the response to his formulation would have been tepid. Other biologists upon reading it would have said, "Yes, of course, and Darwin had a somewhat similar idea, did he not?" And, "Correct me if I'm wrong, but haven't notions of this kind been discussed off and on for a long time?" Yet Hamilton did succeed dramatically (although few learned about the theory until I highlighted it in the 1970s). He did so because he went on to tell us something new about the real world in concrete, measurable terms. He provided the tools for real, empirical advances in sociobiology. As Hamilton told me later, he was able to pull off his feat for three loosely related reasons. First, he was "bothered" by the problem of altruism; was the Darwinian explanation completely sound, or was it not? Second, he had a working knowledge of social insects, to which the altruism problem eminently applied. And third, he was intrigued by the mathematics of kinship, into which—impelled by the first two concerns—he had been guided through reading the work of the geneticist Sewall Wright. The closer the kinship, of course, the larger the fraction of genes shared as a result of common descent. Wright had devised an ingenious way of expressing the exact fraction shared, by a measure he called the coefficient of relationship. Working problems with it is an interesting mental game not unlike calculating the odds in gambling. What, for example, is the fraction of genes shared with a second cousin, or a half-sister's full niece? This number, the degree of kinship, Hamilton saw to be crucial in the evolution of altruism. Even this tributary idea is intuitively straightforward. You may be willing to risk your life for a brother, for example, but the most you are likely to give a third cousin is a piece of advice.

With these points in mind, Hamilton now joined the natural history of wasps and other social insects with the calculus of kin selection. At this point he was aware of two more important pieces of relevant information affected by kinship, this time from entomology. One is that most social insects, including the ants, bees, and wasps, are members of the insect order Hymenoptera. The only exceptions are the termites, composing the order Isoptera. The other important fact is that the Hymenoptera have an unusual sex-determining mechanism called haplodiploidy, in which fertilized eggs, with two sets of chromosomes, produce females, and unfertilized eggs, with only one set of chromosomes, produce males. Turning to the coefficient of relationship (or the "concept of relatedness," as he later named it), Hamilton saw that because of haplodiploidy sisters are more closely related to each other—have more genes in common— than are mothers and daughters. At the same time, they are much less related to their brothers. From the occurrence of haplodiploidy alone, he concluded that all of the following should be true if social behavior has evolved in the insects by natural selection.

- The Hymenoptera should have given rise to many more groups of social species than other orders, very few of which are also haplodiploid.
- The worker caste of these species should always be female.
- In contrast, the males should be drones, contributing little or no labor to the colony and receiving little attention from their sisters.

All these inferences are in fact true, and they admit of no easy explanation except kin selection biased by haplodiploidy.

I first read Hamilton's article during a train trip from Boston to Miami in the spring of 1965. This mode of travel was habitual for me during these years, the result of a promise to Renee that I would avoid trips by air as much as possible until our daughter, Catherine, reached high school age. I found an advantage in the restriction. It gave me, in the case of the Miami run, eighteen hours in a private roomette, trapped by my pledge like a Cistercian monk with little to do but read, think, and write. It was on such journeys that I composed a large part of *The Theory of Island Biogeography*. On this day in 1965 I picked Hamilton's paper out of my briefcase somewhere north of New Haven and riffled through it impatiently. I was anxious to get the gist of the argument and move on to something else, something more familiar and congenial. The prose was convoluted and the full-dress mathematical treatment difficult, but I understood his main point about haplodiploidy and colonial life quickly enough. My first response was negative. Impossible, I thought; this can't be right. Too simple. He must not know much about social insects. But the idea kept gnawing at me early that afternoon, as I changed over to the Silver Meteor in New York's Pennsylvania Station. As we departed southward across the New Jersey marshes, I went through the article again, more carefully this time, looking for the fatal flaw I believed must be there. At intervals I closed my eyes and tried to conceive of alternative, more convincing explanations of the prevalence of hymenopteran social life and the all-female worker force. Surely I knew enough to come up with something. I had done this kind of critique before and succeeded. But nothing presented itself now. By dinnertime, as the train rumbled on into Virginia, I was growing frustrated and angry. Hamilton, whoever he was, could not have cut the Gordian knot. Anyway, there was no Gordian knot in the first place, was there? I had thought there was probably just a lot of accidental evolution and wonderful natural history. And because I modestly thought of myself as the world authority on social insects, I also thought it unlikely that anyone else could explain their origin, certainly not in one clean stroke. The next morning, as we rolled on past Waycross and Jacksonville, I thrashed about some more. By the time we reached Miami, in the early afternoon, I gave up. I was a convert, and put myself in Hamilton's hands. I had undergone what historians of science call a paradigm shift.

That fall I attended a meeting of the Royal Entomological Society of London (crossing on the *Queen Mary*) to give an invited lecture on the social behavior of insects. The day before my session I looked up Bill Hamilton. Still a graduate student, he was in some respects the typical British academic of the 1950s—thin, shock-haired, softvoiced, and a bit unworldly in his throttled-down discursive speech. I found that he lacked the terminal digits of one hand, lost during the Second World War, when as a child he tried to make a bomb in the basement laboratory of his father, an engineer with experience in rock-blasting who invented bombs for the British Home Guard— for use in case of a German invasion. As we walked about the streets of London, rambling on about many subjects of common interest, he told me he had experienced trouble getting approval for his Ph.D. thesis on kin selection. I thought I understood why. His sponsors had not yet suffered through their paradigm shift.

The next day I devoted a third of my hour-long presentation to Hamilton's formulation. I expected opposition, and, having run through the gamut of protests and responses in my own mind, I had a very good idea of what the objections would be. I was not disappointed. Several of the leading figures of British entomology were in the audience, including J. S. Kennedy, O. W. Richards, and Vincent Wigglesworth. As soon as I finished, they launched into some of the arguments I knew so well. It was a pleasure to answer them with simple prepared explanations. When once or twice I felt uncertain I threw the question to young Hamilton, who was seated in the audience. Together we carried the day.

The time was approaching to write a synthesis of knowledge about the social insects. I dreamed of spinning crystal-clear summaries of their classification, anatomy, life cycles, behavior, and social organization. I would celebrate their existence in a single well-illustrated volume. A work of this magnitude had not been attempted in thirty-five years, the last being Franz Maidl's rather opaque *Die Lebensgewohnheiten und Instinkte der staatenbildenden Insekten*, and was badly needed. The literature was scattered through hundreds of journals and books, in a dozen languages, and it varied enormously in quality. The study of social insects had been balkanized for a hundred years: experts on ants seldom spoke to those on termites, honeybee researchers lived in a world of their own, and students of halictine bees and social wasps cultivated their subjects to one side as minor arcane specialties. I wanted to create a showcase for sociobiology using insects and, in so doing, demonstrate the organizing power of population biology. That much, I believe, my book accomplished. *The Insect Societies*, published in 1971, conveyed my vision of the social insects and, in the final paragraph, I looked to the future:

> *The optimistic prospect for sociobiology can be summarized briefly as follows. In spite of the phylogenetic remoteness of vertebrates and insects and the basic distinction between their respective personal and impersonal systems of communication, these two groups of animals have evolved social behaviors that are similar in degree of complexity and convergent in many important details. This fact conveys a special promise that sociobiology can*

eventually be derived from the first principles of population and behavioral biology and developed into a single, mature science. The discipline can then be expected to increase our understanding of the unique qualities of social behavior in animals as opposed to those of man. ★

Where might I go next? Originally I had no intention of extending my studies beyond the social insects. If honeybees are excluded for the moment—apiculture was in 1975 a major applied discipline unto itself, with hundreds of practitioners—the vertebrate animals, comprising fishes, amphibians, reptiles, and mammals, had at least ten times more zoologists attending to their behavior than was the case for insects. The mainstream journals of evolutionary biology tilted toward the natural history of the biggest animals, and vertebrates prevailed among the textbook case studies of ethology. Vertebrate behavior seemed too formidable a subject to enter from the direction of entomology. But I found out I was wrong. After probing a bit,

★ *The Insect Societies* (Cambridge, Mass.: Harvard University Press, 1971), p. 460.

talking with specialists, I had a revelation. Vertebrates weren't difficult at all. Very few zoologists appeared to be aiming toward an integrated sociobiology of these animals, at least not with an emphasis on population biology or with the speed and directness that Hamilton and I and a few others had achieved for the social insects. With my inquiry expanding, I saw that entomology is a technically more difficult subject than vertebrate zoology, partly because insects are so much more diverse—750,000 known species versus 43,000 vertebrates—and partly because they seem so alien to *Homo sapiens*, the giant bipedal vertebrates who can see them clearly only through microscopes. They receive little attention in college curricula, and few students turn to them for a career. Not least, advanced insect societies are more complicated and variable than those of the nonhuman vertebrates. So I reasoned that it should be easier for an entomologist to learn about vertebrates than for a vertebrate zoologist to learn about insects.

Once again I was roused by the amphetamine of ambition. Go ahead, I told myself, pull out all the stops. Organize *all* of sociobiology on the principles of population biology. I knew I was sentencing myself to a great deal more hard work. *The Insect Societies* had just consumed eighteen months. When added to my responsibilities at Harvard and ongoing research program in ant biology, the writing had pushed my work load up to eighty-hour weeks. Now I invested two more years, 1972 to 1974, in the equally punishing and still more massive new book, *Sociobiology: The New Synthesis*. Knowing where my capabilities lay, I chose the second of the two routes to success in science: breakthroughs for the extremely bright, syntheses for the driven.

In fact the years spent writing the two syntheses were among the happiest of my life. In 1969 Larry Slobodkin invited me to join him in a summer ecology course at the Marine Biological Laboratory in Woods Hole, Massachusetts. In late June Renee, Cathy, and I journeyed to the small coastal village and moved into one of the cottages

323

maintained by the MBL at Devil's Lane. One mile away, at the end of a winding country road, sat the spectacular lighthouse on Nobska Point, and beyond the lighthouse hill Little Harbor, and yet farther out, across the sail-dotted sound, the vacation island of Martha's Vineyard. Cathy, just then entering kindergarten age, fell in with a gang of other faculty youngsters. She and I also spent hours gazing at butterflies, birds, and, in the swamp behind our cottage, a colony of muskrats. In the late afternoons and evenings the three of us explored the southern reaches of Cape Cod by car. After lunch, outside class time, I took long runs over the Quissitt Hills along the coastal road to Falmouth. The rest of my free time I wrote, and read, and wrote. We continued to return to Wood's Hole for another eighteen summers, through Cathy's college years. It was a balanced life during that long period, deeply fulfilling.

In the preparation of the vertebrate sections of *Sociobiology*, I was boosted by an exceptional quality of support resulting, I am inclined to think, from sheer good luck. Decisive parts of the bibliographic search and manuscript editing were conducted by Kathleen Horton, who had joined me in 1965 and acquired a high level of expertise in the difficult and sometimes arcane disciplines that feed into sociobiology. Nearly thirty years later, she continues this vital role across a broad range of biological subjects.

Sarah Landry, then as now one of America's best wildlife illustrators, was miraculously available in the early part of her career as I started work on my big books. She depicted animal societies with composites of animals in behavioral acts that could never be brought together in a single photograph. With a passion for accuracy, she went beyond the effort required for an ordinary book on animal behavior, traveling to zoos and aquaria to sketch captive animals and visiting herbaria to render in detail the plant species found in the natural habitats of the animal societies. To Sarah, the bushes among which a mountain gorilla foraged meant as much as the gorilla itself.

My uneasiness about vertebrate zoologists subsided when I found that they were going to treat me as an ally rather than an intellectual poacher. I sold myself, honestly so, as their chronicler and friendly critic. Literally all with whom I communicated encouraged me to go forward. Many showered me with books, articles, and evaluations of the large literature.

Nineteen seventy-four was one of the earliest years in which a critical mass of sociobiological theory could be assembled. Studies of important species such as the Florida scrub jay and whiptail wallaby were in their final stages. And new elements of theory continued to pour in. One of the new theoretical concepts destined to be most influential was the natural selection of parent-offspring conflict, originated by Robert Trivers of Harvard. Like Hamilton, Trivers attained the key concept as a graduate student; I had just finished serving on his Ph.D. review committee. Trivers both benefited and suffered from a case of manic-depressive syndrome (now cured). When he was up he was dazzling; when he was down he was terrifying. We came into contact only during the peaks. He would stride through my office door and sit down, oblivious or uncaring of the old Harvard custom of making appointments. Thereupon I figuratively fastened my seat belt and prepared for swift and rocky travel to some unknown destination. Then would come a flood of ideas, new information, and challenges, delivered in irony and merriment. Trivers and I were always on the verge of laughter, and we broke down continually as we switched from concept to gossip to joke and back to concept. Our science was advanced by hilarity. My own pleasure in these exchanges was tinged with a sense of psychological risk, as though testing a mind-altering and possibly dangerous drug. Nor could I just sit and listen to Trivers, and let his mental productions wash over me. It is my nature, my conceit if you wish, to try to match any person with whom I converse fact for fact, idea for idea, and never quit. This is the reason I get killed in the company of my friends Murray Gell-Mann and Steven Weinberg, Nobel laureates in physics, egocentric, supremely self-confident, and said to be competing for the title of World's Smartest Human. Two or three hours with Trivers left me exhausted for the day.

For five spectacular years, 1971 through 1974, Trivers blazed new paths in sociobiological theory. He generated a model of reciprocal altruism, by which humans and more intelligent animals evolve contract rules that reach beyond self-sacrifice based on kin selection. What is undoubtedly his most important contribution, the theory of the family, and especially its undergirding models of parent-offspring conflict, set the foundation for today's substantial research enterprise on these subjects within behavioral biology. The selection pressures that bear on the evolution of nurturing, he pointed out, are different and sometimes opposite for parent and offspring. Shifting in direction and intensity as the young mature, these pressures account for youthful rebellion and family tensions better than the more proximate, conventional explanations of personal maladjustment and stress. At the least, Trivers provided a plausible argument for the ultimate causation of conflict, which persists regardless of the day-to-day proximate stressing events that trigger it.

It was Trivers who finally found the flaw in Hamilton's argument. Then he fixed it in a way that lent kin selection even greater credence. The flaw is the following. So long as social hymenopterans—ants, bees, and wasps—raise an equal number of males and queens among the brood destined to start the next generation of colonies, there is (contrary to Hamilton) no advantage for sisters to behave toward one another with any unusual degree of altruism. As a result of haplodiploidy they share three-fourths of their genes with sisters and only one-fourth with brothers, instead of one-half with both sexes, which is the case in animals using ordinary modes of sex determination. The imbalance in the Hymenoptera would seem to favor the formation of female colonies: more of a worker's genes will go into the next generation if she raises sisters instead of daughters. But, Trivers noted, if the haplodiploid ants, bees, and wasps rear equal numbers of sisters and brothers, they end up with an average relationship for all the offspring of one-half, canceling the apparent advantage. Mathematically, we can express this conclusion as follows:

$$\frac{1}{2} \text{ (fraction of females)} \times \frac{3}{4} \text{ (genes shared)}$$
$$+ \frac{1}{2} \text{ (fraction of males)} \times \frac{1}{4} \text{ (genes shared)} = \frac{1}{2}$$

One-half of the genes shared on average is the same payoff as from the ordinary production of sons and daughters without haplodiploidy. Only if the workers can raise a higher percentage of sisters in the royal brood can they reap the larger rewards of altruism twisted by haplodiploidy. The best possible overall degree of relationship in the Hymenoptera is five-eighths, reached by investing three-fourths of the resources in sisters:

$$\frac{3}{4} \text{ (fraction of females)} \times \frac{3}{4} \text{ (genes shared)}$$
$$+ \frac{1}{4} \text{ (fraction of males)} \times \frac{1}{4} \text{ (genes shared)} = \frac{5}{8}$$

Five-eighths beats one-half and gives the advantage to colonial existence, if all other conditions are equal. Subsequent studies showed that this is indeed approximately the ratio reared by ants. Somehow ant workers manage to obey the expectations of kin selection worked out in the heads of two zoologists.

I meant *Sociobiology: The New Synthesis* to serve as a network of such theory, as a vade mecum, and, not least, as an encyclopedia. I covered all organisms that could even remotely be called social, from colonial bacteria and amoebae to troops of monkeys and other primates. I recognized four "pinnacles" of social evolution, groups of species whose societies were, first, independently derived in evolution, and second, complex or sophisticated in organization, and, finally, possessed of genetic structures and organizations differing radically from those of the others. The pinnacles are respectively the corals, siphonophores, and other invertebrates; social insects; the social vertebrates (especially the great apes and other Old World primates); and man. Yes, *man*; that is the word I used in 1975, before it became unacceptably sexist and still meant generic humanity, while it still exercised the same resonant monosyllabic authority as earth, moon, and sun.

Perhaps I should have stopped at chimpanzees when I wrote the book. Many biologists wish I had. Even several of the critics said that *Sociobiology* would have been a great book if I had not added the final chapter, the one on human beings. Claude Lévi-Strauss, I was later reminded by his friend the historian Emmanuel Ladurie, judged the book to be 90 percent correct, which I took to mean true through the chimpanzees but not a line further.

Still I did not hesitate to include *Homo sapiens*, because not to have done so would have been to omit a major part of biology. By reverse extension, I believed that biology must someday serve as part of the foundation of the social sciences. I saw nothing wrong with the nineteenth-century conception of the chain of disciplines, in which chemistry is obedient to but not totally subsumed by physics, biology is linked in the same way to chemistry and physics, and there is a final, similar connection between the social sciences and biology. *Homo sapiens* is after all a biological species. History did not begin 10,000 years ago in the villages of Anatolia and Jordan. It spans the 2 million years of the life of the genus *Homo*. Deep history—by which I mean biological history—made us what we are, no less than culture. Our basic anatomy and physiology and many of our elementary social behaviors are shared with the Old World nonhuman primates. Even our unique qualities, the tool-using hand with its bizarre opposing thumb and the capacity for swift language acquisition, have a genetic prescription and presumably a history of evolution by natural selection. It felt appropriate to use provocative language as I opened the final chapter of *Sociobiology*:

> *Let us now consider man in the free spirit of natural history, as though we were zoologists from another planet completing a catalog of social*

species on Earth. In this macroscopic view the humanities and social sciences shrink to specialized branches of biology; history, biography, and fiction are the research protocols of human ethology; and anthropology and sociology together constitute the sociobiology of a single primate species.

chapter seventeen

THE SOCIOBIOLOGY CONTROVERSY

THE SPATE OF REVIEWS THAT FOLLOWED THE PUBLICATION OF *Sociobiology* in the summer of 1975 whipsawed it with alternating praise and condemnation. Biologists, who as a rule had little stake in the human implications, were almost unanimously favorable. They included Lewis Thomas and C. H. Waddington, elder statesmen of the day. Researchers closest to sociobiology were especially supportive, and they grew more so as time passed. In a 1989 poll the officers and fellows of the international Animal Behavior Society rated *Sociobiology* the most important book on animal behavior of all time, edging out even Darwin's 1872 classic, *The Expression of the Emotions in Man and Animals*.

Social scientists already engaged in biology-accented research also leaned in favor. They included Napoleon Chagnon, ethnographer of the "Fierce People," the Yanomamö of Brazil and Venezuela; and the sociologists Pierre van den Berghe and Joseph Shepher, who sought biological explanations of incest avoidance, marriage customs, and other key aspects of human behavior. Paul Samuelson, Nobel laureate economist turned public philosopher, favored the approach in one of his *Newsweek* columns but said *beware*—this subject is an intellectual and doctrinal minefield.

Samuelson was right. A wave of opposition soon rose among social scientists. Marshall Sahlins, a cultural anthropologist, made a strong attempt to exempt human behavior from the tenets of sociobiology in his 1976 book, *The Use and Abuse of Biology*. In November of that year the members of the American Anthropological Association, gathering in Washington for their annual meeting, considered a motion to censure sociobiology formally and to ban two symposia on the subject scheduled earlier. The arguments of the proposers were mostly moral and political. During the debate on the matter Margaret Mead rose indignantly, great walking stick in hand, to challenge the very idea of adjudicating a theory. She condemned the motion as a "book-burning proposal." Soon afterward the motion was defeated—but not by an impressive margin.

Because such events were widely publicized, with some journalists calling the controversy the academic debate of the 1970s, it is easy to exaggerate the depth of the opposition. The serious literature was in fact always strongly disposed toward human sociobiology. In the nearly twenty years since 1975, more than 200 books have been published on human sociobiology and closely related topics. Those more or less in agreement outnumber those against by a ratio of twenty to one. The basic ideas of sociobiology have expanded (their critics might say metastasized) into fields such as psychiatry, aesthetics, and legal theory. Four new journals were created in the late 1970s to accommodate a rising number of research and opinion articles.

Regardless of its real strength, much of the controversy might have been avoided, and for that I must bear the responsibility. I had written *Sociobiology* as two different books in one. The first twenty-six chapters, composing 94 percent of the text, was an encyclopedic review of social microorganisms and animals, with the information organized according to the principles of evolutionary theory. The second, the twenty-nine double-columned pages of Chapter 27 ("Man: From Sociobiology to Sociology"), consisted mostly of facts from the social sciences interpreted by hypotheses on the biological foundations of human behavior. The differences in substance and tone between books one and two give rise to the dual sociobiologies of popular perception. The first is sociobiology as I intended to portray it: a discipline, the systematic study of the biological basis of social behavior and advanced societies. And then there is the evil twin as perceived by Marshall Sahlins and some members of the American Anthropological Association, the scientific-ideological doctrine that human social behavior is determined by genes.

Genetic determinism, the central objection raised against book two, is the bugbear of the social sciences. So what I said that can indeed be called genetic determinism needs saying again here. My argument ran essentially as follows. Human beings inherit a propensity to acquire behavior and social structures, a propensity that is shared by enough people to be called human nature. The defining traits include division of labor between the sexes, bonding between parents and children, heightened altruism toward closest kin, incest avoidance, other forms of ethical behavior, suspicion of strangers, tribalism, dominance orders within groups, male dominance overall, and territorial aggression over limiting resources. Although people have free will and the choice to turn in many directions, the channels of their psychological development are nevertheless—however much we might wish otherwise—cut more deeply by the genes in certain directions than in others. So while cultures vary greatly, they inevitably converge toward these traits. The Manhattanite and New Guinea highlander have been separated by 50,000 years of history but still understand each other, for the elementary reason that their common humanity is preserved in the genes they share from their common ancestry.

It was the commonality of human nature and not cultural differences on which I focused in *Sociobiology*. At this level what I said could by no stretch be considered original; many others had advanced a similar thesis for decades. Darwin, who seems to have anticipated almost every other important idea in evolutionary biology, cautiously advanced theories of genetic change in aggression and intelligence. But no scientist before me had employed the reasoning of population biology so consistently to account for the evolution of human behavior by natural selection. The human genome is there in the first place, I argued, because it enhanced survival and reproduction during human evolution. The brain, sensory organs, and endocrine systems are prescribed in a way that predisposes individuals to acquire the favored general traits of social behavior.

In order to use models of population genetics as a more effective mode of elementary analysis, I conjectured that there might be single, still unidentified genes affecting aggression, altruism, and other behaviors. I was well aware that such traits are usually controlled by multiple genes, often scattered across many chromosomes, and that environment plays a major role in creating variation among individuals and societies. Yet whatever the exact nature of the genetic controls, I contended, the important point is that heredity interacts with environment to create a gravitational pull toward a fixed mean. It gathers people in all societies into the narrow statistical circle that we define as human nature.

Mine was an exceptionally strong hereditarian position for the 1970s. It helped to revive the long-standing nature–nurture debate at a time when nurture had seemingly won. The social sciences were being built upon that victory. But I hoped that even if sociobiology was dismissed by some of the more established scholars, evolutionary biology, including models of population genetics, would prove attractive to a younger generation of researchers in the social sciences, who might then connect their field to the natural sciences.

That expectation was desperately naive. The sociocultural view favored by most social theorists, that human nature is built wholly from experience, was not just another hypothesis up for testing. In the 1970s it was a deeply rooted philosophy. American scholars in particular were attracted to the idea that human behavior is determined by environment and therefore almost infinitely flexible.

If in fact genes did surrender their control sometime back during human evolution, and if the brain simply resembles an all-purpose computer, biology can play no contributory role in the social sciences. The appropriate domain of sociology would then be variation within cultures, interpreted as the product of environment. And cultural anthropology should concentrate on the internal detailed study of alien societies accepted on their own terms, with minimal reference to extraneous Westernized schemes, including those from biology. There were also important political implications. If human nature is mostly acquired, and no significant part of it is inherited, then it is easier to conclude, as relativists do with passion, that different cultures must be accorded moral equivalency. Differences among them in ethical precepts and ideology deserve respect, for what is thought good and true has been determined more by power than by intrinsic validity. The cultures of oppressed peoples are to be specially valued, because the histories of cultural conflict were written by the victors.

The hypothesis that human nature has a genetic foundation called all these assumptions into question. Many critics saw this challenge from the natural sciences as not just intellectually flawed but morally wrong. If human nature is rooted in heredity, they suggested, then some forms of social behavior are probably intractable or at least can be declared intractable by ruling elites. Tribalism and gender differences might then be judged unavoidable, and class differences and war in some manner "natural." And that would be just the beginning. Because people unquestionably vary in hereditary physical traits, they might also differ irreversibly in personal ability and emotional attributes. Some people could have inborn mathematical genius, others a bent toward criminal behavior.

In the 1970s a great many ordinary people believed these hereditarian propositions to be more or less true. But anyone who advanced such ideas in colleges and universities risked the scalding charges of racism and sexism. In contrast, those who attacked the hereditarian position were praised as defenders of truth and virtue. The psychobiologist Jerre Levy parodied the politically correct formula as follows: "Even without supporting evidence, the sociocultural hypothesis is assumed to be true unless proved false beyond any possible doubt. In contrast, the biological hypothesis is assumed to be false unless evidence is completely unassailable in its support."★

Understandably, then, American scholars, in a society grown hypersensitive to its internal divisions, shrank from the word "sociobiology." When American researchers formed a professional association on human sociobiology in 1989, they named it the Human Behavior and Evolution Society, and they used the word "sociobiology" only sparingly thereafter at their annual meetings.

The Europeans were less chary. One circle of researchers formed the European Sociobiological Society, headquartered in Amsterdam. Another established the Sociobiology Group at King's College, Cambridge University. A third began the Laboratory of Ethology and Sociobiology at the University of Paris–Nord. The word "sociobiology" and the ideas behind it were freely used in China, the Soviet Union, and other socialist countries, with articles written both for and against it in a scattering of journals.

What made *Sociobiology* notorious then was its hybrid nature. Had

★Jerre Levy, "Sex and the Brain," *The Sciences* 21, no. 3 (1981): 20–23, 28.

the two parts of the book been published separately, the biological core would have been well received by specialists in animal behavior and ecology, while the writings on human behavior might easily have been dismissed or ignored. Placed between the same two covers, however, the whole was greater than the sum of its parts. The human chapters were rendered creditable by the massive animal documentation, while the biology gained added significance from the human implications. The conjunction created a syllogism that proved unpalatable to many: Sociobiology is part of biology; biology is reliable; therefore, human sociobiology is reliable.

Some of the critics, assuming that I must have a political motive, suggested that the main purpose of the animal chapters was to lend credence to the human chapter. The exact opposite was true. I had no interest in ideology. My purpose was to celebrate diversity and to demonstrate the intellectual power of evolutionary biology. Being an inveterate encyclopedist, I felt an additional obligation to include the human species. As I proceeded, I recognized an opportunity: the animal chapters would gain intellectual weight from their relevance to human behavior. At some point I turned the relationship around: I came to believe that evolutionary biology should serve as the foundation of the social sciences.

Hence my conception of human sociobiology did not spring from any grand Comtean scheme of the relation between the natural and social sciences. I simply expanded the range of the subjects that interested me, starting with ants and proceeding to social insects, then to animals and finally to man. Believing the time ripe for the melding of biology and the social sciences, I used strong, provocative language to start the process. The last chapter of *Sociobiology* was meant to be a catalyst dropped among reagents already present and ready to combine.

Then everything spun out of control. In my calculations I had not counted on the ferocity of the response at my own university. Dur-

THE SOCIOBIOLOGY CONTROVERSY

ing the McCarthy era, Harvard had been a celebrated—if imperfect—sanctuary for academics accused of being members of the Communist Party. It was supposed to be a forum in which people could exchange ideas with civility, protected from defamation by political ideologues. Yet the fact that it was well populated by leftist ideologues put that genteel goal at risk. Shortly after the publication of *Sociobiology*, fifteen scientists, teachers, and students in the Boston area came together to form the Sociobiology Study Group. Soon afterward the new committee affiliated itself with Science for the People, a nationwide organization of radical activists begun in the 1960s to expose the misdeeds of scientists and technologists, including politically dangerous thinking. The Sociobiology Study Group was dominated by Marxist and New Left scholars from Harvard. Two of the most prominent, Stephen Jay Gould and Richard Lewontin, were my close colleagues and fellow residents of the Museum of Comparative Zoology. Three others, Jonathan Beckwith, Ruth Hubbard, and Richard Levins, held faculty posts in other parts of the university.

Although the unofficial headquarters of the Sociobiology Study Group was Lewontin's office, located directly below my own, I was completely unaware of its deliberations. After meeting for three months, the group arrived at its foreordained verdict. In a letter published in the *New York Review of Books* on November 13, 1975, the members declared that human sociobiology was not only unsupported by evidence but also politically dangerous. All hypotheses attempting to establish a biological basis of social behavior "tend to provide a genetic justification of the *status quo* and of existing privileges for certain groups according to class, race, or sex. Historically, powerful countries or ruling groups within them have drawn support for the maintenance or extension of their power from these products of the scientific community . . . [Such] theories provided an important basis for the enactment of sterilization laws and restric-

337

tive immigration laws by the United States between 1910 and 1930 and also for the eugenics policies which led to the establishment of gas chambers in Nazi Germany."

I learned of the letter when it reached the newsstands on November 3. An editor at Harvard University Press called me to say that word about it was spreading fast and might prove a sensation. For a group of scientists to declare so publicly that a colleague has made a technical error is serious enough. To link him with racist eugenics and Nazi policies was, in the overheated academic atmosphere of the 1970s, far worse. But the self-proclaimed position of the Sociobiology Study Group was ethical, and therefore implicitly beyond challenge. And the purpose of the letter was not so much to correct alleged technical errors as to destroy credibility.

In the liberal dovecotes of Harvard University, a reactionary professor is like an atheist in a monastery. As the weeks passed and winter snows began to fall, I received little support from the Harvard faculty. Several friends spoke up in interviews and public radio forums to oppose Science for the People. They included Ernst Mayr, Bernard Davis, Ralph Mitchell, and my close friend and collaborator Bert Hölldobler. But mostly what I got was silence, even when the internal Harvard dispute became national news. I know now after many private conversations that the majority of my fellow natural scientists on the Harvard faculty were sympathetic to my biological approach to human behavior but confused by the motives and political aims of the Science for the People study group. They may also have thought that where there is smoke, there is fire. So they stuck to their work and kept a safe distance.

I had been blindsided by the attack. Having expected some frontal fire from social scientists on primarily evidential grounds, I had received instead a political enfilade from the flank. A few observers were surprised that I was surprised. John Maynard Smith, a senior British evolutionary biologist and former Marxist, said that he disliked the last chapter of *Sociobiology* himself and "it was also absolutely obvious to me—I cannot believe Wilson didn't know—that this was going to provoke great hostility from American Marxists, and Marxists everywhere."★ But it was true. I was unprepared perhaps because (as Maynard Smith further observed) I am an American rather than a European. In 1975 I was a political naïf: I knew almost nothing about Marxism as either a political belief or a mode of analysis, I had paid little attention to the dynamism of the activist left, and I had never heard of Science for the People. I was not even an intellectual in the European or New York–Cambridge sense.

Because of my respect for the members of the Sociobiology Study Group I knew personally, I was at first struck by self-doubt. Had I taken a fatal intellectual misstep by crossing the line into human behavior? The indignant response of the Sociobiology Study Group stood in shocking contrast to the near silence of the other biologists in my department, who failed to offer even casual encouragement during corridor talk. My morale was not helped by the fact that Dick Lewontin, the most outspoken of the critics, was also chairman of the department. I faced the risk, I thought, of becoming a pariah—viewed as a poor scientist and a social blunderer to boot.

Then I rethought my own evidence and logic. What I had said was defensible as science. The attack on it was political, not evidential. The Sociobiology Study Group had no interest in the subject beyond discrediting it. They appeared to understand very little of its real substance.

As my mind settled on the details, anger replaced anxiety. I penned an indignant rebuttal to the New York Review of Books. In a few more weeks anger in turn subsided and my old confidence returned, then a fresh surge of ambition. There was an enemy in the field. An important enemy. And a new subject—which, for me, meant opportunity.

★Quoted in Ullica Segerstråle, "Whose Truth Shall Prevail? Moral and Scientific Interests in the Sociobiology Controversy" (Ph.D. diss., Department of Sociology, Harvard University, 1983).

I set out to learn the elements of Marxism. I was encouraged in my amateur's effort by Daniel Bell, the distinguished sociologist, and Eugene Genovese, a leading Marxist philosopher. Neither of them cared very much for sociobiology, but they disliked even more the aggressive tactics of Science for the People. I expanded my reading into the social sciences and humanities. I acquired a taste for the history and philosophy of science. Two years after the Sociobiology

Study Group published their letter, I wrote *On Human Nature*, which won the 1979 Pulitzer Prize for General Nonfiction (granted, a literary award and not scientific validation). The following year I began an all-out attempt to build a stronger theory to explain the interaction between genetic and cultural evolution.

The sociobiology controversy, I came to realize, ran deeper than ordinary scholarly discourse. The signatories of the Science for the People letter had come to the subject with a different agenda from my own. They viewed science not as separate objective knowledge but as part of culture, a social process compounded with political history and class struggle.

The spirit of their exertions was most clearly embodied, I believe, in the person of Richard C. Lewontin. He was later overshadowed by the scientific and literary celebrity of Stephen Jay Gould, but in 1975 the two men were equally well known and of mostly common political opinion. Gould shared Lewontin's Marxist approach to evolutionary biology, and he afterward maintained a drumfire of criticism in his monthly *Natural History* column and essays published elsewhere. But it was Lewontin who explored more deeply and thoroughly than anyone else every level of the implications of human sociobiology. He was the principal author of the letter in the *New York Review of Books*. Afterward he gave the greatest number of lectures opposing sociobiology, drawing on his extensive knowledge of genetics and the philosophy of science. He devoted the greatest amount of time to rallying opposition among potential converts, and his vigilance never slipped. If there is a truly fatal flaw in the sociobiology argument, he will have explicated it somewhere.

Without Lewontin the controversy would not have been so intense or attracted such widespread attention. He was the kind of adversary most to be cherished, in retrospect, after time has drained away emotion to leave the hard inner matrix of intellect. Brilliant, passionate, and complex, he was stage-cast for the role of contrarian. He possessed a deep ambivalence that kept both friend and foe off balance: intimate in outward manner, private inside; aggressive and demanding constant attention, but keenly sensitive, anxious to humble and to please listeners at the same time; intimidating yet easily set back on his heels by a strong response, revealing a fleeting angry confusion that made one—almost—wish to console him. Robert MacArthur told me, when we three were young men, that Lewontin was the only person who could make him sweat.

Unafflicted by shyness, at committee meetings he almost always seated himself near the head or center of the conference table, speaking up more frequently than others present, questioning and annotating every subject raised. He was the boy prodigy you surely encountered at least once in school, the first to raise his hand, the first reaching the blackboard to crack the algebra problem. His youthful demeanor was preserved into middle age by a round face, easy grin, and knowing stare, a shock of unruly dark hair, and a tieless shirt, always blue, said by amused friends to advertise his solidarity with the working class. Journalists referred to his countenance as owlish, but that was true only in freezeframe. Lewontin was too nervous and active in real life for the strigid image to fit.

He would pivot from one role to another, first the thoughtful and cautious dean, now the lecturer expanding a philosophical idea, then the hearty joking companion, and abruptly, on occasion, the angry radical. To accentuate a point, he would raise his hands above his head with fingers opened, and as his voice evened out and the argument unfolded, slide them back to the table top palms down, at first placed side by side and then eased apart, the mood having turned reflective, then quickly up again to chest level and windmilled one around the other, the subject grown more complex and the listener thereby commanded to pay close attention. He spoke in complete sentences and paragraphs. The stream of words was punctuated at intervals by a slowing delivery, sometimes almost a slurring, to reinforce a key phrase and, finally, the approach of the concluding argument. While he spoke he turned about to make eye contact with each listener within range, flashing the grin, signaling a confidence in his choice of words, revealing an attention to technique as well as to substance.

His self-confidence and style were potent in the academy of the 1960s and 1970s. It was the era when students clamorously asserted their independence and at the same time searched desperately for leaders. Lewontin's lectures at Harvard and abroad were enthusiastically received. His antiestablishment barbs, delivered with the panache of a stand-up comedian, were marvelously witty, even when you happened to be the target; they drew dependable laughter. Here was a scientist, the students knew, and a thinker, drawing from a deep revolutionary wellspring. He impressed journalists, too, who commonly referred to him as "the brilliant population geneticist." Lewontin was an intellectual who preached social change from the temple of hard science.

His scientific credentials were beyond challenge. His genetic research was of the highest caliber. In the mid-1960s, while at the University of Chicago, he collaborated with J. L. Hubby to make the first estimates of gene diversity within populations by means of the electrophoretic separation of closely similar proteins. Their technique soon became standard and inaugurated a new era of quantitative studies in evolutionary biology. He was also one of the first to use computers to study the role of chance in microevolution. Striking out from the same base of expertise, he explored the border area between genetics and ecology by linking the evolution of demography to changes in the rate of population growth.

Very early, at the age of thirty-nine, Richard Lewontin was elected to the National Academy of Sciences, one of the highest honors in American science. Then the contrarian side of his nature emerged. In 1971, amid verbal fireworks, he resigned in protest over the Academy's sponsorship of classified research projects for the Department of Defense. He was one of only twelve members out of the thousands elected during the 130-year history of the organization to quit it for any reason. He had placed himself in distinguished company; the others included Benjamin Peirce, William James, and Richard Feynman.

In the early spring of 1972 a Harvard committee, of which I was a member, recommended to the Department of Biology that Richard Lewontin be offered a full professorship. He was at that time considered the best population geneticist of his generation in the world. Under ordinary circumstances the appointment would have received quick approval and been passed on to the dean and president; but circumstances were no longer normal. Dick by that time was more than just a leading scientist. He had also become a political activist targeting other scientists. At the 1970 annual meeting of the American Association for the Advancement of Science he had been one of a small group who disrupted a session on a politically sensitive topic.

Several of the senior professors, alarmed by what they saw as a trend in his personality, were prepared to vote against Lewontin's candidacy. Wouldn't he be disruptive in his own department, they asked, if brought to Harvard? At the critical meeting of the tenured professors Ernst Mayr and I defended him. We argued (rather stuffily it seems in retrospect) that political beliefs should not influence faculty appointments. Some of the members remained unpersuaded: beliefs are one thing, they said, but what about personal attacks and disruption? I badly wanted Lewontin to come to Harvard. I said, let me call a friend in his department at the University of Chicago and ask if Dick has attacked his own colleagues there on ideological grounds. The proposal was accepted, and the decision postponed. In the interim George Kistiakowsky, one of Harvard's most respected senior professors and wise adviser to the university administration, got wind of the proceedings and telephoned me from the Department of Chemistry. He said in effect, you're going to be sorry if Lewontin comes. I was committed; I made my own call and was assured that Lewontin had not created problems at the University of Chicago. At the next meeting we voted unanimously to recommend him for a professorship. President Derek Bok approved his appointment on November 8, 1972, and the following year he came to Harvard.

Once he was installed, and increasingly after the sociobiology controversy began, I realized that we were opposites in our views of the proper conduct of science. Lewontin was the philosopher-scientist, tightly self-constrained, critical at every step, a stern guardian of standards who opposed—indeed, would have banned, if given the opportunity—plausibility arguments and speculation. I was the naturalist-scientist, in agreement on the need for strict logic and experimental testing but expansive in spirit and far less prone to be critical of hypotheses in the early stages of investigation. A collector and pragmatist by lifelong experience, I believed that every scrap of information and reasonable hypothesis should be put on record, then kept or discarded as knowledge grows. My notebooks were an indiscriminate hodgepodge. To be restrictive in the early stages, to make a moral issue of plausibility arguments, was in my view antithetical to the spirit of science. I wanted to move evolutionary biology into every potentially congenial subject, roughshod if need be, and as quickly as possible. Lewontin did not.

By adopting a narrow criterion of publishable research, Lewontin freed himself to pursue a political agenda unencumbered by science. He adopted the relativist view that accepted truth, unless based upon ineluctable fact, is no more than a reflection of dominant ideology and political power. After his turn to activism he worked to promote his own accepted truth: the Marxian view of holism, a mental universe within which social systems ebb and flow in response to the forces of economics and class struggle. He disputed the idea of reductionism in evolutionary biology, even though it was and is the virtually unchallenged linchpin of the natural sciences. And most particularly, he rejected it for human social behavior. "By reductionism," he wrote in 1991, "we mean the belief that the world is broken up into tiny bits and pieces, each of which has its own properties and

345

which combine together to make larger things. The individual makes society, for example, and society is nothing but the manifestation of the properties of individual human beings. Individual properties are the causes and the properties of the social whole are the effects of those causes."★

This reductionism, as Lewontin expressed and rejected it, is precisely my view of how the world works. It forms the basis of human sociobiology as I construed it. But it is not science, Lewontin insisted. And according to his own political beliefs, expressed over many years, it could not possibly be true. "This individualistic view of the biological world is simply a reflection of the ideologies of the bourgeois revolutions of the eighteenth century that placed the individual at the center of everything."† Lewontin sought instead laws that were transcendent, beyond the reach of natural science. "There is nothing in Marx, Lenin, or Mao," he wrote in collaboration with Richard Levins, "that is or can be in contradiction with the particular physical facts and processes of a particular set of phenomena in the objective world."‡ Only antireductionist, nonbourgeois science would help humanity attain the ultimate, highest goal, a socialist world.

That a distinguished scientist could advocate an approach to science guided by a radically sociocultural version of Marxism in the service of world socialism may seem odd today, and perhaps most of all in the former republics of the Soviet Union. But it helps to explain the distinctive flavor of the controversy at Harvard in the 1970s. In the standard leftward frameshift of academia prevailing then, Lewontin and members of Science for the People were classified as progressives, admittedly a bit extreme in their methods, while I—

★Richard C. Lewontin, *Biology as Ideology: The Doctrine of DNA* (New York: HarperPerennial, 1991), p. 107.
†Ibid.
‡R. C. Lewontin and R. Levins, "The Problem of Lysenkoism," in Hilary Rose and Steven Rose, eds., *The Radicalisation of Science* (London: Macmillan, 1976), pp. 34, 59.

Roosevelt liberal turned pragmatic centrist—was cast well to the right.

After the Sociobiology Study Group exposed me as a counterrevolutionary adventurist, and as a result of it, other radical activists in the Boston area conducted a campaign of leaflets and teach-ins to oppose human sociobiology. As this activity intensified through the winter and spring of 1975–76, I grew fearful that it might reach a level embarrassing to my family and the university. I briefly considered offers of professorships from three universities—in case, their representatives said, I wished to leave the physical center of the controversy. But it all came to very little. For a few days a protester in Harvard Square used a bullhorn to call for my dismissal. Two students from the University of Michigan invaded my class on evolutionary biology one day to shout slogans and deliver antisociobiology monologues. When it became apparent that they had not read *Sociobiology* and were more interested in using it as a stick to beat the Harvard ruling class, they were heckled by my own students. I received almost no hate mail, and never a death threat.

The most dramatic episode was the water dousing in Washington in 1978. On February 15 I arrived at the Sheraton Park Hotel to speak at a symposium on sociobiology planned as part of the annual meeting of the American Association for the Advancement of Science. The largest organization of scientists in the world, the AAAS was and remains especially concerned with the relation of science to education and public policy. A large crowd was expected at the symposium, which featured a half-dozen of the principal researchers on human sociobiology, as well as one of its most articulate critics, Stephen Jay Gould.

The moderator was to be Margaret Mead, and I looked forward to meeting her for the second time. A year before, at a conference on human behavior in Virginia, she had invited me to have dinner with her to discuss sociobiology. I was nervous then, expecting America's mother figure to scold me about the dangers of genetic determinism.

I had nothing to fear. She wanted to stress that she, too, had published ideas on the biological basis of social behavior. One was that each society contains an array of people genetically predisposed toward different tasks, say artist or soldier, and this differentiation creates a more efficient division of labor. Over roast beef and red wine (I was too mesmerized by her presence to taste either) she recommended several of her own writings that she thought I might want to read.

Sadly, I was not to see her again. Shortly before the AAAS meeting, she was stricken with the cancer that would soon take her life.

As the time approached for the symposium to begin, the atmosphere in and around the meeting hall grew tense. I was told that some kind of demonstration was planned by the International Committee Against Racism (INCAR), a group known for violent action. Its leaders, on learning that a session on human sociobiology was scheduled and that I would be present, had alerted members throughout the country. On hearing this news I walked by the INCAR booth to collect the literature they were distributing and to pick up a lapel button. As the crowd of several hundred began to settle in the nearby lecture hall, two INCAR members moved about distributing copies of a protest leaflet. I reached for one, but the young woman offering it recognized me and snatched it away.

Nothing happened as the substitute moderator, Alexander Alland, Jr., an anthropologist from Columbia University, opened the session and several other speakers presented their papers. When my turn came I chose to stay in my seat rather than stand at the lectern; my right leg was in a cast from an ankle fracture incurred while jogging over black ice two weeks previously. As soon as I was introduced, about eight men and women—I never managed an exact count—sprang from their seats in the audience, rushed onto the stage, and lined up behind the row of speakers. Several held up anti-sociobiology placards, on at least one of which was painted a swastika. A young man walked to the lectern to take the microphone away from Alland. AAAS officials had earlier issued instructions to session chairs to surrender their microphones if demonstrators demanded them, to avoid physical scuffling, and then to inform the protestors that if the microphones were not returned within two minutes, hotel security would be called. Alland announced that he was following the AAAS official procedure and turned over the microphone. Meanwhile, some of the members of the audience, fearing a riot, began to move out of their seats and away from the stage. They made little progress, however, because all the seats were filled and the aisles were crowded. Napoleon Chagnon, seated in a middle row, struggled to move the other way, determined to reach the stage and eject the protestors, but his way was also blocked. With several other audience members he shouted back at Alland and the protestors: the surrender of the microphone was wrong; no group should be allowed to take over a session by force. But this was the era of parity and equivalence, and every form of expression was considered free speech. The crowd began to settle down.

Then, as the INCAR leader harangued the audience, a young woman behind me picked up a pitcher of water and dumped the contents on my head. The demonstrators chanted, "Wilson, you're all wet!" In a little over two minutes they left the stage and took their seats. No one asked them to leave the premises, no police were called, and no action was taken against them later. After the symposium, several stayed behind to chat with members of the audience.

As I dried myself off with my handkerchief and a paper towel someone handed me, Alland, in possession of the microphone again, expressed his regret to me for the incident. The audience then gave me a prolonged standing ovation. Of course they did, I thought. What else could they do? They might be next. Before I could proceed with my brief lecture, other members of the panel rose to condemn the INCAR action. Steve Gould seemed to be speaking to the demonstrators when he quoted Lenin on the inappropriateness of violence for mere radical posturing, as opposed to the attainment of worthy political goals. Gould referred to the AAAS incident, using Lenin's words, as an "infantile disorder" of socialism. In that he was correct. It was the grown-up intellectuals I knew I had to worry about.

How did I feel during the incident? Calm—dare I say icy cold, as I let the protestors' anger wash over me? That evening I joined Napoleon Chagnon for dinner and then debated Marvin Harris on human sociobiology at the Smithsonian Institution, with another large audience in attendance—no takeover by radicals this time. Afterward I taxied to Union Station to catch the Night Owl sleeper to Boston. There I ran into the physicist Freeman Dyson, who was on his way home to Princeton. Well, I said, I've had quite a day. I had water dumped on me by protestors at the AAAS sociobiology symposium. Well, he said, I've also had quite a day. I was just in a train wreck. The engine had derailed a few miles north of Washington and the passengers had been ferried back to the station to await a later northbound train.

By this time it was obvious to me that human sociobiology would remain in trouble, both intellectually and politically, until it incorporated culture into its analyses. Otherwise the critics could always cogently argue that since semantically based mind and culture are the defining traits of the human species, explanations of human social behavior without them are useless. This shortcoming was on my mind when Charles Lumsden, a young theoretical physicist from the University of Toronto, arrived in early 1979 to work with me as a postdoctoral research fellow. His interests had lately turned to biology, and he saw great opportunity in the analysis of social behavior. We talked at first about a collaboration on social insects, but soon our conversation gravitated to the subject of heredity and culture. I said, the possible payoff justifies the high risk of failure; let's give it a try. So two or three times a week for eighteen months we sat together and framed the subject piece by piece.

We reasoned as follows. Everyone knows that human social behavior is transmitted by culture, but culture is a product of the brain. The brain in turn is a highly structured organ and a product of genetic evolution. It possesses a host of biases programmed through sensory reception and the propensity to learn certain things and not others. These biases guide culture to a still unknown degree. In the reverse direction, the genetic evolution of the most distinctive properties of the brain occurred in an environment dominated by culture. Changes in culture therefore must have affected those properties. So the problem can be more clearly cast in these terms: how have genetic evolution and cultural evolution interacted to create the development of the human mind?

No doubt we went out of our depth in embarking upon this subject. But so was everyone else, and no one can be sure of anything until the attempt is made. Undaunted then, we sifted through a small mountain of literature in cognitive psychology, ethnography, and brain science. We built models in population genetics that incorporated culture as units of learned information. We studied the properties of semantic thought to make our premises as consistent as possible with current linguistic theory.

We were looking for the basic process that directed the evolution of the human mind. We concluded that it is a particular form of interaction between genes and culture. This "gene-culture coevolution," as we called it, is an eternal circle of change in heredity and culture. Over the course of a lifetime, the mind of the individual person creates itself by picking among countless fragments of information, value judgments, and available courses of action within the context of a particular culture. More concretely, the individual comes to select certain marital customs, creation myths, ethical precepts, modes of analysis, and so forth, from among those available. We called these competing behaviors and mental abstractions "culturgens." They are close to what our fellow reductionist Richard Dawkins conceived as "memes."

Each time an individual modifies his memories or makes decisions, he entrains intricate sequences of physiological events that run first from the perception of visual images, sounds, and other stimuli, then to the storage and recall of information from long-term memory, and finally to the emotional assessment of perceived objects and ideas. Not all culturgens are treated equally; cognition has not evolved as a wholly neutral filter. The mind incorporates and uses some far more readily than others. Examples of heredity-bound culture that Lumsden and I found from the research literature include the peculiarities of color vision, phoneme formation, odor perception, preferred visual designs, and facial expressions used to denote emotions. All are diagnostic of the human species, all part of what must reasonably be called human nature.

Such physiologically based preferences, called "epigenetic rules," channel cultural transmission in one direction instead of another. By this means they influence the outcome of cultural evolution. It is here, through the physical events of cognition, that the genes act to shape mental development and culture.

The full cycle of gene-culture coevolution as we conceived it is the following. Some choices confer greater survival and reproductive rates. As a consequence, certain epigenetic rules, those that predispose the mind toward the selection of successful culturgens, are favored during the course of genetic evolution. Over many generations, the human population as a whole has moved toward one particular "human nature" out of a vast number of natures possible. It has fashioned certain patterns of cultural diversity from an even greater number of patterns possible.

Lumsden and I presented our scheme in several technical articles and two books.* The reviews were mixed; some were enthusiastic, but those in several key journals were unfavorable: Edmund Leach

*C. J. Lumsden and E. O. Wilson, *Genes, Mind, and Culture* (Cambridge, Mass.: Harvard University Press, 1981) and *Promethean Fire* (Cambridge, Mass.: Harvard University Press, 1983). The summary of the theory of gene-culture coevolution presented here is drawn, with minor changes, from our article "Genes, Mind, and Ideology," *The Sciences* 21, no. 9 (1981): 6–8.

was enraged in *Nature*; Peter Medawar was contemptuous in the *New York Review of Books*; Richard Lewontin, by his own later description, was nasty in *The Sciences*. The subject of gene-culture coevolution simply languished, mostly ignored by biologists and social scientists alike. I was worried, and puzzled. The critics really hadn't said much of substance. Had we nevertheless failed at some deep level they saw but we failed to grasp? During the 1980s a handful of other researchers investigated the subject along conceptual pathways of their own devising. Gifted scientists with diverse expertise from genetics and anthropology, they included Kenichi Aoki, Robert Boyd, Luigi Cavalli-Sforza, William Durham, Marcus Feldman, Motoo Kimura, and Peter Richerson. They too met with only limited success, at least as measured by the spread and advance of the total research enterprise. Kimura, Japan's foremost geneticist, told me that he had received almost no requests for his article on the subject.

It is possible that gene-culture coevolution will lie dormant as a subject for many more years, awaiting the slow accretion of knowledge persuasive enough to attract scholars. I remain in any case convinced that its true nature is the central problem of the social sciences, and moreover one of the great unexplored domains of science generally; and I do not doubt for an instant that its time will come.

chapter eighteen

BIODIVERSITY, BIOPHILIA

IN 1980 THE EDITORS OF *HARVARD MAGAZINE* ASKED SEVEN Harvard professors to identify what they considered to be the most important problem facing the world in the coming decade. Four cited poverty arising from, variously, overpopulation, the influx of rural masses into cities, and capitalism. Another, focusing on the United States, cited the welfare state and excessive governmental control. The sixth chose the global nuclear threat.

None of these scholars mentioned the environment. None gave more than fleeting attention to the impact that problems of the 1980s might have on future generations. As the only natural scientist I chose a radically different subject, and a broader time scale: species are going extinct in growing numbers, I wrote; the biosphere is imperiled; humanity is depleting the ancient storehouses of biological diversity. I was thinking like an evolutionary biologist, in evolutionary time. "The worst thing that can happen, *will* happen," I said, "is not energy depletion, economic collapse, limited nuclear war, or conquest by a totalitarian government. As terrible as these catastrophes would be for us, they can be repaired within a few generations. The one process ongoing in the 1980s that will take millions of years to correct is the loss of genetic and species diversity by the destruction of natural habitats. This is the folly our descendants are least likely to forgive us."*

This article marked my debut as an environmental activist. I was, I will confess now, unforgivably late in arriving. Biodiversity destruction had troubled my mind for decades, but I had made little overt response. In the 1950s, as I worked my way around bare red-clay gullies in Alabama and sought the vanishing rain forests of Cuba, I knew something was terribly wrong. My apprehension grew as I pored over the list of extinct and endangered animal species in the Red Data Books of the International Union for Conservation of Nature and Natural Resources. In the 1960s the picture darkened further when Robert MacArthur and I found that a reduction of habitat is inexorably followed by a loss of animal and plant species. Very roughly, we learned, a 90 percent reduction of forest cover—or prairie, or river course—eventually halves the number of species living there.

Adding to my concern was the Dream. It was literally an anxiety dream, and one that I occasionally experience to this day. I am on an island near an airport or in a town. I recognize the place immediately: from one night to the next, either Futuna or New Caledonia, both in the South Pacific. I've been there alone for weeks, and now, as my

*"Resolutions for the 80s," *Harvard Magazine*, January–February 1980, pp. 22–26.

355

surroundings take increasingly detailed form, I remember that the hour of my departure is approaching. I realize that I have not examined the fauna and flora of the island, nor have I made any attempt to collect the ants, most of whose species remain unknown to science. I begin a frantic search for native forest. In the distance I see what looks like the edge of a copse and run to it, only to find a row of exotic trees planted as a windbreak, with more houses and fields stretching beyond. Now I am in an automobile. I speed down a country road; nothing but houses and fields appear on either side. There are mountains far to the north—in every dream always to the north. Perhaps some forest remains in the mountains. I fumble with a map and locate the access road, but I cannot go; my time has run out. The dream ends, and I awaken knotted with anxiety and regret.

Knowledge and dreams notwithstanding, I hesitated, confining myself in the waking world almost entirely to research and writing on other subjects. As the 1970s passed I wondered, at what point should scientists become activists? I knew from hard experience that the ground between science and political engagement is treacherous. I was gun-shy from the sociobiology controversy. Speak too forcefully, I thought, and other scientists regard you as an ideologue; speak too softly, and you duck a moral responsibility. I hesitated on the side of caution, taking some relief from knowledge that nonacademic organizations were already active in the conservation of biological diversity. They included the World Wildlife Fund and the International Union for the Conservation of Nature, global in their outlook and highly competent and respected. There was also the Organization for Tropical Studies, a consortium of universities and other institutions dedicated to the training of young biologists, which I had helped found in 1963. Many of these new professionals, I knew, were going into conservation science. I thought, let the next generation do it. Still, the movement needed the voices of senior biologists.

The decisive impetus for me came when, in 1979, the British ecologist Norman Myers published the first estimates of the rate of destruction of tropical rain forests. After adding up data country by country, he calculated the global loss of cover to be a little under one percent per year. This piece of bad news immediately caught the attention of conservationists around the world. The rain forests were and are of crucial importance as reservoirs of diversity. They teem with the greatest variety of plants and animals of all the world's ecosystems, yet at the time of Myers' report they occupied only 7 percent of the world's land surface. Their area was thus about the same as the contiguous forty-eight United States, and the amount of cover removed each year was about equal to half the area of the state of Florida. The reduction in area translated, in terms of the general relation between habitat area and diversity worked out in other ecosystems, to roughly one-quarter of a percent of species extinguished or doomed to early extinction each year. The cutting and burning appeared to be accelerating as a result of incursions by land-hungry rural populations and the increasing global demand for timber products.

Primed by Myers' report, I was finally tipped into active engagement by the example of my friend Peter Raven. A distinguished scientist and director of the Missouri Botanical Garden, increasingly a public figure, Peter was determined and fearless. He had no qualms about activism. By the late 1970s he was writing, lecturing, and debating those still skeptical about the evidences of mass extinction. In 1980 he chaired a National Research Council study of research priorities in tropical biology, putting stress on the urgent problems of deforestation and biological diversity. More than anyone else Raven made it clear that scientists in universities and other research-oriented institutions must get involved; the conservation professionals could not be expected to carry the burden alone. One day on impulse I crossed the line. I picked up the telephone and said, "Peter, I want you to know that I'm joining you in this effort. I'm going to do everything in my power to help." By this time a loose confeder-

NATURALIST

ation of senior biologists that I jokingly called the "rain forest mafia" had formed. It included, besides Raven and myself, Jared Diamond, Paul Ehrlich, Thomas Eisner, Daniel Janzen, Thomas Lovejoy, and Norman Myers. We were to remain in frequent communication from then on.

A short time later I joined the Board of Directors of the World Wildlife Fund–U.S. and became their key external science adviser. I encouraged the staff to strengthen further their programs in scientific research while broadening the organization's coverage to include entire ecosystems and not just individual star species such as the giant panda and bald eagle. I joined in promoting the "new environmentalism" being formulated within WWF. This more pragmatic approach combines conservation projects with economic advice and assistance to local populations affected by efforts to salvage biological diversity. Nature reserves, we knew and argued, cannot be protected indefinitely from impoverished people who see no advantage in them. Conversely, the long-term economic prospects of these same people will be imperiled to the degree that their natural environment is destroyed.

I lectured and wrote widely on the problems of ecosystem destruction and species extinction, and on possible socioeconomic solutions. In 1985 I published an article in the policy journal of the National Academy of Sciences titled "The Biological Diversity Crisis: A Challenge to Science," which received widespread attention.* The following year I gave one of several keynote addresses at the National Forum on BioDiversity, held in Washington under the combined auspices of the National Academy of Sciences and the Smithsonian Institution. I then served as the editor of the proceedings volume, *BioDiversity*, which became one of the best-selling books in the history of the National Academy Press. The forum was the first occasion on which the word "biodiversity" was used, and after the publication of the book it spread with astonishing speed around the

*In *Issues in Science and Technology* 2(1) (Fall 1985):20–29.

358

world; by 1987 it was one of the most frequently used terms in conservation literature. It became a favorite subject of museum exhibitions and college seminars. By June 1992, when more than a hundred heads of state met at the Earth Summit in Rio de Janeiro to debate and ratify global protocols on the environment, "biodiversity" approached the status of a household word. President Bush's refusal to sign the Convention on Biological Diversity on behalf of the United States brought the subject into the political mainstream. Finally, the continuing controversies over the Endangered Species Act and the northern spotted owl made it part of American culture.

Biodiversity, the concept, has become the talisman of conservation, embracing every kind of living creature. So what exactly does it mean? The definition soon agreed upon by biologists and conservationists is the totality of hereditary variation in life forms, across all levels of biological organization, from genes and chromosomes within individual species to the array of species themselves and finally, at the highest level, the living communities of ecosystems such as forests and lakes. One slice of biodiversity among the near infinitude possible would be the variety of chromosomes and genes within one species of freshwater fish found in Cuba. Another would be all the freshwater fish species of Cuba, and still another would be the fishes and all other forms of life living in each river in Cuba studied in turn.

Because I edited the volume *BioDiversity* in 1988, it is widely thought that I also coined the term. I deserve no credit at all. The expression was put into play by Walter Rosen, the administrative officer of the National Academy of Sciences who organized the 1986 Washington forum. When Rosen and other NAS staff members approached me to serve as editor of the proceedings, I argued for "biological diversity," the term I and others had favored to that time. Biodiversity, I said, is too catchy; it lacks dignity. But Rosen and his colleagues persisted. Biodiversity is simpler and more distinctive, they insisted, so the public will remember it more easily. The subject surely needs all the attention we can attract to it, and as quickly as possible. I relented.

I am not sure now just why I resisted the word at all, in view of the quickness with which it acquired both dignity and influence. After all, in 1979 I had invented a very similar term, "biophilia," for use in a *New York Times* article on conservation.★ Later, in 1984, I employed it as the title and pivotal idea of my book *Biophilia*. It means the inborn affinity human beings have for other forms of life, an affiliation evoked, according to circumstance, by pleasure, or a sense of security, or awe, or even fascination blended with revulsion.

One basic manifestation of what I called biophilia is a preference for certain natural environments as places for habitation. In a pioneering study of the subject, Gordon Orians, a zoologist at the University of Washington, diagnosed the "ideal" habitat most people choose if given a free choice: they wish their home to perch atop a prominence, placed close to a lake, ocean, or other body of water, and surrounded by a parklike terrain. The trees they most want to see from their homes have spreading crowns, with numerous branches projecting from the trunk close to and horizontal with the ground, and furnished profusely with small or finely divided leaves. It happens that this archetype fits a tropical savanna of the kind prevailing in Africa, where humanity evolved for several millions of years. Primitive people living there are thought to have been most secure in open terrain, where the wide vista allowed them to search for food while watching for enemies. Possessing relatively frail bodies, early humans also needed cover for retreat, with trees to climb if pursued.

Is it just a coincidence, this similarity between the ancient home of human beings and their modern habitat preference? Animals of all kinds, including the primates closest in ancestry to *Homo sapiens*, possess an inborn habitat selection on which their survival depends.

★"The Column: Harvard University Press," *New York Times Book Review*, January 14, 1979, p. 43.

It would seem strange if our ancestors were an exception, or if humanity's brief existence in agricultural and urban surroundings had erased the propensity from our genes. Consider a New York multimillionaire who, provided by wealth with a free choice of habitation, selects a penthouse overlooking Central Park, in sight of the lake if possible, and rims its terrace with potted shrubs. In a deeper sense than he perhaps understands, he is returning to his roots.

Balaji Mundkur, an anthropologist and art historian at the University of Connecticut, has suggested a parallel explanation for another peculiarity of human taste: our fascination with snakes. These reptiles are among the features of mankind's ancient environment for which people can easily acquire phobias. Other strong phobia inducers are spiders, wolves, heights, closed spaces, and running water. Just one frightening experience with snakes—as mild as a scary story—is enough to instill the aversion in a child. The fear experienced thereafter is marked by the onset of panic, nausea, and cold sweat, reactions of the autonomic nervous system beyond ordinary rational control. The responses are quickly acquired, yet strangely difficult to eradicate.

The highly directed reaction against snakes appears to have a genetic foundation. In evidence is the remarkable fact that people rarely acquire phobias toward the objects of modern life that are truly dangerous, such as guns, knives, electric sockets, and speeding automobiles. Our species has not been exposed to these lethal agents long enough in evolutionary time to have acquired the predisposing genes that ensure automatic avoidance.

People everywhere are not just repelled by snakes. They are fascinated by them, and if they can do so safely, they draw close to inspect them. Snakes are the wild animals that appear most often in dreams, and, designated as mystical serpents, in religious symbolism. Variously hybridized with humans or other animals, plumed, twinned, grown gigantic and swift and all-seeing, the dream-mutants are gods who both avenge and transmit wisdom according to the vagaries of mood and circumstance. The caduceus, the staff entwined by a pair of serpents and carried by Mercury as messenger of the gods, now serves as the emblem of the medical profession.

The ultimate source of our attention to snakes may be the same as that of the fear and fascination they excite in other primates: their deadly nature. Poisonous species occur throughout the world, in the Northern Hemisphere as far north as Canada and Finland, and are an important source of mortality in most places where people live close to natural environments. The chain of biophilic evolution, as I interpreted it in 1984 from Mundkur's evidence, runs as follows. The deadliness of some kinds of snakes resulted through evolutionary time in an innate aversion and fascination among human beings. Hence they regularly disturb our dreams with ambiguous symbolism. Shamans and prophets report their own dreams as divine revelation and install the imagery in mythology and religion. From these sacred redoubts the glittering transformed serpent has invaded story and art.

By the ordinary standards of natural science, the evidence for biophilia remains thin, and most of the underlying theory of its genetic origin is highly speculative. Still, the logic leading to the idea is sound, and the subject is too important to neglect. In 1992 a conference of biologists, psychologists, and other scholars meeting at Woods Hole, Massachusetts, reported and evaluated a great deal of ongoing research. Some of it was experimental, consistent with earlier data, and persuasive.★

In my opinion, the most important implication of an innate biophilia is the foundation it lays for an enduring conservation ethic. If a concern for the rest of life is part of human nature, if part of our culture flows from wild nature, then on that basis alone it is fundamentally wrong to extinguish other life forms. Nature is part of us, as we are part of Nature.

★The proceedings of the conference were published as *The Biophilia Hypothesis*, ed. Stephen R. Kellert and E. O. Wilson (Washington, D.C.: Island Press, 1993).

Biophilia is the most recent of my syntheses, joining the ideas that have been most consistently attractive to me for most of my life. My truths, three in number, are the following: first, humanity is ultimately the product of biological evolution; second, the diversity of life is the cradle and greatest natural heritage of the human species; and third, philosophy and religion make little sense without taking into account these first two conceptions.

In this memoir I have described, for myself and for you, how I arrived at this naturalistic view of the world. Although the tributary sources extend far back in memory, they still grip my imagination, as I write, in my sixty-sixth year. I am reluctant to throw away these precious images of my childhood and young manhood. I guard them carefully as the wellsprings of my creative life, refining and overlaying their productions constantly. When obedient to the rules of replicable evidence, the knowledge obtained is what I have called science.

The images created a gravitational force that pulled my career round and round through epicycles of research. They still define me as a scientist. In my heart I will be an explorer naturalist until I die. I do not think that conception overly romantic or unrealistic. Perhaps the wildernesses of popular imagination no longer exist. Perhaps very soon every square kilometer of the land will have been traversed by someone on foot. I know that the Amazon headwaters, New Guinea Highlands, and Antarctica have become tourist stops. But there is nonetheless real substance in my fantasy of an endless new world. The great majority of species of organisms—possibly in excess of 90 percent—remain unknown to science. They live out there somewhere, still untouched, lacking even a name, waiting for their Linnaeus, their Darwin, their Pasteur. The greatest numbers are in remote parts of the tropics, but many also exist close to the cities of industrialized countries. Earth, in the dazzling variety of its life, is still a little-known planet.

The key to taking the measure of biodiversity lies in a downward adjustment of scale. The smaller the organism, the broader the frontier and the deeper the unmapped terrain. Conventional wildernesses of the overland trek may indeed be gone. Most of Earth's largest species—mammals, birds, and trees—have been seen and documented. But microwildernesses exist in a handful of soil or aqueous silt collected almost anywhere in the world. They at least are close to a pristine state and still unvisited. Bacteria, protistans, nematodes, mites, and other minute creatures swarm around us, an animate matrix that binds Earth's surface. They are objects of potentially endless study and admiration, if we are willing to sweep our vision down from the world lined by the horizon to include the world an arm's length away. A lifetime can be spent in a Magellanic voyage around the trunk of a single tree.

If I could do it all over again, and relive my vision in the twenty-first century, I would be a microbial ecologist. Ten billion bacteria live in a gram of ordinary soil, a mere pinch held between thumb and forefinger. They represent thousands of species, almost none of which are known to science. Into that world I would go with the aid of modern microscopy and molecular analysis. I would cut my way through clonal forests sprawled across grains of sand, travel in an imagined submarine through drops of water proportionately the size of lakes, and track predators and prey in order to discover new life ways and alien food webs. All this, and I need venture no farther than ten paces outside my laboratory building. The jaguars, ants, and orchids would still occupy distant forests in all their splendor, but now they would be joined by an even stranger and vastly more complex living world virtually without end. For one more turn around I would keep alive the little boy of Paradise Beach who found wonder in a scyphozoan jellyfish and a barely glimpsed monster of the deep.

acknowledgments

I am indebted to a number of persons for important assistance in reconstructing the events of my early childhood. They were, in Biloxi and Gulfport, Mississippi, William B. Carlin II; Edward B. Kitchens, Brigadier General (Ret.); and Murella Powell; in Pensacola, Florida, Frank Hardy, Sr., Barbara McVoy, and Patricia Shoemaker; and in Washington, D.C., Ellis G. MacLeod. I obtained some details of my ancestry from Elizabeth Wilson Covan, our family's genealogist; my mother, Inez Linnette Huddleston; and William M. P. Dunne, professor at the State University of New York, Stony Brook, and an expert on the history of Gulf Coast pilotage. Life at the

NATURALIST

University of Alabama and Harvard University during my student years was reconstructed with the aid of information from my friends William L. Brown and Thomas Eisner; from Joyce Lamont, librarian at the University of Alabama; and from Aaron J. Sharp, my mentor at the University of Tennessee, who helped me gain admission to Harvard.

I am also grateful to the following friends and colleagues for reading portions of the manuscript and generously providing help and advice: Alexander Alland, Jr., Gary D. Alpert, Stuart Altmann, George E. Ball, George W. Barlow, Herbert T. Boschung, Napoleon Chagnon, Franklin L. Ford, Stephen Jay Gould, William D. Hamilton, Bert Hölldobler, Robert L. Jeanne, Ernst Mayr, Basil G. Nafpaktitis, William Patrick, Reed Rollins, Ullica Segerstråle, Daniel Simberloff, Lawrence B. Slobodkin, Frederick E. Smith, Kenneth Thimann, Robert L. Trivers, Barry D. Valentine, and James D. Watson. My wife Irene (Renee) discussed the work in progress and provided help and encouragement throughout. John P. Scott sent background materials on the earliest days of sociobiology, while Michael Ruse provided wise counsel and advice over the years that enriched my perception of the sociobiology controversy. None of these consultants, of course, is in any way responsible for errors of fact that may have survived, or for my interpretations.

The service at Pensacola's First Baptist Church in 1943 described in Chapter 3 is a composite pieced together, respectfully and I trust without distortion, from my fifty-year-old memories, from conversations with my fellow member (still active) Barbara McVoy, and from *On the Bay—On the Hill*, a history of the Pensacola church by Toni Moore Clevenger and a 1986 publication of the First Baptist Church, Pensacola.

The portion of Langston Hughes's poem "Daybreak in Alabama" that opens Part I is from *Selected Poems of Langston Hughes* (New York: Alfred A. Knopf, 1959) and is reprinted by permission of the publisher. My account of the capture of the cottonmouth moccasin (Chapter 6), together with the reconstruction of early conversations on island biogeography with Robert MacArthur and the description of MacArthur's personality (Chapter 13), is taken with slight modification from *Biophilia* (Cambridge, Mass.: Harvard University Press, 1984). The summary of Konrad Lorenz's 1953 lecture at Harvard (Chapter 15) is based upon an imperfect memory. I may have combined my recollections with some details from reading and discussion conducted soon afterward, but the spirit and main themes I believe to be accurate.

As for all my books in the past, back to *The Theory of Island Biogeography* with Robert MacArthur in 1967, I am grateful to Kathleen M. Horton for her invaluable editorial assistance and advice.

index

adaptive demography, 313–314
aggression, 315–316, 333
Akihito, Emperor of Japan, 204
Alland, Alexander, 348, 366
Allee, Warder Clyde, 311
allometry, 312–314
Alpert, Gary D., 284, 366
Altmann, Stuart, 253, 308–312, 366

altruism, see kin selection
American Anthropological Association, 331–332
American Association for the Advancement of Science (AAAS), 307–308, 344, 347
amphiuma, 104
ancestry, 62–67, 127–129
Aneuretus (primitive ant), 198–199

Animal Behavior Society, 330–331
ant castes, 312–314
Antarctic biogeography, 170
Ants (by W. M. Wheeler), 94
ants, 48–50, 52–53, 59–60, 71, 94–
    97, 104–105, 109, 115–117, 132–
    135, 141, 148–150, 152, 173–
    174, 176–178, 182–196, 203, 242,
    282–306, 312–314, 318–319
Aoki, Kenichi, 353
arachnophobia, 188
area-species formula, 216–217
army ants, 96–97, 104–105
army, enlistment, 98–99
Arnold Arboretum, 231
art, definition, 245
Associated Institutions, Harvard,
    231
Atkins Gardens, Cuba, 147
Australia, field research, 175–181,
    197

Baker, John Harvard, 136–137
Ball, George E., 108–109, 366
ballooning, spiders, 275–276
Bannister, Roger G., 118
Baptism (religion), 33–46
baptism (rite), 43
Barlow, George W., 366
barracudas, 50
Beatty, Joseph, 270
Beckwith, Jonathan R., 337
Beebe, William, 139, 239–240
beetles, 104–105
Bell, Daniel, 340

Bergmann, G., 192
BioDiversity (book), 358
biodiversity, 60–61, 189–191, 209–
    210, 354–364; origin of term,
    359
biogeochemistry, 236
biogeography, see dominance, in
    faunas, and island biogeography
biology, recent history, 225–227
Biophilia Hypothesis (book), 362
biophilia, 360–363
bird watching, 14–15, 183, 245,
    263
Blanco's Woods, Cuba, 147–148
Bok, Derek, 306, 345
Bonner, John Tyler, 258
Boorman, Scott A., 258
Boschung, Herbert T., 102, 108,
    366
Bossert, William H., 122, 257, 266,
    297–298, 314
Botanical Museum, Harvard, 231
Boy Scouts of America, 73–80
Boyd, Robert, 353
Bradley, Philip H., 82
Brewton, Alabama, 80, 82–91
Brinton, Crane, 145
broken stick model, 246–247
Brown, Doris, 135–136
Brown, William L., 132–136, 206–
    209, 215, 366
Bryant, Paul W. ("Bear"), 105
Buck, Frank, 139
bull ring, military school, 21–22
bulldog ants, 177–178

INDEX

Bundy, McGeorge, 202
Buren, William F., 117
bush flies, 177
Butenandt, Adolf, 288
butterflies, 58, 67–69, 93, 183

Camp Bigheart, Pensacola, 84
Camp Pushmataha, Mobile, 77–
79
Cape Cod, Massachusetts, 323–
324
Carlin, William B., 365
Carpenter, C. Ray, 308
Carpenter, Frank M., 136, 200–
201
Carr, Archie F., 277
Carson, Rachel, 12–13
Carthy, J. D., 288
Castro, Fidel, 149
Cavalli-Sforza, L. L., 353
cave ants, 242
cave exploring, 93–115
Cayo Santiago, Puerto Rico, 308–
310
Ceylon, 197–199
Chagnon, Napoleon A., 331, 349–
350, 366
chameleons, 150–151
character displacement, 208–209
Chermock, Ralph L., 108–110, 113
Chetverikov, Sergei, 111
Chomsky, A. Noam, 146
citronella ants, 59–60
Civil War, 65–67, 101–102, 128
Clark, John, 178

Clevenger, Toni Moore, 366
Climate and Evolution (book), 21
Cohen, Joel E., 257
Cole, Arthur C., 129–130
Committee on Evolutionary Biol-
ogy, Harvard, 227
Committee on Macrobiology,
Harvard, 225
Comstock, John Henry, 110
concept formation, evolutionary
biology, 205–206, 210–211,
213–214
Congressional Medal of Honor,
26–27, 67
Connell, Joseph H., 255
Cornell University, 109–110
Costa Rica, 304–305
Counter, S. Allen, Jr., 45
courage, 25–27, 54–55
Covan, Elizabeth Wilson, 365
Crane, Jocelyn, 239–240
creativity, evolutionary biology,
205–206, 210–211, 213–214
Creighton, William S., 95
Crick, Francis, 223–224
Crimson Confidential Guide, 256–
257
Crocker, Mrs. A. E., 178
crocodiles, 30–31
Crompton, A. W. ("Fuzz"), 232
Crow, James F., 257
Crowley, L., 192–193
Cuba, 29, 146–151
cultural evolution, 350–353
Curtis, Bob, 183–188

dacetine ants, 109, 132–135

Darlington, Philip J., 28–31, 163–164, 211–212, 215, 217, 244, 249, 257

Darwin, Charles, 131, 166, 209, 313, 317, 331, 333

Darwin's finches, 209

daughter, see Wilson, Catherine (Cathy)

Davis, Bernard D., 338

Dawkins, Richard, 317, 351

Death Valley, 143–144

Decatur, Alabama, 92–99

Deevey, Edward S., 236

depression, mental, 242

DeVoto, Bernard A., 146

Diamond, Jared M., 358

dingoes, 180

distance running, 118–121

divorce, parents, 16–17

DNA structure, 223–224

Dobzhansky, Theodosius, 112, 215

doctoral research, 140–144, 288

dominance, in faunas, 211–217

Double Helix (book), 219

Douglas, Bob, 178

Doyle, Arthur Conan, 139

Dressler, Robert L., 147–152

Dry Tortugas, Florida, 265–266

Dunlop, John T., 301

Dunne, William M. P., 365

Durham, William H., 353

Dyson, Freeman J., 350

Eads, James H., 116–117

Earth Summit, Rio de Janeiro, 359

earthquake, 174

Ecological Society of America, 239, 310

ecology, at Harvard, 219–220, 233

Edmondson, W. Thomas, 236

Edsall, John T., 220

Ehrlich, Paul R., 358

Eisner, Thomas, 141–144, 279, 358, 366

Eliot, T. S., 146

Emerson, Alfred E., 215, 311

Emery, Carlo, 199

Endangered Species Act, 359

ethology, 285–288, 299–300

Europe, museum tour, 199–200

European Sociobiological Society, 335

evolutionary biology, origin of term, 226–227; research strategy, 166–167

Expression of the Emotions in Man and Animals (book), 331

eye injury, 13–14

Fallacy of Affirming the Consequent, 251

Farragut, Admiral David, 65–66

father, see Wilson, Edward O., Sr.

Feldman, Marcus W., 353

fights, boyhood, 54–55

Fiji, 165–169

fire ants, 48–49, 71, 115–117, 288–295

fish biology, 93, 204

Fisher, Ronald A., 111

fishing, 10–11, 13, 53–54

fistfights, 54–55

flies, scientific study, 93–94

Florida Audubon Society, 279

Florida Keys, 262–281

fly catching, 76

Folsom, Governor James E. (Sr.), 107

football, 82–84, 93

Ford, Franklin L., 366

Freeman, Martin, 66–67

Freeman, Robert, Jr. (great-grandfather), 128

Frisch, Karl von, 285, 299, 304

frogs, 15, 113–115, 196

Galápagos Islands, 209

Gell-Mann, Murray, 325

gene-culture coevolution, 350–353

Genetics and the Origin of Species (book), 112

Genovese, Eugene D., 340

Geographical Ecology (book), 255, 258

GI Bill of Rights, 101–102

"Glossary of Phrases in Molecular Biology," 229–230

Gödel, Escher, Bach (book), 294

Goodall, Jane, 308

Gould, Stephen Jay, 337, 341, 347, 349–350, 366

Grant, Peter R., 209

Grant, Rosemary, 209

Gressitt, J. Linsley, 183

Griffin, Donald R., 228–229

Growth and Regulation in Animal Populations (book), 233

Gulf Coast Military Academy, 16–25, 31–32, 73

Hägg, Gunder, 118, 120

Haiti, 29–30

Haldane, J. B. S., 111

Hall, Donald, 146

Hamilton, William D., 253, 315–321, 366

Handbook for Boys, 73–77, 79

Hardy, Frank, Sr., 365

Hardy, G. H., 244–245

Harris, Marvin, 350

Harvard Forest, 231

Harvard Magazine, 354–355

Harvard University, appointment procedure, 227; Wilson's career, 129, 132–138, 140–146, 200–203

harvester ants, 52–53

Haskins, Caryl P., 170–181

Hawkins, Mary Ann (ancestor), 64

Hawks, Howard, 162

Heinrich, Bernd, 121

heroes, 26–32

Hofstadter, Douglas R., 294

Holden Green, Harvard University, 200

Holland, W. J., 58

Hölldobler, Bert, 259, 299–306, 338, 366

Horton, Kathleen M., 324, 366

housing, Cambridge and Lexington, 200, 242–243
Hubbard, Ruth, 337
Hubby, J. L., 343
Huddleston, Harold H. (stepfather), 128, 136
Huddleston, Inez Linnette Freeman (mother), 6–7, 16–17, 38, 52, 97, 101, 127–129, 136, 365
Hughes, J. M. Langston, 4, 366
Human Behavior and Evolution Society, 335
human evolution, 130–131
hunting, 8–9
Huon Peninsula, 183–196
hurricanes, 266, 271–272
Hutchins, Robert Maynard, 221
Hutchinson, Arthur, 235
Hutchinson, G. Evelyn, 209–210, 235–237, 239, 244, 257
Hutchinsonian niche, 236
Huxley, Julian S., 313
Hymenoptera, 318–321, 326–327

illness, 174
Indonesia, 248
Insect Societies (book), 321–323
International Committee Against Racism (INCAR), 348–350
International Union for the Conservation of Nature (IUCN), 355–356
island biogeography, 166–167, 216–217, 244, 248–253, 255–256, 260–281, 312

Janzen, Daniel H., 358
Jeanne, Robert L., 284, 366
jellyfish, 5–6
Jones, Quentin, 147–152
Joyner, Anna Amelia (great-grandmother), 64
Joyner, James Eli (great-grandfather), 64
Junior Fellow, Society of Fellows, 144–145

Karlson, Peter, 288
Kennedy, Donald, 141
Kennedy, J. S., 321
Kiester, Ross, 257
Kimura, Motoo, 353
kin selection, 315–321, 326–327
King, Martin Luther, Sr., 45–46
Kipling, Rudyard, 240
Kistiakowsky, George B., 334
Kitchens, General Edward B., 365
Klopfer, Peter, 236
Knoxville, Tennessee, 129–132
Krakatau, 252, 260–261

Lack, David, 209, 239, 287
Ladurie, Emmanuel, 328
Lamont, Joyce, 366
Landry, Sarah, 324
Law, John H., 292–293
Lawrence, T. E., 240
Leach, Edmund, 352–353
leeches, 186, 194
Leibniz Prize, 301

Leigh, Egbert G., 236, 252–253, 312

Levenson Prize, Harvard College, 203

Lévi-Strauss, Claude, 328

Levine, Paul, 220–221

Levins, Richard, 253, 312, 337, 346

Levy, Jerre, 335

Lewontin, Richard C., 253, 259, 312, 337, 341–347, 353

Lignumvitae Key, 246, 277–279

Lindauer, Martin, 304

Lindroth, Carl, 215

Livingstone, Katherine, 258

lizards, 150–151, 271–272

Lorenz, Konrad, 277, 285–287, 299, 315, 366

Lost World (book), 139

Louis, Joe, 54, 70

Lovejoy, Thomas E., 236, 358

Lowell, Abbott Lawrence, 145

Lumsden, Charles J., 122, 350–353

Lüscher, Martin, 288

Lutz, Frank, 58

Lysenko, Trofim D., 44

MacArthur, Betsy, 259

MacArthur, Robert H., 122, 236, 238–239, 243–260, 312, 342, 366

MacLeod, Ellis G., 58–59, 71, 365

magic, 314

Maidl, Franz, 321

Mammoth Cave, 128

Man and Beast symposia, 315

Mann, William M., 60, 149–150

Marine Biological Laboratory, 323–324

Marlboro Circle, 252–254, 312

mathematical ability, 122–123, 242, 244–245

Matthew, William Diller, 211–212, 244

Maximin, George, 254

Maynard Smith, John, 338–339

Mayr, Ernst, 44–45, 110, 112, 192, 215, 228, 232, 338, 344, 366

McVoy, Barbara, 365–366

Mead, Margaret, 331, 347–348

Medawar, Peter B., 353

Meinertzhagen, Richard, 240–241

memory, its peculiar qualities, 5, 50–51

Mercer Award, Ecological Society of America, 280

Meselson, Matthew S., 220–221

Methuselah (Cuban lizard), 150–151

Mexico, field research, 151–157

Michener, James A., 175

mile run, 118–123

military code, 18–19, 26–27

military school, 16–25, 31–32

Mill, John Stuart, 219

Mitchell, Ralph, 338

Mobile Press Register, 71–73, 115, 138

Mobile, Alabama, 54, 62–81, 124–127

Mobile-Tensaw delta, 140

moccasins (snakes), 89–91

Modern Synthesis, evolutionary theory, 110–112, 286
molecular biology, at Harvard, 218–237
monkeys, 307–312
Mother Raub, see Raub, Belle
mother, see Huddleston, Inez Linnette
movies, 48
Mundkur, Balaji, 361–362
Murphy, Pearl, 14
Museum of Comparative Zoology, 28, 231–232, 259, 301
Myers, Jacob (great-great-grandfather), 65
Myers, Norman, 356–358
Myers, Sarah Solomon (great-great-grandmother), 65

Nafpaktitis, Basil G., 366
National Academy of Sciences, 343–344
National Forum on BioDiversity, 358
National Medal of Science, 257–259, 307
National Museum of Natural History, 56–61, 94–96
National Science Foundation, 305
National Zoological Park, 56–61
natural selection, 111, 300, 315–321
naturalist's prayer, 171
Nature Conservancy, 279
Nature, as concept, x–xi
Neo-Darwinism, 110–112

neophilia, 171
Nevins, Ralph, 275
New Caledonia, 169–174
New Guinea, 30, 31, 163, 181–196
New Hebrides (Vanuatu), 174–175
New York Review of Books, 337–339, 341
newspaper route, 71–73
Niedhauk, Russell and Charlotte, 277–278
Nobel Prize, 222, 285
North America, field work 1952, 143–144
Northington Campus, 102, 118–119
Nothomyrmecia (primitive ant), 176–181

Odum, Eugene P., 257
Odum, Howard T., 236
Oluwasanmi, Hezekiah, 138–139
On Aggression (book), 277, 315
On Growth and Form (book), 313
On Human Nature (book), 26, 341
Oppenheimer, J. Robert, 44, 146
Organization for Tropical Studies, 304–305, 356
Orians, Gordon H., 360
Orizaba, mountain, Mexico, 153–157
Orlando, Florida, 52–54
Oster, George F., 122, 314

Paradise Beach, Florida, 5–15
parent-offspring conflict, 326

Patrick, William, 284–285, 366
patriotism, 25–26
Patterson, Floyd, 306
Pensacola, Florida, 34–52
Perry, Mr., 85–86
Peterson, Roger Tory, 14
pets, 39, 150–151
Pharaoh's ant, 283–285
pheromones, 287–299
Phi Beta Kappa, 106
phobias, 361
Picasso, Pablo, 245
Pico de Orizaba, Mexico, 154–157
pinfish, 13
poison oak, 69
population biology, 233–234, 238–
    239, 299–300, 312
porpoises, 9
Powell, Muriella, 365
priority, in science, 210
Problems of Relative Growth (book),
    313
Ptashne, Mark S., 232, 283
Pulitzer Prize, 306, 341

Rabi, Isador I., 146
race, in Old South, 70, 80–81
rain forest mafia, 358
rain forests, 152–153
Ratard, Aubert, 175
rattlesnakes, 78–79
Raub, Belle (Mother Raub), 38–
    43, 84
Raven, Peter H., 357–358
Rawls, Hugh C., 102, 108, 113

Red Data Books, 355
religion, 33–46, 191–192
Reserve Officers Training Corps
    (ROTC), 106
rhesus monkeys, 308–312
Richards, O. W., 321
Richards, Thomas, 279
Richerson, Peter J., 353
Robertson, William, 265, 269
Robinson, Michael, 60
Rock Creek Park, Washington,
    D.C., 58
Rogers, Wallace Roland, 34–38,
    42–43
Rollins, Reed C., 366
Roosevelt, Franklin Delano, 22–
    23, 70
Rosen, Walter, 359–360
Rosovsky, Henry, 146
Roughgarden, Jonathan, 257
Royal Entomological Society of
    London, 320
running (sport), 118–121, 324
Ruse, Michael, 366

Sahlins, Marshall, 331–332
salamanders, 104
Samuelson, Paul A., 331
Sanderson, Ivan, 139
Sarawaget Mountains, New
    Guinea, 183–196
Schneiderman, Howard A., 141
Schoener, Thomas W., 257–258
Schrödinger, Erwin, 44
Science for the People, 337–341

science, culture of, 27–28, 210–211; social value, 114

Scopes trial, Tennessee, 130

Scott, John P., 311, 366

sea nettle, 5–6

sea, love of, 11

Second World War, 69–71, 91

Segerstråle, Ullica, 339, 366

selfish gene, 317

Serventy, Vincent, 178

Seven Pillars of Wisdom (book), 240

sex, education and humor, 79–80

sharks, 9, 177, 272

Sharp, Aaron J., 132, 366

Shoemaker, Patricia, 365

Silberglied, Robert E., 276–279

Simberloff, Daniel S., 257, 266–281, 366

Simla, 239–240

Simpson, George Gaylord, 112, 228, 249

Skinner, B. F., 286

Slobodkin, Lawrence B., 229, 233–239, 243, 253–255, 258, 312, 323, 366

Smith, Frederick E., 219–220, 366

Smith, Marion R., 94–96, 116–117

snake bite, 78–79, 90–91

snakes, 69, 77–79, 86–91, 177, 361–362

Snodgrass, R. E., 58

social insects, 317–322, 326–327, see also ants

Society of Fellows, 144–146

Sociobiology (book), 323–329, 332–339

Sociobiology Study Group, 337–341

sociobiology, history, 225, 253, 281, 300, 307–353

Solomon, Jacob (ancestor), 65

southern manners, 25

spiders, 188, 270, 275–276

Spirals (book), 284–285

Spring Hill, Trinidad, 239–240

Sri Lanka, 197–199

Stanford University, 201–202

Stanley, G. A. V., 181

Stebbins, G. Ledyard, 112

Sterling, Wallace, 201–202

stingrays, 8–11

Stockdale, Admiral James B., 26–27

subspecies concept, 206–208

Suriname, 241

Systematics and the Origin of Species (book), 44–45, 110, 112, 232

Szent-Györgyi, Albert v. N., 317

Szent-Ivany, Joseph, 181, 183

Tales of the South Pacific (book), 175

Talmud, 51

taxon cycle, 213–217

taxonomy, 203–205

Taylor, Robert W., 180

teaching, 77–79, 200–203

Tempo and Mode in Evolution (book), 112

Tendrich, Steve, 268–269, 272–275

Tennessee evolution law, 130

Tennessee Valley Authority, 93

Tennessee, travels in, 130

Terman, Frederick, 201–202
The Ants (book), 306
The Nature Conservancy, 279
Theory of Island Biogeography (book), 256, 319
theory of the family, 326
Thimann, Kenneth V., 366
Thomas, Lewis, 330
Thompson, D'Arcy W., 313
Tinbergen, Niko, 285, 299
toadfish, 11
track (sport), 118–121
Trinidad and Tobago, 239–242
Trinidad Mountains, Cuba, 148–151
Trivers, Robert L., 325–327, 366
tropical biology, field research, 139–199

University of Alabama, 100–120, 140
University of Chicago, 344
University of Florida, 201
University of Michigan, 201
University of Tennessee, 129–132, 140
University of Würzburg, 301, 305–306
Use and Abuse of Biology (book), 331
Uxmal, Yucatán, 152

Valentine, Barry D., 108–110, 113, 366
vampire bats, 240–241
Van Valen, Leigh, 253

Vander Meer, Robert K., 293
Vanderbilt University, 98
Vanuatu, 174–175
Variation and Evolution in Plants (book), 112
Vietnam War, 267
vision, impaired, 13–15

Waddington, Conrad Hall, 330
Wald, George, 220, 222, 266
Walker, J. Henry, 103
Wallace, Alfred Russel, 163
Walsh, Christopher T., 292–293
Washington, D.C., 56–61
Watson, Doc, 302
Watson, Jack, 269
Watson, James D., 218–225, 366
Webster, Grady L., 147, 215
Weinberg, Steven, 325
Weisskopf, Victor F., x
West Indies, biogeography, 244, see also Cuba
Weston, William H. ("Cap"), 200, 202
What Is Life? (book), 44
Wheeler, William M., 94, 149
Whitehead, Alfred North, 114
wife, see Wilson, Irene (Renee)
Wigglesworth, Vincent B., 321
Williams, Bert, 103–104
Williams, Carroll M., 229, 284
Wilson, Catherine (Cathy) (daughter), 261, 263, 319, 323–324
Wilson, Edward O., Sr. (father), 6–7, 16–17, 52, 55–56, 62–64, 84, 97–98, 101, 124–127

NATURALIST

Wilson, Herbert (uncle), 62–63,
125
Wilson, Inez Linnette (mother),
see Huddleston, Inez Lin-
nette
Wilson, Irene Kelley (Renee)
(wife), 164, 200, 239–242, 261,
263, 319, 323–324, 366
Wilson, Jack, 127
Wilson, Maria Louise Myers
(great-grandmother), 65
Wilson, Mary Emma (May)
(grandmother), 62–64
Wilson, Pearl (stepmother), 52,
56, 69, 84, 91–92, 97–98,
125
Wilson, Renee, see Wilson, Irene
(Renee)

Wilson, William Christopher (Black
Bill) (great-grandfather), 65–67
Wolff, Sheldon M., 143
Woods Hole, Massachusetts, 323–
324
World War II, 69–71, 91
World Wildlife Fund, 356, 358
Wright, Asa, 239–240
Wright, Sewall, 111
Wylie, Philip, 106

Yanomamö, 225, 331
Yucatán, field research, 151–152

Ziebach, Bill, 115
Zimmerman, Elwood C., 215
Zoogeography (book), 211
zoos, 57–61